Praise for *Published! The Complete Guide to Nontraditional Publishing*

"Read *Published!* before you start writing. Read it before you finish writing. Read it again when you think you're finished. And if it's too late for you, read it before you pay another red cent to anyone for publishing your masterpiece!" – W. Ron Drynan,
Author of *Power Split – A Philosophical Thriller*

Many writers get wrapped up in the excitement of getting published, only later to face bitter disappointment for having made naive decisions along the way.
Published! delivers vital information and caveats to writers, so they can understand the upsides, downsides, and insides of getting published. Every writer who wants to get a book published should read this valuable book. --Bobbie Christmas, owner of Zebra Communications and author of *Write In Style*

"I have never seen a more comprehensive guide to the ins and outs of non-traditional publishing. For anyone considering self-publishing, this is a great place to start!" --
Melinda Copp, executive editor, The Writer's Sherpa, LLC

A great resource for writers to "comparison shop" the self-publishing and subsidy options while navigating a course to publication. This information will protect you from the heartbreak of having a (seemingly) great publishing deal go bad. Read. Learn. Publish!
Susan Carter, Author & Publisher
www.WriterProfits.com

"A great primer on the basics of self-publishing"
	Mark Levine,
		Author of *The Fine Print of Self-Publishing*

"Here's the situation: You're a writer, the shoebox in your closet is filled to overflowing with rejection slips, but you _know_ what you've written is good... So what are your options now? Think you've tried everyplace and everything? You haven't. All those other markets are here, in PUBLISHED!, a compendium of publishing options from hiring your own printer to going through Amazon to locating good subsidy publishers (as well as places you wouldn't touch with someone else's ten-foot pole). This book will tell you which sorts of publishers will get you where you want to go, list who's out there from A to Z in depth, and give you some firm, no-nonsense guidelines for finding the RIGHT solution for your book. – "
	Holly Lisle, Author, Instructor

About the Authors

Author Bio's:

Al Musitano, the author of several books including *Published! A Complete Guide to Nontraditional Publishing*, has been published in anthologies and he wrote a local newspaper column. He found his background in art and engineering blended perfectly to design book covers and graphics on websites. Samples can be viewed on his site, www.PersonalCovers.webs.com.

Dona Lee is the author of both fiction and nonfiction books. She is an editor, coach, ghostwriter, bookstore owner, and now an "author's services provider" and subsidy publisher. Her short stories have been included in numerous anthologies, she writes features for local magazines and newspapers and leads the Florida Writer's Association of Manatee as well as writing and publishing the monthly newsletter for the Sarasota Fiction Writers, "Plotting Success."

Published!
The Complete Guide to
Nontraditional Publishing

By
Dona Lee
&
Al Musitano

Published! An Affiliate of Village Voices Gallery

1010 10 Avenue West, Bradenton, FL 34205

Copyright 2012 by Dona Lee & Al Musitano

All rights reserved, including the right to reproduce this book or portions thereof in any form whatsoever. For information address Published! An Affiliate of Village Voices Gallery,
1010 10th Avenue West, Bradenton, Fl 34205

ISBN-13: 978-0-98468272-0
ISBN-10:   0-98468272-4

Front cover illustration by Al Musitano

Manufactured in the United States

Acknowledgements:

We wish to thank all our Florida Writers who supported us during this endeavor. Special thanks to Bill Carrigan, our editor and grammarian as well as all the authors, both published and un-published, who told us how necessary a book like this is for all writers.

In loving memory of our greatest supporter,
T. Diane Allard 1964-2012

Foreword

by Dan Poynter

I have been advising writers for many years on how to put their ideas into words, their words into print, and to print their own books.

Yet some writers do not have the necessary "tools" to accomplish publishing on their own; others would rather not be bothered, preferring to concentrate on writing their next book or moving on to other projects.

This book, *Published! The Complete Guide to Nontraditional Publishing*, advises readers of the many subsidy publishers and author services available, giving them insight into costs, and providing them with service/cost comparisons in order to help them decide the best path for their circumstances and their book.

In addition to the information on the author service providers and subsidy printers, *Published!* provides warning signs, the red flags to heed in order to avoid scams and disappointment. You will find detailed information on how you can now publish either ebooks or POD's for free if you are willing to do all the work yourself. *Published!* authors strongly suggest you hire a freelance editor and in this book they'll show you how to locate qualified editors who don't change your style. If you aren't an artist, they tell you how to locate illustrators for your cover or picture book at costs ranging anywhere from a couple hundred dollars up to thousands. Interested in book trailers? Or publishing Audio books? You will know how to find them and have an estimate on how much they should charge. If you can't figure out how to format your book, yet you don't want to pay three hundred dollars to Amazon for their professional formatting? *Published!* supplies alternates to overcome this obstacle as well.

If you lack computer skills to publish yourself, Published! suggests alternatives, companies who are willing to help you out for a fee, sometimes low, sometimes exorbitant.

You are an expert in the subject matter of your book. Book publishing is a business and a different business. The most expensive parts of book publishing are the mistakes. You do not have to make them. This book is full of information to help you choose the best path for YOUR book.

Considered by many to be the guru of self publishing, **Dan Poynter** is the author of more than 120 books and has been a successful publisher since 1969. His Self-Publishing Manual propelled him to notoriety in the publishing industry. Each year he addresses scores of groups on the subject of publishing. He is the founder of Para Publishing and has been featured in many major media outlets, including *Entrepreneur, U.S. News and World Report, Christian Science Monitor, The Wall Street Journal, The Washington Post, Writer's Digest* and the *The New York Times.*

Table of Contents:

Chapter Four: Subsidy Publishing—
                    The Unknown Underdog
          Who is best served by this option and
          what should you consider when
          choosing a publisher to best suit
          your needs. What have you written?
          Fiction? Nonfiction? Poetry? Memoirs?
          A Cookbook? Children's Book? Do you
          need photos? Do you need an illustrator?
          How many pages do you have? Have
          you already hired a professional editor?
          Interviews with an author and a
          publisher of a subsidy press

Chapter Five: Reality Check
          Break-even-point calculation. Are you
          willing to market your book? The bitter
          truth—statistics versus unrealistic
          expectations.

Chapter Six: Warning—Danger Ahead
          The warning flags to look out for. When to run,
          not walk away, sites to check for legitimate
          publishers, other books to research.

Chapter Seven: Edit, edet, edite!
                    Everyone should use an outside
          independent editor.

Chapter Eight: To Market, to Market
                    Promoting, platforms, and networking

Chapter Nine: Distribution. It costs WHAT???

Chapter Ten: e-Publishing

Introduction: The Decision

"I love being a writer. What I can't stand is the

paperwork."

— Peter De Vries

Members of our writing groups regularly asked,
"Who's the best subsidy publisher?" We looked for a book
or guide to answer their question. Imagine our amazement
when we discovered no one has written a comprehensive,
comparative guide on subsidy publishers.

And a book was born.

"I was so frightened." Carly W.
"When it was over, I was happy to have survived." Bill C.
"I couldn't believe what happened." Dale F.
"I just wanted it to be over." Cheryl C.
"Afterward, I couldn't believe how little there was left."
                                        Frank M.
"I was devastated, destroyed. I lost everything." Amber L.

This isn't a horror writers group, nor an appointment at the dentist. These are writers who utilized a subsidy publisher without doing their research to find the best company for their book. These writers chose a publisher who had a different vision for the writer's book—the publishing equivalent of buying a sports coupe when you have a large family.

Many unpublished writers view the traditional publishing world as an angry, self-righteous giant, stomping his feet and yelling, "Fee, fie, foe, fum! I smell the blood of an amateur." A coded door, accessible only to elite members, denies entry to all but the famous, confirmed best-sellers, or the magically lucky who miraculously land an AAR agent. Traditional publishers don't give a hoot if you've written one book or twelve—if you're an unknown author without a following, you're a financial risk—one that traditional publishers aren't willing to take on. Writers are forced to turn to other avenues to be published.

> "Writing is not necessarily something to be ashamed of,
> but do it in private and wash your hands afterward."
> --Robert Heinlein (1907 – 1988)

Most authors try to break into traditional publishing first. They send out queries, synopses, and even their completed manuscripts. Then they wait, and wait, and wait some more, wading through a mountain of rejections, or sweating the silence of no replies. The writer must decide.

Do I wait until I break through to the traditionals? What if it never happens? How long should I give it? Our recommendation—take control. If you are vacillating, still hoping to be discovered before you choose to self or subsidy publish—draw your own line. Set a date, *six months, a year, five rejections, until my next birthday.* The waiting period, while you anxiously hope to hear a request to read the entire manuscript, drives many authors close to insanity. This intermission is akin to watching a teapot, hoping for a quick boil. While waiting, occupy yourself with another project—perhaps a sequel to the first book, or even a whole new genre. Keep writing. No matter which path you choose, once your book is published, you'll be spending a large portion of your time marketing and promoting and will miss and relish these days of peace. Practice a little patience, examine your alternatives, take a deep breath—relax.

Once you've cried over the last rejection you ever want to see and have reached your deadline it's time to make your next decision. Self-determination—take your destiny into your own hands. When your self-imposed deadline arrives, you need to make your next decision; to publish your book yourself, to utilize experts for part of the task, or to pay to have a subsidy publisher do all the work.

You must first understand the differences between them, including all the recent additions to the field that blur the lines.

This guide is laid out to show you what each subsidy publisher offers. We make no judgments, good, bad, or horrible. Each individual author must decide which features best suit his or her personal needs.

"I'm all in favor of keeping dangerous weapons out of the

hands of fools.

Let's start with typewriters."— Frank Lloyd Wright (1867

– 1959)

The recent surge in subsidy publishing has filled the field with the good, the bad, and the downright ugly, offering neither guidance nor quality control. The uninformed author is like a lamb, alone in the wild among the wolves.

According to Bowker's Books in Print, almost 300,000 titles were self or subsidy published in 2008—in just a single year! This was a whopping 132% increase over 2007, which had triple-digit growth over 2006. In 2009 that more than tripled with over a million self and subsidy titles published. Even in the poor economy of 2010, it increased almost threefold with a whopping 2,776,260 titles assigned ISBN's. These luckless writers had no comprehensive guide to help them make an informed decision.

YOU DO.

We have researched and written *Published! The Complete Guide to Nontraditional Publishing* to save you time, energy, and most importantly—money. *To Self or Subsidy Publish—That Is the Question* is a comprehensive guide that lays out all the major options available to you

We provide unpublished authors with the tools they'll need to make the best choice for their book and to help it grow to its full potential. We push aside the clouds of advertising confusion and allow you to see the facts about subsidy publishers without imparting our judgment or opinion.

Our first step is to clear up the confusion between all the names used by subsidy publishers. Commercial publishers, subsidy publishers, vanity/subsidy publishers, self-publishing—what's the difference?

A **commercial or trade publisher** (often called a traditional publisher) purchases the right to publish a manuscript (usually along with other rights, known as subsidiary rights). Most pay an advance on expected royalties. Commercial publishers are highly selective, publishing only a tiny fraction of the manuscripts submitted. They handle every aspect of publication—from editing, cover, even the title, as well as distribution and marketing. There are no costs to the author, although in recent years commercial publishers have left their midlist and lower-tiered authors to handle most of the promotion and marketing costs.

A **vanity or subsidy publisher** charges a fee to produce a book. There are many models for vanity/subsidy publishing. Some companies do little more than produce a print run and ship it to the author. Other companies provide an a la carte menu including design, editing, distribution, and marketing services in addition to the book production. Vanity/subsidy publishers may or may not be selective. A few specialize and will only accept nonfiction, inspirational, or Christian-based books. They will not turn down a book simply because it is poorly written. And this is the primary reason that subsidy publishing carries a stigma. Some will make a claim on authors' rights. Marketing and distribution, if provided, are usually limited to their own webpage. The burden of promoting and selling falls solely on the author. Costs for vanity/subsidy publishing can rise into the five-figure range, with some companies charging over twenty grand. In these cases it is virtually impossible to recoup your costs, let alone make a profit.

A few fee-based publishers will attempt to convince you that they are NOT a vanity publisher. Their spiel hinges on convincing the writer they are far more respectable. They may claim they are a "joint venture," "co-op," "partner," or "equity" publisher in order to suggest they're contributing their own resources to the relationship. Don't be taken in. Fee-based publishing is fee-based publishing, and whatever you're paying, it covers 100% of the cost and their profit. Period. If you are willing to pay for their services and have a reasonable idea of your book's potential for profit or loss, they might provide exactly what you desire.

Self-publishing service providers fall somewhere between vanity/subsidy publishing and true self-publishing. Unlike vanity publishers, they don't present themselves as publishers. Writers are offered packages that usually include limited distribution (wholesale only). Because most self-pub services are digitally based, the upfront expense can be low—but most promote costly extras such as marketing options AND take a hefty percentage of the gross sales.

True **self-publishing**, like vanity publishing, requires the author to bear the entire cost of publishing, distribution, and marketing. However, rather than pay for a pre-set package of services, the author chooses the services desired. Because each step can be separated in self-publishing, the writer can decide how much to spend on editing, cover design, distribution, printing, and marketing. Done correctly, it is far more cost effective than vanity publishing and can result in a superior publication. Most importantly, all rights and all profits remain with the author.

When Is Vanity or Subsidy Publication the Right Choice?

And, yes, it can be the right choice for the right project. For projects where the number of books required is small, and marketing and profit aren't a concern, an honest, straightforward vanity or subsidy publisher can be a reasonable alternative. If you are planning to sell your books directly through a website or via speaking engagements, a POD (Print On Demand) publisher may be exactly what you need. For writers with niche nonfiction projects, where they're able to reach their audiences directly—say a church cookbook, or a family genealogy— yet they don't want to take the time and effort to self-publish, it is a viable option. If you have been turned down by all avenues of traditional publishers and refuse to change a word of your book, and you have no wish to struggle through learning how to publish your book, subsidy publishing will be your best choice.

If you're hoping to start a career as a writer, however, or if you actually want people you don't know to buy and read your book, vanity/subsidy publishing will probably cause you disappointment and heartbreak. Neither bookstores nor libraries will buy POD books. Subsidy publishing can cost an enormous amount of money. Some authors mortgaged their homes to finance publishing. Don't make that mistake. In order to ensure their profit, vanity publishers charge far more than the actual production cost of a book. They are trying to support not only themselves, but all the people they hire. It's very difficult for authors to recoup their investment, since vanity/subsidy publishers rarely offer meaningful distribution or marketing. They have no economic incentive to do so—their principal source of income isn't the sale of books to the public, but rather the sale of services to authors, and they have little desire to cut into that. Most writers who vanity/subsidy or self-publish lose money. And for writers who wish to start a career, subsidy publishing can be the kiss of death. There is a stigma attached to vanity/subsidy publishing. While it has lessened slightly in recent years due to the growth of self-publishing services and the wild success of a few authors, it still exists. You will have trouble getting any legitimate reviewers to look at a POD book, and most bookstores will not order it, even if you're a local author (especially if your publisher doesn't offer standard discounts, doesn't accept returns, or has shoddy production standards). As for building a writing resume…agents, editors, publishers, and reviewers generally do not consider vanity-published books as professional writing credits.

Another important point to consider: while honest vanity publishers who fulfill contractual promises exist, there are also many that engage in a wide range of unethical or fraudulent practices, including misrepresenting themselves as commercial publishers, grossly overcharging for their services, reneging on contract obligations, producing shoddy books, failing to print the number of books contracted for, providing kickbacks to agents who refer manuscripts…the list goes on.

The Wolf in Sheep's Clothing

As writers become more aware of the pitfalls of vanity/subsidy publishing, many less-than-honest, pay-to-publish operations are trying to dodge the vanity label by omitting to mention their fees on their websites or other public materials, or by shifting their charges to areas other than printing and binding. I often hear from writers who are confused because they've been offered a contract by a publisher that describes itself as "traditional," "independent," or "small press" but wants its authors to make some sort of financial commitment to be published. During the past two years of our research, this problem has grown. Many sites that previously listed their fees, now advise they can no longer do so unless you first send them the manuscript. This is in order to set you up for the hard sell. Once they have your information, the barrage of calls offering you a special deal if you sign up RIGHT NOW begins.

If asked, some publishers vehemently deny that they are subsidy publishers. After all, they claim, they don't accept everyone who submits! They don't require money for publishing—just to finance the necessary editing. Often they require a commitment to pre-selling a certain number of books. But whether you're laying down cash for book production, finished books, or adjunct services, the bottom line is the same: You are paying to see your book in print. A publisher that turns its authors into customers has little incentive to get books into the hands of readers.

True self-publishing—where the author him/herself handles every aspect of publication, from editing to cover art to interior design to printing and binding—is a more reputable alternative to vanity/subsidy publishing. You have far greater control over the process (which can result in a superior product), and you retain full ownership of your rights. Authors can function as their own distributors (although it is very difficult and time-consuming), offering standard discounts and returnability to bookstores, which may entice stores to stock a self-published book. (Literary agents and commercial publishers often become interested in self-published books that sell a large number of copies. It has happened more frequently in the last two years as more books are e-published and purchased by thousands of the author's fans.)

Self-publishing is not a breeze. It takes work. You have to change hats. You become a business person and must handle all aspects of publishing, distributing, and promoting your book, a process that eats up not just time but money and requires a huge amount of energy, creativity, and determination.

Self-publishing works best for nonfiction. With self-publishing, you, the publisher, knows who the readers are and how to reach them with marketing. A book about dogs would do well at dog shows, in pet magazines, and even at veterinarians' offices. A book about sailing the world would sell at yacht clubs, boating magazines, and travel agencies. Even some fiction, if it has a specific audience, can be sold this way. A book about the "Haunting of Don Caesar" would sell well in St. Petersburg gift shops. H. Terrell Griffin sold thousands of his mystery "Longboat Blues" in gift shops and hotels along Longboat Key. The chef at Euphemia Hayes sells his cookbook right out of his five-star restaurant and has recouped his investment, made a small profit, and best of all reaped immense publicity for his restaurant. Public speakers can provide a book to each attendee, include the cost in the ticket, and increase their sales number with every ticket sold at every seminar. The book improves the speaker's persona as an expert in his field, and each book is another sale.

General fiction, memoirs, and autobiographies do not fare as well in self-publishing. That is not to say that there aren't a few success stories, but they are few and far between, representing only a tiny fraction of all self-published authors. Your odds of success with a self-published novel are much steeper than with a commercially published novel. Or… at least they were.

We won't make false promises, but the explosion of ePublishing over the last two years has changed the landscape of publishing. Forever. We watched and wondered how an unknown author could possibly come to the notice of a fan base without the promotion and marketing of the big traditional publishing houses. But the truth is, except for a very select few, traditional publishers spend only a minute amount of time or money on midlist and lower-level authors. They withhold their marketing dollars for their top ten writers. Their other writers must hire PR people, advertising, and marketing. Recently, a number of ePublished authors marketed well, making waves and coming to the notice of the masses.

Often this is done through Amazon and the way they categorize the books. If you are considering ePublishing, study the chapters dealing with this new phenomenon. Even if you aren't considering ePublishing, read the chapters on Amazon and their marketing method.

Given the prevalence and relative inexpensiveness of self-publishing services, there's little reason to hire a subsidy publisher—especially one that misrepresents itself. If however, you don't want to be bothered and don't want to devote the energy and tenacity to publish it yourself, be careful. Heed the red flags. Choose wisely, Kemosabe.

We start our guide with definitions for some of the jargon found in the publishing world. We'll explain some of the high-pressure sales tactics that are full of nothing but hot air, and advise you of warning flags—what you should avoid. We will show the necessary calculations so each author can determine the total cost per book and the quantity they will need to sell if they want to break even.

Chapter One: Learning the Lingo

The glossary of terms listed here is the foundation of the industry. They are utilized throughout the book. These are listed in no particular order of importance.

POD: Print on Demand has revolutionized the self-publishing industry. A publisher no longer needs to order 5000 books. The electronically formatted book is sent to the printer of choice and kept on file until the book is ordered. Then the printer prints the book out and ships it to the buyer. There is no more need for storage fees, shipping to the author/publisher and then again to the buyer. It saves money. It saves space. And it saves trees.

ISBN: An **I**nternational **S**tandard **B**ook **N**umber is just that: standard. It enables a bookstore to locate your book. If you wrote your book for family and close friends without any intention of trying to sell it to others, you won't need one. A few of the ePublishers also do not require one, but if you want global distribution, or to appear on Amazon, it's required. All online, POD, and subsidy publishers need the ISBN in order to track sales of your book. Most bookstores will not accept a book without one.

ISSN: An **I**nternational **S**tandard **S**erial **N**umber is similar but set for serial literature in an ongoing episodic story. After the number for the first part of the serial is granted, the rest of the numbers are granted for no extra charge.

Bar Code: Most of us have encountered and know the purpose of a barcode. It is not a necessity if you want the book for your own gratification to provide to friends and family, but it is required to sell your book in stores. Also know as a UPC, a barcode is an optical machine-readable representation of data. It is necessary for ordering, inventory control, and in our electronic age, many computer systems interact sales and inventory programs.

LCCN: An LCCN (Library of Congress Control Number) is a unique identifier assigned to your book by the Library of Congress that is used for cataloging purposes throughout the library systems. While related to the numbers you see in the nonfiction sections of your local library, it is different as it covers all registered books, fiction and nonfiction. These are the basis behind the LCCN. Registering with the Library of Congress is free to publishers and should be included in any subsidy packages. However, if you self-publish you are ineligible for a CIP (Cataloging In Publication). You may be eligible for a PCN (Preassigned Control Number). You may apply for the PCN at http://pcn.loc.gov/ This is not to be confused with an ISBN or a copyright registration. It

Books in Print: Touted as the largest independent book database, Bowker's *Books in Print* provides information to the publishing industry in the United States. They are also the official U.S. agency responsible for assigning the ISBN. They list nearly all books currently available in English. Registering your book with Bowker is an important step if you self-publish. This is done for free at www.bowkerlink.com.

Color: Usually refers to 4-color. Covers printed in 4-color look like the books you see in the stores. Unless you are aiming for a dark, dreary "feel" to your book, we highly recommend your cover be in color. The best covers draw the reader to pick it up.

Embossing: Since tactile contact is important to many people, embossing is a nice feature to add a certain professionalism to your work. Embossing entails raising portions of the cover picture for a 3-dimensional look and feel.

Binder Printing: Most companies include this feature, even on hardcovers. Printing the name on the binder of a book allows them to be stacked on a bookshelf and still be identified. Most bookstores display books binder out, making this a necessity.

Bindings: There are several different kinds of binding.

1) Case binding or adhesive binding (sometimes called perfect binding) is most common for paperbacks.

2) Punch binding and machine binding (also called spiral binding) is used infrequently and not accepted in most bookstores except by special arrangement. These are used generally for pamphlets, children's books, and instructional manuals. They can be very handy in reference books, such as when you display pictures of guitar chords, or recipe cooking instructions, or any instance where it is practical for the book to lay flat as it is used.

3) Finally, stitching or saddle stitching is the most common method for hardbacks.

Some companies may offer other unique methods. Approach these with caution, since bookstores tend to be quite fussy about the bindings they accept. It's always good to check.

Printed Price: The downside to placing the selling price on the cover of the book is that you can't change it when you sell it at different venues, although you can discount it. The big chain bookstores require a printed cover price and a UPC bar code. If your book hasn't sold in a year, the bookstores will return it to the distributor and it ends up in a discounter's warehouse at a drastically lowered price.

Small-Run/Medium-Run/Large-Run Presses: Presses are the companies who print quantities of your book when you supply them with a pre-formatted disc set up for printing. These printers are utilized by self-publishers and book brokers. A short-run press deals with quantities as small as 25 copies and you pay a set price per book. For a lower price per book, a medium- run press will usually start a print run at 100-book minimums. A larger run press tends to charge considerably less per book but requires runs beginning at 1000 or more.

Offset Printing: Offset printing is a commonly used printing technique in which the inked image is transferred (or "offset") from a plate to a rubber blanket, then to the printing surface. Printers "set" the book.

Book Broker: An individual or company that does some or most of the legwork involved in self-publishing.

They may do editing, arrange a custom cover, format for printing, and/or locate a printing company.

Editing: There are a number of different types of editing.

1) **Content editing:** Focuses on general accuracy and continuity. Usually done in conjuncture with style editing. However—subsidy publishers rarely provide content editing.

2) **Style editing:** Style editing checks for style issues, such as showing rather than telling, passive verbs rather than active, point-of-view issues, and syntax.

3) **Copy/Line editing:** Can go by either name. Copy editing checks spelling, capitalization, punctuation, grammar, sentence structure, subject/verb agreement, consistent verb tense, and word usage. A good copy editor will catch your use of a wrong word as well as many grammatical problems that software programs will miss. Copy editing is the type most subsidy publishers provide. Generally a clerical worker runs it through a software program that suggests changes.

4) **Manuscript Evaluation:** This should be your first step after self-editing. A good professional editor can read the manuscript or even a portion of the manuscript and advise you of style

problems, point-of-view problems, and overall issues of tension, characterization, plot, and timing.

5) **Ghost Writing:** Many good editors will ghost write, but be advised, this is expensive. Ghost writers charge anywhere from three thousand to fifteen thousand dollars, and occasionally even more. They need to be paid for their time and experience and will not do it as a percentage of book sales. They are best used for nonfiction where a book is required to help present a platform and has built in-sales, or for a celebrity tell-all.

We will discuss editing in detail in Chapter Seven.

Q. How many editors does it take to screw in a light bulb?
A. Only one, but first they have to rewire the entire building.

Q. How many managing editors does it take?
A. You were supposed to have changed that light bulb last week!

Q. How many art directors does it take?
A. Does it HAVE to be a light bulb?

Q. How many copyeditors does it take?
A. The last time this question was asked, it involved art directors.
   Is the difference intentional? Should one of the other instances
   be changed? It seems inconsistent.

Q. How many proofreaders does it take?
A. Proofreaders aren't supposed to change light bulbs.
   They should just query them.

Q. How many writers does it take?
A. But why do we have to change it?

Q. How many publishers does it take?
A. Three. One to screw it in and two to hold down the editor.

Cover Design: Okay, you write. But can you draw? Design? Most writers need a little assistance in this department. You may have a basic idea of what you want on the cover, or maybe you know dxexactly what you want, but don't have the ability to design it well. If you want something special, contact a graphic designer in your area, or visit the nearest art school. Many of the subsidy presses have people on hand to assist in designing a cover, but most companies we contacted use templates. If you want a custom cover they charge extra. You will probably be happier if you work with a local artist and get exactly what you envisioned for your masterpiece.

"Anyone who says you can't judge a book by its cover has never met the buyer from Barnes & Noble."
                    --Terri Lonier, *Working Solo*

Illustrations: If you plan to sell your illustrated book to a traditional publisher, they usually insist on using their own artists. Unless you're writing a children's book, this feature is unnecessary and very expensive. If you are self-publishing or subsidy-publishing children's books, if you can't draw, you'll need to find an illustrator. Don't scrimp, a great illustrator will reward you in the long run. You can look for an artist locally at area art schools, maybe even contact high school art teachers and ask if they have any students who might be interested. Some of the subsidy publishers have a stable of artists and illustrators you can contract for an extra fee. You go through their portfolios looking for a style you feel goes with your story and then work back and forth online.

Endorsements: Endorsements come in many forms, some serious, a few humorous, or even negative. An endorsement is simply someone saying they found your book fascinating and couldn't put it down. It usually helps if the person providing it is someone of note, maybe a well-known author, a major newspaper editor, a celebrity, a political figure, or an expert in your field. A note from your mom won't cut it (unless your mom is Sarah Palin or Meryl Streep).

Copyright: Copyright registration is not necessary unless you fear your work will be stolen or plagiarized. In most cases, theft is not a serious problem when submitting a manuscript to an agent or publisher. If it makes you feel more comfortable, it will not hurt the sale of your book. However, do NOT apply for one if you are still attempting to contract with a traditional publisher. It interferes with their copyright when they publish and implies that you don't trust them. And while you may be the suspicious type, please consider—why would anyone steal the work of an unknown author? If it's that good, they'd rather buy it. Besides, in this age of electronics, it really is extremely easy to prove original authorship when necessary. If you are self or subsidy-publishing, a copyright is easy and inexpensive to procure. To register a work, submit a completed application form, a nonrefundable filing fee, which is $35 if you register online (or $65 if you register using Form CO); and a nonreturnable copy or copies of the work to be registered at http://www.copyright.gov/eco. Be aware that as of July 2, 2012 the Copyright Registration office will no longer accept printed hardcopy CO forms.

The 1976 Copyright Act generally gives the owner of copyright the exclusive right to do and to authorize others to do the following:
- reproduce the work in copies or Phonorecords prepare derivative works based upon the work
- distribute copies or phonorecords of the work to the public by sale or other transfer of ownership, or by rental, lease, or lending
- perform the work publicly, in the case of literary, musical, dramatic, and choreographic works, pantomimes, and motion pictures and other audiovisual works
- display the work publicly, in the case of literary, musical, dramatic, and choreographic works, pantomimes, and pictorial, graphic, or sculptural works, including the individual images of a motion picture or other audiovisual work
- perform the work publicly (in the case of sound recordings*) by means of digital audio transmission

Copyrights are not eternal. As a general rule, for works created after January 1, 1978, copyright protection lasts for the life of the author plus an additional 70 years. For an anonymous work, a pseudonymous work, or a work made for hire, the copyright endures for a term of 95 years from the year of its first publication or a term of 120 years from the year of its creation, whichever expires first.

Sales Results: One of the important factors to look at when choosing a subsidy publishing company are their sales results. Obviously you want a company that gets the books sold. Remember, don't be fooled into thinking that a higher up-front cost means more book sales. In some cases you may find the more money you pay up front, the less incentive they have to sell your books. After all, they already made their money.

Formatting: All printers and most publishers have strict requirements for formatting (often PDF). Before you can submit you have to set your manuscript up in the manner they require. This usually includes page numbers, margins, white space, and file format. Many subsidy companies and self-publishing services offer to do this for you at an additional cost or incorporate the cost into their package fee.

Distribution: Most products have a distributor between the producer and the retail outlet. And they usually charge big bucks. In publishing, distributors have an amazing network across the country, supplying bookstores, small and large, with the newest releases. They stock books, deliver them, pick up the unsold copies, bill and collect the money. It's important to note that even if you are with one of the large distributors (Ingram or Baker & Taylor), it doesn't mean your book will get on the shelves at the big bookstores. Their shelf space is limited and valuable. The distributors send the bookstores a catalog and the stores select the books they wish to carry. Only books believed to be top sellers get the premium space. For more information on distributors, please see Chapter Nine.

Niche Marketing: When your book is about specific information such as a pet or a sport, you can aim the majority of your advertising at that market. Other people who enjoy the same music or drive the same car will read the appropriate publications, hang out in the same kinds of places, and have similar hobbies. Advertising your book to them affords you the best opportunity to sell your work to the largest group of people in the shortest amount of time.

Online Registration: At the time of this printing, we found that most of the subsidy publishers register their new books with Amazon.com and several other online venues. If you self-publish, the traffic visiting the site makes it imperative to have your book registered with Amazon. Your own website will garnish the highest profit per book, but most purchasers go to Amazon.   If you are self or subsidy published, it is expensive to be listed on Amazon. Amazon charges a whopping 55% of the "cover" price for print books. Your profit goes way up if you ePublish, an incentive Amazon offers, as they virtually monopolize the ePublishing market. In many cases you must ship your book to Amazon unless you have a POD arrangement with a subsidy publisher. After you subtract shipping and printing costs from your 45%, there isn't much net profit left. Subsidy publishers pay the same 55% distribution fee, so when your book sells on Amazon, your royalty payment is decreased accordingly. With the addition of CreateSpace there is now an alternative dropping your fee to a mere 30%. We discuss this option in detail in Chapter Thirteen. Amazon.com is one of the largest internet destinations, with tens of millions of customers world-wide. There is no bigger community of book-hungry customers anywhere in the world. Amazon also has the ability to proactively put titles in front of the most qualified and receptive potential buyers. They have software that recognizes their customers' preferences and offers them similar books, whether it's a top selling book or the most obscure title, self, subsidy or traditionally published. On Amazon everyone is equal.

To register with Amazon you must have an ISBN and a barcode. Then list your book with Amazon Advantage at http://advantage.amazon.com/gp/vendor/public/join-advantage-books. The cost is $29.95 annually.

Royalties: Many people have misconceptions about this term. Royalties are NOT your net profit. Royalties are the percentage of sales a publishing company pays you when someone purchases your book. Most subsidy companies have their own online stores in addition to selling through Amazon and Barnes & Noble. When a book is purchased through their site you do not need to pay the 55% distributors fee and should earn a higher royalty. What they pay you is called a "royalty." Most companies calculate their fees differently, which is how so many manage to tout "highest royalties paid in the business." Traditional publishers pay very low royalties (generally 2.5% to 15%) because they take on the entire financial risk of printing and distributing. Therefore, they reap the largest rewards. Subsidy companies offer royalties anywhere from 20% to 100%. Yet statistics can be deceiving. There are many ways they manipulate the costs, and it is spelled out in their contracts. Are they paying royalty on the gross or net? When it is net, you must compare what costs are deducted. Printing costs can be and often are inflated, and distribution and shipping costs may be deducted as well. For a clear understanding of what you will actually receive you should read Mark Levine's, *The Fine Print of Self-Publishing*. If you are self-publishing, all your earnings after paying for your printing, shipping, distribution, and marketing costs are your net profit.

Timeline: The length of time it takes to get your book in your hands differs drastically between traditional, subsidy, and self publishing. With traditional publishers, it is generally from eighteen months to two years from the signing of the contract until the release of the book. With subsidy publishers it can be a week to two months, occasionally longer. While this feature may be of less importance when you subsidy or self publish, you should be aware of it when you need to order books for a show or a signing. You need to order far enough in advance to receive your copies, so understand your printer's or publisher's standard timeline.

Book Pricing: The cover price of your book is set by the subsidy publisher. If they tell you they allow authors to choose a price, they refer to ABOVE their preset minimum price. Always attempt to price your book according to the market and other similar books. We have seen one self-published book with photographs selling for $65.00. To date (over two years), none have sold in the local book store they occupy.

Author Purchases: Many companies have a specialized price guide for author purchases. Calculate how many books you will need for yourself. If you want your book reviewed, you need copies (usually reviewers prefer hardback). When you schedule signings and seminars, you need copies. If you rent a booth at the local book fair or flea market, you need copies. If you plan to order a large number of your books, be aware of author purchase costs BEFORE you sign the contract. In fact, if you need a large quantity of books, we advise you to use self-publishing services or self-publish.

Warranties: These are guarantees the author gives the publisher within the contract. This part is usually written in complicated legal language. However, the author should not be frightened. This refers to your right to publish the materials you've sent. This is how it breaks down. *Author is the sole proprietor of the work*—which means you now own it. If you co-wrote, both authors must sign. *Author owns all rights to the work*—this expands the first concept, promising that no one else can ever make claim to the work. This is particularly important if someone is suing you for copyright infringement and the case is ongoing. *The work is original and has not been previously published.* You can publish with a different company, even if you've published the same work before. BUT, it's necessary to inform the new publisher. In some cases a contract bars you from republishing with another publisher without paying a penalty. *For work not in public domain*—This clause refers to any work that still has copyrights, and it claims you've procured permission to use it. Obviously, if the copyright has expired and the work has become public domain, no permission is needed. *No part of the work, including the title, contains any matter which is defamatory, unlawful, or which in any way infringes, invades, or violates any right, including privacy, copyright, trademark, or trade secret of any person*—Long-winded, but necessary. Put simply, you can't falsely accuse your neighbor of robbing the grocery store last year. You can't instruct people how to blow up government buildings. You can't use Frodo as a character. You can't print the

Colonel's secret recipe, although you can say someone ate at KFC. And sorry, but you can't print your girlfriend's diary. *The publication doesn't breach any oral or written agreement the author has made with anyone else*—This one is obvious. If another company has claimed the rights to your work, you're stuck with their contract agreement. *The warranties are in full effect on the date of publication*— Simply, to the best of your knowledge, on the date signed, all the above is true. *All warranties survive the term of the agreement*—If someone comes back years later to sue because of something in your book, even after the agreement with the publisher has expired, you are still liable for whatever legal action is taken to uphold the warranties you've made.

Indemnification: There are usually three clauses of indemnity to any contract. They state that the author accepts all responsibility for any legal action against the work. Also, the publisher can extend the benefit of the author's statements to any party affected by a breach. This means, if you sell your book through a bookstore and someone tries to sue that bookstore for defamation of character, the suit falls back to the author. Lastly, the author incurs all legal fees, including fees to protect the publisher, against any libel action brought to them for the author's breach of any warranty.

Releases: The author may be required to obtain a release from any real business used in the book, even if the author was unaware of it at the time of writing. In other words, if you create a fictitious gas station and it turns out to be a real place with the same name, the owner of the business could demand to be removed from the story. Advanced permission from these businesses is usually best.

Author Likeness: The publisher will also require a written release from the author for the publisher to use the author's name and picture in the sale, promotion, and advertising of the novel.

Rights and Contracts: The most complicated part of the process. In the warnings section, we mention confusing contracts. These should simply be avoided. Some of the common contract pitfalls are listed in the rest of the definitions. But whenever possible, have a professional evaluate the contract for all its subtleties. Again, we suggest Mark Levine's *The Fine Print of Self Publishing* for detailed information on how to avoid these slippery slopes.

Imprint: When a publishing company "sets up" your book in their computers and printers, they have to set pages, font, margins, page numbers, extra page information (table of contents, bibliography, etc.), front and back cover art and text, and much more. This is called making an imprint, and that's what you are paying their fee for. Sometimes, according to contract, this expires. It simply means that after a defined amount of time, they delete your book from their computer and files and you have to start over again, often paying the entire fee once again. If you are fortunate, the price hasn't gone up since you paid the first time.

Ownership: If your book is a family memoir or genealogy, it's unlikely to become a bestseller and Hollywood won't be knocking on your door. There's no need to worry about retaining your rights. But if you have higher aspirations for your tome, and hope to publish elsewhere, attract a movie production company, or even cut a deal with a traditional publisher, you need to retain ALL your rights or have them revert to you in minimal time (six months or less). If the publisher owns the rights, you will not be allowed to make ANY changes or use excerpts for anthologies or collections. You won't even be able to quote yourself. One publisher keeps your rights for seven years with an option for seven more if THEY choose. Another subsidy contracts for the life of the copyright, which is a very, very long time. ePublishing has brought another consideration to the table. Do not give away your ePublishing rights. This is an entirely new area of contention between authors and publishers. A few of the traditionals have realized the money involved in out of print books being available in eBook format. There is money in this field. Big money. Please see the chapter on ePublishing for more information in this lucrative field.

Subsequent Publications: Some subsidy publishers demand that if you write another book, you must use them again for your next book. Many authors, thinking the company believes they are wonderful and about to become a great success, fall for this ruse. What happens if you aren't happy with their services? Even worse—what if a traditional publisher takes notice and wants to sign you up. You have committed to pay the subsidy instead. The company will not allow you out of the contract without another payment. Ouch!

No Escape: Many publishing houses do not offer an opportunity to be released from their contract under any circumstance or for any reason. If you get a great offer from somewhere else, and you can't get out of the contract, you can only hope the new offer remains until you get your rights back. These are legal contracts you are signing. Be sure to read them carefully and understand what you are signing. Don't let the excitement of seeing your book published blind you to the reality of the binding agreement. If any point is unclear or unacceptable, do not sign the contract. There are other subsidies that will provide you with the features you require.

Length of Copyright: NEVER enter into a contract where the publisher retains the rights to your work for the length of the copyright. This may sound reasonable. But a copyright is good for the life of the author plus 70 years. That's not a misprint. The rest of your life plus seventy years after you die. That means even your kids cannot regain the rights to your work! If authors stop utilizing companies with nasty clauses like this, the companies might eventually concede and stop using them.

Parties of Contract: You will be referred to as "Author." The publisher is called "Publisher" or "Company," rarely by its name. And your manuscript will be referred to as the "Work." This is common, as most contracts are standard forms with fill-in-the-blank spots. This is not a reason to be concerned.

Termination: Some publishers have their contracts written so they retain rights even after the contract is terminated. This shouldn't be confused with the publisher's right to sell off any remaining stock.

Automatic Renewal: Beware of contractual elements that automatically renew without your consent. These are occasionally attached to the marketing extras purchased after publication. An internet sweep sending out mass emails and notices to blogs and social networks can cost you a thousand dollars and up. Six months later, they may do it again and send the bill to you because you failed to notice the automatic renewal clause. This can also apply to retaining your rights. A few companies may advise that you have to opt out of renewal of the contract in writing at a specific time or it renews without consent.

Further Clauses: There should be a clause stating that if the publishing company goes out of business, claims bankruptcy, or in any way becomes something other than a publishing company that can carry out the terms of the contract, then all rights and materials shall return to the author. Also, there should be a clause that if the contract is terminated by either party, all rights and materials return to the author. That means if you paid for a custom cover and then terminate the contract, you should be provided your cover imprint. You paid for it. And the clause where you keep the rights to your work should include the rights to all derivatives of said work. In this way, no one else can write a sequel or an offshoot, produce a movie, or market any after-publication products based on your original work.

Remember, if you find the contract different from what you expected, incomplete, or confusing in any way, do NOT sign it!

eBook: A book in digital form read on an
          eReader, tablet, computer, or phone.
ePub: A format that can be read on many
          eReaders, including Nook, iPad, and

Sony. It does NOT work with KDP.

DTP: Digital Text Platform allows authors to self publish eBooks on Amazon.

eReader: Any device which allows you to read eBooks.

Tree-Book: Any book published on paper, made from trees. They are headed for extinction.

PDF: Portable Document Format created originally by Adobe. It was officially released as an open standard on July 1, 2008, Basically it is a software fixed layout form that has blanks that can be filled in by the person accessing the form. PDF is now the de facto standard for printable documents on the web (a standard web document).

Part Two:
The Championship Match

Three Publishing Choices an Author Faces:

Many writers complete their book before realizing how difficult it is to break into publishing. When their book is finished, they begin the process of contacting agents and publishers only to find themselves sinking deeper into depression with each subsequent rejection. They start reading the writers magazines, joining writers groups, and attending conferences. Some decide to stick it out and continue trudging the path, waiting to break through. Others turn to self-publishing, and still more turn to those wonderful advertisements in the writer's magazines shrilling "Get published now" or "Publish traditionally!"

All three options are valid choices, but you need to understand who they are and which path best suits your needs.

ePublishing is the newest challenger. It is a component that every writer needs to be aware of and decide how it fits into their own path to publication. ePublishing rights are a new bone of contention with traditional publishers; subsidies are including it in their offerings; and it can go hand in hand with self-publishing or be the sole route to a completed publication.

Chapter Two: Trade/Traditional Publishers—The Champion

We have listed the large traditional houses and their imprints. For a complete list of the traditional publishers, small and large, you should check the most recent edition of *Writer's Market*. The large houses are much more difficult for a new author to breach. Medium-sized publishers are those who publish more than six titles a year and include most university presses. Small publishers publish six or less titles a year and often don't have the marketing resources to distribute nationally, but may be a great place for a regionally directed book.

These publishers offer authors the brass ring. Most of us aspire to be read by others, to share our work with the multitudes of people out there who will enjoy what we have to say. Sadly, only a small fraction of us will ever pass into the golden circle. Even worse, those that do are often disappointed because they never go higher than midlist and need to retain their day jobs in order to survive. However, if we don't at least attempt to breach the walls of the mighty titans, we never know if we could have been the exception, the stand out, the next Nora Roberts, James Patterson, or Stephen King.

Large Publishing Houses:
(Also known as Commercial or Traditional Publishers)

Hachette Book Group USA
www.hachettebookgroupusa.com

Center Street

FaithWords

Little, Brown and Company
Back Bay Books

Grand Central Publishing
Business Plus
5-Spot
Forever
Springboard Press
Twelve
Vision
Wellness Central

Hachette Book Group Digital Media
Hachette Audio

Little, Brown Books for Young Readers
LB Kids
Poppy

Orbit

Yen press

Harlequin Enterprises
www.eharlequin.com

Harlequin
Harlequin American Romance
Harlequin Bianca
Harlequin Blaze
Harlequin Deseo
Harlequin Everlasting Love
Harlequin Historical
Harlequin Intrigue
Harlequin Jazmin
Harlequin Julia
Harlequin Medical Romance
Harlequin NASCAR
Harlequin NEXT
Harlequin Presents
Harlequin Romance
Harlequin Superromance

HQN Books

Luna

Mira

Kimani Press
Kimani Press Arabesque
Kimani Press Kimani Romance
Kimani Press Kimani TRU
Kimani Press New Spirit
Kimani Press Sepia

Red Dress Ink

Silhouette
Silhouette Desire
Silhouette Nocturne
Silhouette Romantic Suspense
Silhouette Special Edition

SPICE
SPICE Books
SPICE Briefs

Steeple Hill
Steeple Hill Café
Steeple Hill Love Inspired
Steeple Hill Love Inspired
  Historical
Steeple Hill Love Inspired
  Suspense
Steeple Hill Women's Fiction

Worldwide Library
Rogue Angel
Worldwide Mystery

HarperCollins
www.harpercollins.com

HarperCollins Australia
Angus & Robertson
Collins
Fourth Estate
Harper Perennial
HarperCollins
Harper Sports
Voyager

HarperColllins Canada
Collins Canada
HarperCollinsPublishers
HarperPerennial Canada
HarperTrophy Canada
Phyllis Bruce Books

HarperCollins Children's Books Group
Amistad
Bowen Press
Eos
Greenwillow Books
HarperCollins Children's Audio
HarperCollins Children's Books
HarperFestival
HarperEntertainment
HarperTeen
HarperTrophy
Joanna Cotler Books
Julie Andrews Collection
Katherine Tegen Books
Laura Geringer Books
Rayo

HarperCollins General Books Group
Amistad
Avon
Avon A
Avon Inspire
Avon Red
Caedmon
Collins
Collins Design
Ecco
Eos
Harper Mass Market
Harper Paperbacks
Harper Perennial
Harper Perennial Modern
HarperAudio
HarperCollins
HarperCollins e-Books
HarperEntertainment
HarperLuxe
HarperOne
Morrow Cookbooks
Rayo
William Morrow

HarperCollins India

HarperCollins New Zealand

HarperCollins UK

Zondervan
Vida
Zonderkidz
Zondervan

Macmillan US

http://us.macmillan.com

Bedford, Freeman & Worth Publishing Group
Bedford/St. Martin's
Hayden-McNeil
Pulgrave Macmillan
W.H. Freeman
Worth publishers

Farrar, Straus & Giroux
Books for Young Readers
Faber & Faber, Inc.
Hill & Wang (division)
North Point Press

Felwel & Friends
First Second
Henry Holt
Books for Young Readers
Christy Ottariano Books
Metropolitan Books
Owl Books

Times Books

Macmillan Audio

Picador

Priddy Books

Roaring Book Press

Square Fish

St. Martin's Press
Griffin Books
Let's Go
Minotaur
St. Martin's Paperbacks
St. Martin's Press
Thomas Dunne Books
Truman Talley Books

Tom Doherty Associates
Forge
Tor Books

Penguin Group (USA), Inc.

www.penguingroup.com

Penguin Adult Division
Ace
Alpha
Avery
Berkley
Dutton
Gotham
HPBooks
Hudson Street Press
Jeremy P. Tarcher
Jove
NAL
Penguin
Penguin Press
Perigree
Plume
Portfolio
Putnam
Riverhead
Sentinel
Viking

Young Readers Division
Dial
Dutton
Firebird
Frederick Warne
Grosset & Dunlap
Philomel
Price Stern Sloan
Puffin Books
Putnam
Razonbill
Speak
Viking

Random House, Inc.
www.randomhouse.com

Bantam Dell Publishing Group
Bantam Hardcover
Bantam Mass Market
Bantam Trade Paperback
Delacorte Press Hardcover
Dell Mass Market Paperback
Delta Trade Paperback
The Dial Press Hardcover
The Dial Press Trade Paperback
Spectra

Crown Publishing Group
Clarkson Potter
Crown
Crown Forum
Harmony
Potter Craft
Potter Style
Shaye Arehart Books
Three Rivers press

Doubleday Broadway
Broadway Books
Currency
Doubleday
Doubleday Image
Doubleday Religious Publishing
Harlem Moon
Main Street Books
Morgan Road Books
Spiegel & Grau
Nan A. Talese

Knopf Publishing Group
Alfred A. Knopf
Anchor Books
Schocken Books
Vintage Books

Random House Publishing Group
Ballantine Books
Del Rey
Del Rey/Lucas Books
Fawcett
IVY
The Modern Library
One World
Random House Trade Group
Random House Trade Paperbacks
Reader's Circle
Striveer's Row Books
Villard Books
Wellspring

Random House Audio Publishing Group
Listening Library
Random House Audio
Random House Audio Assets
Random House Audio Dimensions
Random House Audio Price-less
Random House Audio Roads
Random House Audio Voices

Random House Children's Books
Bantam Delacorte -
  - Dell Books for Young Readers
Knopf/Crown Books for Young Readers
Wendy Lamb Book
Random House Books for Young Readers

Spiegel & Grau
Schwartz & Waote Books

Random House Direct, Inc.
Bon Apétit
Gourmet Books
Pillsbury

Random House Information Group
Fodor's Travel Publications
Living Language
Prima Games
Princeton Review
Random House Español
Random House puzzles & Games
Random House Reference publishing

Random House International
Areté
McClelland & stewart Ltd.
Plaza & Janés
Random House Australia
Random house Canada Ltd.
Random House Mondadori
Random House South Africa
Random House South America
Random House United Kingdom
Transworld UK
Verlagsgruppe Random House

Random House Large Print

Random House Value Publishing

Waterbrook Press
Fisherman Bible Study Guides
Shaw Books
Waterbrook Press

Simon & Schuster
www.simonsays.com

Simon & Schuster Adult Publishing
Atria Books
  -Washington Square Press
Free Press
Howard Books
Pocket Books
Scribner
Simon & Schuster
Strebor
The Touchstone & Fireside Group

Simon & Schuster Audio
Pimsleur
Simon & Schuster Audioworks
Sound Ideas

Simon & Schuster Children's Publishing
Aladdin Paperbacks
Atheneum Books for Young Readers
Libros para Niños
Little Simon
Little Simon Inspirations
Margaret K. McElderry Books
Simon & Schuster Books for Young Readers
Simon Pulse
Simon Scribbles
Simon Spotlight
Simon Spotlight Entertainment

Simon & Schuster International
Simon & Schuster Australia
Simon & Schuster Canada

Chapter Three: Self-Publishing—The Contender

The most important definition in this guide is "Self-Publishing." Self-Publishing is the process where, just as the name implies, you do it ALL yourself. For a new author it may seem like a gargantuan task, but there are many books and resources available to guide you through the steps. Step one if you are determined to do it all yourself is to purchase the ISBN number and register it in YOUR name or that of your personal publishing company.

The best reason to self-publish?—YOU have the most control. No one can tell you to change your title, your cover, your price, your spelling, or your ideas. It's all yours, good or bad. A reflection of your vision.

Another reason to self-publish is financial. Both traditional and subsidy publishing pay you royalties, and they are ultimately a minimal percentage of the gross. If your book has the possibility of selling over 500 copies, self-publishing is probably your best choice to make a profit. If you have written a novel and do not know more than fifty people who will purchase your book, this is probably not the best path to take. The average subsidy or self-published book sells less than 200 copies. Consider ePublishing.

In this chapter we'll discuss the nuts and bolts of getting it done. You decide if you are up to the task and if this is the path you wish to pursue.

The work load may seem monumental. Don't be frightened. Most people manage to muddle through it with a little effort. Becoming a self-publisher does not mean you'll have any obligation to deal with anyone else's manuscripts. We've known several authors who self-published, including Terry Griffin, who simply will not touch anyone else's work, though they own a publishing company and have published several titles of their own under their imprint.

In most states, starting a self-publishing company requires a business license. This may be as simple as registering the business name and paying a small fee, often less than a hundred dollars. No insurance, no specialized licensing, no formal education is required. You will need to decide whether to be a sole proprietorship, partnership, or limited liability corporation.

Once you've become a company, what's next? You might want to celebrate, dance in the streets, and play loud music, but now comes the *real* work. Imagine (or research) what a publishing company does behind the scenes.

First you need to edit. If you want a quality product, hire a professional editor. (See our chapter on editing.) Next you decide on a title and cover design.

When you have this information and have decided which company to use for the printing, it is time for formatting. The website of your printer should advise you as to which format they accept. Some accept PDF. Many accept doc. Some have their own programs to download and use. Be sure to check prices, especially shipping costs, which can be exorbitant. Find a printer who will provide the quantity you desire at a cost you can afford. Check a few printers before you commit. And don't hesitate to ask for samples of their work. Any printer worth their name should be proud of their work. There are a few non-web printers listed in Part Three as offset printers. Generally, short, medium, and large-run offset printers will charge you considerably less than your local printer.

You may have to purchase or download software that formats your manuscript to the printer's requirements. If you lack computer savvy, many printers will perform this function for you at an additional cost. However, the manuscript must be electronically digitalized. If you have a handwritten or typewritten paper copy, a printer will not accept it. You will need to hire a typist to enter it into a computer. You can usually find typists locally, possibly on Craigslist, or in the classified section of a writer's magazine.

Unlike P.O.D., offset printers will only print quantities of your book. Most offer discounts for larger runs. Don't buy more than you believe you can sell, or they will be sitting around in your garage. Sales are not guaranteed. (See chapter on marketing.) Do your cost calculations. Just as you would with any business plan, determine the size of your market. Determine your break-even point before you order. If Company A will sell you 5000 books at $1.41 each and Company B will sell you 1000 for $3.45 each you still need to enter other factors into the equation. Say you decide to sell your books for $8.00 each.

	Company A (5000)	Company B (1000)
Printing	$ 7029.00	$3450.00
Shipping to you	2100.00	500.00
Storage yearly	1200.00	N/A
Editing	1000.00	1000.00
Marketing	1000.00	1000.00
Total	$12,329.00 ÷ 5000	$5950.00 ÷ 1000
Cost is	$2.47 per book	$5.95 per book
Profit per book	$5.53	$2.05

With Company A you will make $40,000 minus your cost of $12,329.00, IF you sell all of your books. Your profitability will not start until after you have sold 1542 books. With Company B you will need to sell 744 books before you reach profitability. To reach this calculation, you take your total cost and divide by the book cover price. Round upward and you have the quantity of books you must sell before you are making a profit. Research the market and determine how many sales you can realistically make. Remember, the average self-published book sells fewer than 200 copies.

Okay, you're sure of your success. You pay the printer, borrow someone's truck, and bring home all the boxes of books you've just paid for. Now you can't park your car in the garage any longer, your wife is upset at the mess, the neighbors are whispering behind your back, and the kids complain because they can't reach their bicycles anymore. What do you do now? The first thing we recommend is that you buy a pair of quality earplugs and forge ahead.

Marketing can be the most daunting part of the "publication" process. We've devoted a chapter to selling your book. Remember, it's all up to you.

As a self-publisher, you should associate with other publishers. Many publicity companies will only speak with publishers. As a self-publisher, you qualify. National book reviewers are familiar with most of the subsidy/vanity publishers and generally refuse to review any book published by them or interview the author. But local reviewers will often consider a new self-published author. Publisher's Weekly has been making some changes in the past year, reviewing books that make "best-seller" status on Amazon or Barnes & Noble regardless of the publisher.

The entire task is in your hands. You can get radio interviews for free, the social networks are free, and press releases are free. But you have to do all the legwork. Just remember, in most cases, even the marketing plans of traditionals and subsidies leave it up to the author to initiate and execute.

If you want more in-depth information on starting your own self-publishing firm, we suggest you read Dan Poynter's *Self-Publishing Manual.*

Self-publishing is not a choice for the timid or the lazy. But if you're up to the challenge, this path can be very rewarding.

Longboat Blues Isn't Blue Anymore.
An interview with a successful self-publisher,
Terrell Griffin

H. Terrell Griffin finished his first book, *Longboat Blues*, and began sending queries to agents all over the country. Time passed. He became disgusted with one rejection after another and considered the subsidy publishing world.

His first choice cost him a couple thousand dollars, and they did exactly what they said they would. After a short time, Mr. Griffin realized it didn't amount to very much and it wasn't what he had envisioned for his book. "They did what they promised, but it was a bunch of crap." He has sold less than 300 copies through the subsidy publisher to this day.

He altered course and chose to self-publish instead. Luckily, (he is a lawyer, after all) he had retained all the rights to his book. In the truest sense of the term, Mr. Griffin formed his own publishing company and, with a little help designing his cover, published his book under his own imprint. He has sold over 5000 copies and is on his fourth edition.

He copied his success with his second novel in the Matt Royal series, *Murder Key,* and it fared well. His third, *Blood Island*, was contracted by a traditional small press, which has signed him for a three-book deal. His fourth thriller in the series is *Wyatt's Revenge.* He hopes his new publisher will reprint his previous novels when the series takes off.

Mr. Griffin sees the publishing world slowly moving forward toward electronics but retaining a certain "old-world" charm by continuing to print books the old-fashioned way for the elder generations. While what lies ahead may be more efficient and "green," real books still offer a certain smell, and there's a sense of pride in displaying your own personal library.

His advice to new and upcoming authors: Always write and rewrite. It's never going to get done if you don't sit yourself down in the chair and put your fingers on the keys. You have to start if you ever want to see the finish.

Interview with a Self-publisher, Chinese Style

One of the Village Voices best-selling local books is a cookbook-autobiography written by Chef Ray Arpke, the owner of the only five-star restaurant in the Sarasota-Manatee area. The book blends his early beginnings and classic signature recipes in an anecdote-filled autobiography highlighting his background that defines the word 'unique', with credits to mentors and masters, from the large institutional kitchens where he learned the basics to Sarasota's superlative Cafe L'Europe.

Because the book is full of high-quality photographs, I asked how he kept the price so reasonable. Chef Ray advised that after a bit of research, he discovered that a Chinese printer could complete the book at one third the cost of local printers and publishers.

After writing the book and choosing the recipes, Chef Ray decided he was better at creating culinary masterpieces than becoming a publisher, so he enlisted the help of Jeff Litzler, a graphic designer and computer whiz who was recommended by a neighbor.

Jeff advised that during his preliminary research for a printer, a friend recommended he try overseas, starting with China. His research quickly led him to a Chinese publisher with a branch office in San Diego, California. The contact spoke excellent English, and the company behaved professionally and quickly, fulfilling all promises. He was extremely impressed with their service.

He never reached the point of checking costs of Canadian or other international printers because he knew after all his research that the Chinese firm was an excellent bargain.

The entire printing process, including the photo-shoot, took less than three months from inception to the cookbook's timely delivery.

The firm does not handle print on demand. They are an offset printer. They set the book, sent a proof copy, and when it was approved, they created 5000 copies of *You Don't Have To Be Crazy, But It Helps.*

An ISBN number was required, and Jeff handled all the details during the entire process. Even with shipping, the 190-page, color-photographed book cost less than 50% of the cost of using local publishers. The total was nearly $50,000. This included the cost of the photo-shoot, Jeff's services, the printing, shipping, and marketing. Having sold over 4000 copies to date, Chef Ray has recouped his investment and made a profit. But by far his biggest payoff has been the publicity and renown the book has brought him. Would he do it again? "Absolutely."

Jeff Litzler is also willing to do it again. If you have a book that requires color photographs or pictures, and would like to get a quote on your project, you may contact Jeff Litzler at: JeffL@pulp2data.com. Prices will be based on your project: how many pages your manuscript is, how many pages in color, do you already have them or does he have to arrange the photo-shoot, how many hours must he invest in the process, and the printers current charges and shipping costs. Chef Ray endorsed Jeff's work and highly recommends him as a book broker experienced in dealing with foreign printers.

Chapter Four: Subsidy Publishing—Vanity Be Thy Name

Subsidy publishing appeals to the writer's desire to become a published author, and the vanity publishers make their money from fees for the services rendered rather than from book sales. This is an option many authors are turning to, and with good reason. With the explosion of subsidy publishing in recent years, there have been a number of breakout successes. Still—the vast majority of subsidy-published authors will never recoup their investment.

Subsidy publishers today produce quality finished products—complete with all the legal requirements—for a fraction of what it cost in past decades due to the advent of print-on-demand. The per-book unit cost remains the same whether one book is printed or one thousand books are printed.

A writer can find a company to fit almost any specific need. Price ranges are just as varied. Subsidy publishing manages the nuts and bolts of publishing your book. When they finish, your book is a complete work—ready to sell. All you have to do is market it. (See the chapter on marketing.)

The subsidy publishing option is for those who have given up on landing a contract with a traditional publisher because they are unknown, their topic is obscure, controversial, of interest only to a small select group, or they have been repeatedly rejected. In addition, the option may be preferable if the author desires complete artistic control and wants nothing altered, or for the author who cannot or will not perform the publishing work for himself.

> "Many books require no thought from those who read them, and for a very simple reason. They made no such demand upon those who wrote them
> —Charles Caleb Colton (1780 – 1832)

Perhaps you don't have the time to research your publishing options or to commit to the process, or maybe you're afraid you'll encounter legal headaches. Maybe you'd simply prefer to focus all your energies on your marketing campaign. However, we want you to be aware that the cost of subsidy publishing will likely exceed the expectations you have for sales. If your preliminary calculations suggest sales of less than 500 books, choosing a low-cost POD subsidy is your best option if you aren't going to self-publish. In any case, subsidy publishing is one of the fastest growing industries in the United States and hasn't been negatively affected by the struggling economy. In fact, overall unemployment appears to have swelled their business.

Many authors are turning to subsidies more frequently, often without even attempting the traditional route. And with the growing number of success stories from people who have followed this path, the field thrives.

To get started you have to ask yourself what you really want and how much money you have available to spend. Nothing is free! Let's get over that lie right away.

This is going to cost you money. Our mission is to provide you with all the options and let you choose which is best for YOU.

Feel free to contact the subsidies found in this guide, and compare their features and costs for yourself. Always remember—unethical people inhabit all kinds of business, and a few bad companies should not ruin it for the reputable subsidies. When you send your manuscript to a subsidy publisher, expect to receive a response advising you of how magnificent your writing is: Incomparable! Wonderful! The next Great American Novel! Pulitzer Prize material!

No offense, but quality control is missing in most subsidy publishing companies. It is not the purpose of this book, nor do the authors make any suggestions as to which companies are of good quality or have used underhanded tactics.

In many cases the horror stories we've heard were due to poor matches. An author who hoped to move on to a traditional publisher after his book sold enough copies, signed on with a subsidy publisher who kept his rights for years. Another author signed on with a company that charged an exorbitant retail price for the book without offering an author discount, and he needed books to sell at seminars and book signings.

Some companies are more than adequate for an author who is publishing a copy of their family genealogy and wants fewer than 100 copies. If that is your goal, we suggest you spend as little as possible getting your book published, even if it entails a higher cover price. Figure out the total cost of different options and chose the one that is lowest for you.

Obviously if you aspire to sell a few thousand copies or more, you need to consider the importance of a lower cover price which may require you to pay more up front. The subsidy publishing companies are a business and must cover their expenses AND make a profit—from you. They are providing a service and lending you their expertise. Once they make it up front, they may be less likely to spend anything on the actual sales of your book. Any non-required marketing would cut into their overall profit.

Please consider all your options and personal circumstances carefully before placing yourself into financial hardship. And remember—never, ever sign a contract you do not understand or are not completely satisfied with. One author has subsidy-published five titles over the last eight years at a cost of nearly $5,000.00. To date he has sold just over one hundred copies at $16. per book—a net loss of $3,400.00.

Another important subject to consider when you examine a contract from a subsidy publisher is the use of a pseudonym. If you plan to use one, make sure the contract allows your royalties to be paid to your legal name. Establishing a fictitious name for payment can become a legal quandary. Using a pseudonym for writing, however, is completely legitimate and quite common. When you self-publish, you set up the company that receives the money. If you have doubts, ask the subsidy for clarity.

We are going to delve into marketing in greater depth in Chapter Eight, but a quick mention is appropriate here. Someone once said, "Even bad publicity is publicity." We've all heard stories about controversial books becoming best-sellers. But one thing to beware of is how subsidy publishers do their marketing.

The best way to describe this is to note how packages work. A subsidy publisher may offer to set you up on all the social networks like FaceBook and Twitter. They usually charge a nominal fee like $50.00. But you can do these things yourself for free. They may also offer to send your name to radio stations to help generate interviews. You can do this as well.

Publishing companies often combine the freebies into a package, charging you exorbitant fees for minor marketing that sounds like a deal. Ask for a breakdown of the costs of different package components.

It is important to note that none of the publishers we spoke to have a publicist working on staff. They had email lists and a connection to some people in radio, but little more. And some of these marketing packages cost thousands of dollars. Buyer beware! Read the chapter on marketing and do your own research—no matter which option you chose.

We interviewed the owner of a local subsidy publishing house as well as one of her pleased clients. Not everyone is willing to take the self publishing route.

Peppertree Press

Interview with an author, Barb Alpert

While Peppertree Publishing began small, they've grown quickly. One extremely happy customer, Barb, had this to say when asked if she had any negative experiences.

"I felt Julie Ann might be getting too busy to offer the personal assistance she once did. Perhaps she could hire on more associates to assist fledgling authors so we don't feel so much like a number."

When Barb first stepped into the mire of publishing, she gave herself a year, sending queries the traditional way, contacting one agent after another. With the big publishers completely out of reach, she chose to use a subsidy publisher. The first one she tried only printed plain black letters on white paper, like a regular novel.

But Barb had a children's book in her hands. She needed lots of pictures in lots of colors to appeal to her younger audience. She withdrew from that subsidy company and stumbled across the Peppertree Press. They not only offered what she needed; they offered a gentle hand to show the way. Barb instantly became a huge fan.

The first thing Peppertree did was hand Barb a packet with all the information she needed to get started and be prepared. Barb found the packet complete and informative. But when the Peppertree Press suggested Barb change the title of her book, you could hear a pin drop.

However, in the end, the sensible reasons and gentle suggestion for a new title won Barb over, and the book now has a more child-friendly title. She said she'd use Peppertree again for her future projects without hesitation. The company responded to her calls and emails quickly and in a friendly manner.

As for other writers looking for a publishing outlet, Barb highly recommends Peppertree. Before you get that far, she has one other piece of advice to give. "If you write and you think you're ready, bring your piece to a writers' critique group where many voices and points of view can see your material and help you make it the best it can be.

"If you can't pass the test of a room full of like-minded writers, how will you ever stand against hundreds of readers (or more)? How can you be accepted by even one scrutinizing, hard-nosed critic from a major magazine or newspaper?"

Peppertree Press

Interview with publisher Julie Howell

We recently had the opportunity to speak directly with the owner of a subsidy press and hear her point of view. While each one may be different and the answers that follow can hardly be considered "the norm," I believe this interview offers writers a unique perspective from the other side of the business.

Julie Ann Howell from the Peppertree Press sat down with us in an informal business atmosphere that immediately put us at ease. We made her aware of our project and she was more than happy to help. Like us, she wants the truth to be known so writers can make informed decisions.

Julie Ann refers to the Peppertree Press as a 'stepping stone' for writers. In her opinion, the world of publishing is changing. As traditional publishers become more exclusive, writers are turning to the subsidy publishers rather than give up all hope of ever seeing their completed work in print. By publishing with a subsidy first, a writer can work at marketing and sometimes catapult themselves into enough fame for the big houses to take notice.

"This is no easy task," Julie Ann says with emphasis. "You can't come in here with two-thousand dollars and expect to get a spot on Oprah. What you can expect is a finished book and some direction on what to do next. From then on, it's up to the author."

As you've seen throughout this book, it's about money, time, and connections. If you've got them or can get them, you can sell your book. If you don't, even people who might be very interested in your work will never hear about it.

When a manuscript is sent to Peppertree Press, Julie reads the first thirty pages or so and makes an evaluation. If it needs work, she tells you what you need. Generally, they need editing. But as you may remember from the interview with Barb, it can be as simple as a title change. In fact, with a writer creating the entire work, almost anything can be unappealing enough for Julie Ann to offer suggestions. After all, a writer can hardly be expected to draw.

However, a writer is also not expected to know about the inner workings of the publishing world and that's why some companies take advantage. For example, Julie Ann tells us that a Library of Congress Registration number is free and yet some companies charge a substantial fee for it—several hundred dollars, in some cases.

Julie Ann prefers honesty and integrity. She will tell you everything you need to know up front. And she'll answer your questions appropriately. Let's look at this from a straightforward perspective.

A book costs money to print and promote. Everyone working for the publishing company wants to earn a paycheck. How do you expect any company to publish you for free? The traditional publishers put up the money as an investment in your work, which is why they are so picky. And any money they pay may you in advance is taken out of the royalties you earn from book sales. In most cases, a traditionally published author earns less than 10% of the cover price. The other 90% goes to the publisher.

When a subsidy publisher says they're not going to charge a fee, you need to scrutinize how they're getting paid. A percentage of sales is usually not enough, they won't promote you, and they don't know how well you can market. So where do they get their money from?

Julie Ann tells you up front what she charges and what she's giving you in return. In this manner she presented a business plan that made us feel comfortable. If you don't feel comfortable with a publisher, perhaps you should question them further.

Chapter Five: Reality Check— Don't Quit Your Day Job

As mentioned in the last chapter, one author we interviewed is still in the red after eight years of hawking his books. He spends his Saturday mornings sitting at a booth at the farmers market, has his novels on local bookstore shelves, and even on Amazon, all to little avail. He is retired, so it (obviously) isn't his source of income.

If you want your book just to see your name on the cover, or you'd like to have copies to hand out to friends and family on the holidays, then the following information is of little use to you. However, if you'd like to make money, please read on.

You don't have to be a math wizard to know you need to earn back all the money you spend up front before you can claim a profit. So you need to complete your calculations before you mortgage the house and quit your day job.

As we've discussed, different subsidy companies offer vastly different pricing for publishing, printing, and distribution. All these aspects affect your net profit.

Here is a simplified understanding of how to calculate your monies before you head to your local loan shark. In the end, if you don't understand what is offered by a company or it confuses you, BEWARE. Take a step back and reconsider what you're doing before you throw good money away on a shady deal or on a deal that doesn't suit YOUR personal needs.

There is no simple one-formula-fits-all, so we will offer you a few calculations. Use the ones that best fit your choices. Nothing cut-and-dried exists. We are using a sample figure of a 100-page book that we paid Company C $1,000.00 to publish. We have priced our sample book at $10.00 on the cover. Keeping it all in the decimal system helps to simplify the explanation.

You must understand, in most cases even after paying to have your books published, you don't own them. You may be "given" a few with a particular package, but unlike self-publishing, you do not own your books. The publisher owns the books. You will be doled out a "royalty" for each copy sold. Even to acquire any for promotion, you will need to purchase copies of your own book over and above the price you already paid to have them published.

So if company A pays you 50 % royalties on NET sales, you need to know how they arrive at what they mean by net sale. Remember, statistics are easily manipulated. First, they will deduct the price of actual printing. This is usually done through Lightning Source. At the time of printing, Lightning Source charged subsidy printers $.90 per cover and $.015 per page to print, bind, and ship to the customer. Our sample book would cost a subsidy publisher $2.40. They might also legitimately charge a minimal handling fee, up to 5%, which would be around $.50, for a total cost of $2.90. Now, you have already paid them for set-up and cover design, so they should not be padding the printing cost. However, most of them do. This is something you must negotiate BEFORE you sign the contract. If they did no cost manipulation and sold your book from their website, your net price should be $7.10. At 50% royalty, you just earned $3.55. Remember, they are receiving the other 50%, so they are still making a profit.

But wait! It gets complicated. That book sold from the publisher's in-house website and should not have incurred any trade discount. No distribution charges were incurred. However, most books are sold through Amazon and Barnes & Noble or other distributors. These distributors generally charge 55% ($5.50 on our sample book). The handling fee disappears since it is included in the trade discount. Now your net sale stands at a mere $2.10. You just earned a whopping $1.05 plus your 50% royalty. If your subsidy publisher pads his costs and essentially double-charges you on anything, you will make even less. And if your book sells at a brick-and-mortar bookstore, the distributors charge between 45% and 55% as well, so there is no escaping this fee unless you sell the book yourself, and then you usually incur shipping fees or a booth rental cost.

Let me make this simple. To earn back the $1000.00 you originally paid, you must sell 953 books on Amazon before you can start earning a profit. Or 282 books if sold directly from your subsidy publisher's site. In all likelihood it will be a combination of both and your breakeven point lies somewhere in between. Again, a reminder…most titles sell less than 200 copies.

Your basic calculations will be:

1) If sold from the subsidy publishers website:

cover price <u>- subsidy charge per book for printing and admin fees</u>

> = net price
> <u>x royalty %</u>
> = your income per book

2) If sold through a distributor, online or brick-

and-mortar:

> Cover price
> - subsidy charge per book for printing
> <u>- trade discount/distribution percentage</u>
> = net price
> <u>x royalty %</u>
> = your income per book

3) And the last calculation should be to determine how many books you must sell to recoup your initial subsidy payment and leave the red ink behind: Original (total) cost to subsidy publish ÷ your income per book = breakeven point

These formulas will not work when you choose a subsidy publisher who backloads the deal rather than having you pay up front. If you choose to pay little-to-nothing up front and give up a large percentage of the cover price upon each sale and are required to purchase a set number of books at the inflated price, you will probably not recoup your money until much farther into the future. When you calculate the royalty you earn, it is generally so small (less than $.25 per book) that you must sell thousands before you are able to recoup the cost of your required, overpriced purchases. These backload deals are enticing for those who have no funds to pay up front and, for some purposes, are the best choice. If you have a specific number of sales in mind, say fifty advance orders for a $25.00 book, and the publisher requires no other funds, just a guaranteed order of fifty copies—go for it. You have published the book, your audience is glad to have it, and you aren't out any money. Our only caveat with the backload deal is—"don't expect to make money."

Questions to consider asking yourself and the prospective subsidies regarding royalties are:

1) Based on retail cover price or net sales?
2) Are net sales based on actual hard costs or ephemeral handling fees?
3) How much have they padded their costs?
4) What is the royalty percentage? Is it at least 50% or higher.
5) Do they offer an author discount of at least 30%?

Other costs you must consider before you reach your breakeven point are: Editing, Shipping (if you ship out books, you pay for it; if you request a quantity from your subsidy, you pay shipping), Storage costs (if you have any quantities to store, these costs need to be included), Marketing and Promotion, not just advertising, but the cost of a booth at a trade show or convention, the cost of space at the local farmers market, travel costs to go to book signings, book marks and postcards, your website, and any other promotional costs you incur. On the good side, you can write most of these costs off on your taxes. Keep all of your receipts.

Don't forget to consider your market as well as your wallet. Remember, until you're making enough money to live on, don't quit your day job.

"Twenty years from now," said a poor writer who was having trouble with his landlord, "people will come by and look at this house and say, 'Phillips, the famous writer, had a room here.'"

The landlord was unimpressed. "Phillips, I'm telling you that if you don't pay your rent, they'll be saying that the day after tomorrow!"

Chapter Six: Warning! Danger Ahead!

While the intent of this book is not to recommend any publishing house over another, there are warning signs, big red flags, to look for in order to avoid unethical practices. Unless you are aware of the sandbars, you might run aground. We are informing you of as many unscrupulous practices as we can uncover in order to provide you with a map so you can navigate around them or negotiate through them. As quickly as we learn of them, the connivers alter the game enough to tempt others. You may have to read the companies FAQs or possibly even contact someone within the company to verify facts, but at least you'll know what to look for, what questions to ask.

If you sell a large quantity of books (in self and subsidy publishing, generally at least 2000, in some cases over 5000) and have a great book and marketing plan, a traditional publishing house might contact you and make an offer. It is even possible a novel might draw the interest of someone in movies or television. They might offer to "option" the book. (An option is not an offer to produce. Generally it gives a production company a set amount of time to decide IF they want to produce the story. These options for unknown writers usually pay under $2000 and cover a period of a year. If they want to renew the option, they pay again.) If you retain your rights, you will be free to negotiate with them. If your subsidy publisher keeps your rights, even for a limited time, any contact from a production company will be useless to you.

In fact, a subsidy company holding the "rights" to your book could negotiate with an interested party and reap the profit. Be very careful not to sign away your rights to a subsidy company unless you are sure the book will be of no interest to anyone but you.

When you pay your subsidy publisher, they create an imprint of your book. They lay it out in the format necessary for printing. This takes time and effort. A large portion of their fee is for this service. Some companies only keep your imprint on file for a year, a few even less. When the year is up you must pay a fee to re-up, in some cases you have to pay the full amount again to have a new imprint made. A reader who orders the book online is told it is no longer in print. It's important to note here that the amount of time the subsidy publishing company keeps the imprint and the amount of time they keep your rights usually have little to do with each other. You may find that when the imprint runs out, you still cannot simply go elsewhere because the rights have not returned to you. It would behoove you if you work with a subsidy to make sure you deal with a company that keeps the imprint indefinitely. Many do, especially as the electronic versions take very little storage space. This way, if years later you need more printed books, you can contact the company, give them your ISBN, and request as many copies as you need.

Most of the salesmen in subsidy publishing can sell ice to the Eskimos. They have spiels designed to have you signing up before you have time to think about other options. They will charm and flatter you and tell you all about the successes in the business.

Most of it is hot air. When they tell you they only publish a small percentage of the authors submitting to them, it's generally because that is the percentage who were willing to sign up and pay their fee. The others moved on. A couple of the Christian subsidies may turn down anything that isn't clean and family oriented. But none of them will turn you down because you write poorly. So take a deep breath—good or bad, they will accept you and your money. Don't sign with the first subsidy you speak to; contact at least three and compare them. They may word it in different ways, "We refuse X% of the work sent to us because it doesn't meet our standards." They are stroking your ego, suggesting to you that your work is superior because they are accepting it. It also hints that they only publish quality work. They are in the business of making money. They won't do that if they turn people away.

Some of the things you need to watch out for can be quite subtle. Sales pitches often come in the guise of offering you a better deal than another publisher. Be aware of anything that sounds suspicious or toadying.

Then there is the claim, "We pay the highest royalties in the business." You can search and compare the percentages if you like, but they are manipulating statistics. Five different companies say the same thing, so how can they all be true? One might pay the highest royalty on gross, another on net minus true production, and yet another on net minus inflated production. You must consider all their calculations when looking at royalties. Yes, it is important—make sure you understand **their** definition of NET.

Another consideration you must decide on is the pricing of your book. A few subsidies announce that you can price your book. All subsidies set a minimum price, some will allow you to set any price you want above their minimum; others just set the price based on market expectations. If your book is priced too high, it is unlikely anyone will purchase it. If it is priced too low, you will make no money. You must attempt to price it at fair market value. If your book is $16.95 and Grisham's new best seller is $14.99, who do you think most people will select?

Appearance is another type of pitch. They will extol how wonderful their finished books appear, surpassing the other companies. Most of them use Lightning Source, so all their books will be of the same quality. Generally, it is good. We have seen some poor-quality books arrive from Chinese off-set printing firms, but they are contracted by self-publishers.

This type of hard-sell is little better than used-car salesmanship. Our recommendation is "buyer-beware." It is best to clearly define your own needs and goals first, then approach three compatible companies based on those factors.

If you have specific needs—for example, color illustrations, old photographs, or children's pop-ups—and your favorite choice subsidy doesn't handle your needs, you have to keep looking.

Make sure you have a clear understanding of what copies of your book will cost you. Distributors require large discounts (big book stores, online stores), but your subsidy should be able to offer you an author's discount when you order books for events, since the distributor discount is not applicable. Since they are saving the discount, a portion of the savings should be passed on to you. But don't expect a royalty on author-purchased discounted books!

A few subsidy publishers require that their authors buy a minimum bulk quantity of their own books. Fees can range from a few hundred dollars to more than $25,000. This is where they make their profit—from the author. It is a backside arrangement rather than an upfront fee.

Watch for conflicts of interest. These arise where a publisher is associated with an agent, editor, broker, publicist, or any other aspect of publishing that charges you a fee, while the publisher claims to remain "free". Any fee-charging literary agency that directs clients to a subsidy publisher under the guise of having made a "sale"—often without revealing the financial and personnel links between the two businesses—is inappropriate and unethical. Literary agents should NEVER charge a fee.

Editors should be hired independently from your subsidy publisher. See Chapter Seven for a more in-depth explanation.

Contracts that are not author-friendly—that may include rights grabs, taking copyright, restrictive option clauses, substandard royalty provisions (including reverse-accounted royalties), inadequate reversion clauses, draconian "defamation clauses," and a host of other inappropriate and abusive contract terms—are all too common in the subsidy publishing world.

A few subsidy companies have breached their contractual obligations, including nonpayment of royalties, refusal to provide royalty statements, incorrect accounting, publication delays, ARCs (Advance Review Copies) not sent out as promised, failure to ship books or fulfill orders, failure to make author changes in proofs, and failure to respond properly to author queries and communications. Some of these publishers have been the focus of successful litigation and other legal actions by authors. You can check with the Better Business Bureau in the area your company operates. Other places to check on the credentials of your choices are online sites.

Our favorites are:
www.anotherealm.com/prededitors;
www.sfwa.org/beware; and
http://www.absolutewrite.com/forums.

There may be others, but these three sites give you the lowdown on almost every aspect of publishing—who's ethical, who's legit, and who's not.

Beware of advertising that deliberately misleads—including those directly soliciting authors, misrepresenting services to authors in an effort to masquerade as a commercial publisher, hiding the fact that they are vanity operations, and making false claims about distribution and bookstore presence. We have written Chapter Nine on distribution in order to help you understand its importance in selling your book.

At least one subsidy/vanity company, possibly more, claim to be "traditional" publishers. They even offer a nominal "advance." (in most cases $1.00). They attempt to mimic traditional companies by tricking you into signing a two-book contract. Since they charge for many required "other" services and then charge a cover price twice the fair market value, they are NOT traditional. This does not necessarily make them a bad choice for your book; it just makes their sales practices inappropriate for most authors. And, once signed, you may be committed and contracted to writing and **paying** for a second publication, even if you manage to snare the attention of a true traditional. Do your math. Do your research. We have put as much research as possible right here at your fingertips. In the long run you will have a much happier and more rewarding experience in the publishing world.

Chapter Seven: Edit, edet, edite!

Edit: *to collect, prepare, arrange, expunge, or eliminate. – Webster's New Universal Unabridged Dictionary, 2003.* Editing, as opposed to writing, is about polishing and preparing to make a finished product. The necessity to edit is required at all levels, including best-selling authors.

A good editor can help you not only with spelling and grammar but content as well. There's a saying in the industry. You can't self-edit. You know what you meant to write, and when rereading you tend to see what you meant to write, not what is actually on the page. Another problem occurs because you know your character and their back history. Sometimes you'll mention a place or a person you never introduced to the reader. You may use an incorrect name for a character, maybe using the ex's name when the protagonist is speaking to her current beau. Oops. A content editor catches these problems. A software program edit will not. If you do not know an editor you can work with, you should check your local area. Many editors can be found on Craigslist or in the classifieds. Check at your local college, especially if they have any creative writing classes. You can also find editors in the classified sections of the writing magazines. The ones found in the writers' magazines may be top of the line, but they are very expensive and a few impose their voice or writing style to your work.

When you agree to hire the editor, be sure there is a cancellation clause in case you do not like the way they edit. The clause should state they will edit the first 25 pages and get back to you. If it isn't a good match, you pay for 25 pages, no more. As a last resort, most subsidy presses can provide an edit; however, they generally do not staff qualified editors. They tend to perform edits with a simple computer word-processing program (like spell-checker). Quality editing is necessary if you want to sell *quality* work.

> Do you know the difference between God and an editor?
> God doesn't think he's an editor.

Why do you suppose well-known bestselling authors still need editors? Because everyone makes mistakes. We commonly catch a multitude of errors when reading certain best-selling authors. It seems the traditional publishers have been leaving the editing up to the agents, and some of the agents assume their bestsellers don't need editing. The poor quality work slips through. The grammar and spell-checker can't catch it all. You might use the wrong word, but it's still a real word; for example, *with* instead of *will*. This is an obvious mistake and easily missed by the writer. But quality editing goes deeper than that. Examine the following statements.

As the car came to the corner, the pedestrian, seemingly harmless, thrust his hand in the open driver's window and pointed the gun.

And:

Harold came to a stop as the red octagon glared its single command. Always punctual, he knew he'd be late when he saw the arm come through his open window and point a gun in his face.

In the first example you might wonder how the pedestrian could keep up with a moving car. The author, on the other hand, KNEW there was a stop sign. This kind of thing may seem minor, even insignificant, but a few of these incongruities may cause readers to struggle through the story, becoming so confused they eventually toss the book aside without reading any further. When they examine the cover to find out what to avoid in the future, they don't look at the publisher's name. An author can gain a terrible reputation putting out poorly edited work.

As you can see, self-editing will not eliminate all the problems. This does not mean you shouldn't try. In fact, we recommend you set your finished manuscript aside for a few weeks and then read it again as if it were new. In this way you may find errors you previously missed.

It's also a great idea to consider reading some of the material available on self-editing. A number of editing books, or a course at your local college, might also help with the grammar. Our favorite self-editing book, *Write in Style* by Bobbie Christmas, instructs the reader on style editing. The book shows how to use your computer to find style problems and offers solutions to fix them. She also has a book, *Purge Your Prose of Problems*. Her reference manual combines the most important information on creative writing and editing books. It's a must for all serious fiction and nonfiction writers or for anyone who wants to learn how to edit books. You can also sign up for her free newsletter, "Ask the Book Doctor," @ www.zebraeditor.com/newsletter.shtml.

Even after all the self-editing and readings by friends, you still need a final professional edit. All writers need an editor schooled in grammar and style with an eye for detail. Don't use your mother unless she's an English teacher, professional editor, or other similar expert.

While a professional edit may be costly, it is considered the single wisest use of money spent in the publishing journey. If you have not properly edited your work, traditional presses will not publish it, legitimate agents will reject it, and the only positive reviews or endorsements you'll receive will be from friends and relatives.

There are several different types of edits. It's important to know what each accomplishes and how to utilize them.

Your first step after completing your book is to find a **Manuscript Evaluator**. This is the least expensive option. In addition to advising you of possible plot problems or unfinished story lines, the Evaluator will advise you of serious style issues, such as the overuse of passive voice, point-of-view inconsistencies, redundancy, and telling rather than showing. An evaluation is NOT an edit. An evaluation is when a professional reads your manuscript and notes major problems. They do not fix the problems. That is YOUR job.

Content Editing: This focuses on the general accuracy and continuity of the overall story. You certainly don't want someone parking a blue car when they started the trip driving a red van. This type of edit is also useful in finding style issues. The cost generally ranges from three to five cents a word. You should seek content editing before copy/line editing, as this step requires rewrites throughout the manuscript. Editing punctuation, grammar, or spelling at this point will simply be a waste of time and money when you may have to rewrite entire sentences.

Copy/Line Editing: Copy-editing is old-fashioned, basic editing—correcting errors in spelling, grammar, punctuation, and syntax. This shouldn't cost more than a penny a word. Line editing is copy editing with closer scrutiny, checking everything—line by line. This usually costs two to four cents a word. There are editors who will do both together for up to five cents a word, BUT if you need to make serious changes due to content problems, it really should be a two-step process.

We strongly urge you to use an independent editor as any affiliation with your publisher might work against you. Let's be hypothetical for a moment. Say an editor works for the subsidy publisher. They only want your money and don't care about content. This compromises the editor's work. Such an editor will bend over backwards to applaud the customer, and is unlikely to mention legitimate problems in an attempt to avoid hurting the author's feelings by suggesting the manuscript isn't perfect thereby insulting and losing the customer. After all, if the author's nose is bent by editing suggestions, he/she might go somewhere else. If you don't care about the quality of your work and only want to see it in print, a subsidy edit will work. If you have higher hopes for your creation, you need an independent, freelance editor.

As you write, consider the basic staples of writing. Use active voice (not passive), use strong verbs, don't rely on adverbs, and limit your passive verbs. **Show** what's going on, **don't tell** the reader. If you write: *She was beautiful*, the reader knows the author thinks she's beautiful. Instead, you should write a description of how and why she is beautiful: *Her golden hair gently swept her shoulders, and the sapphire earrings accented the sparkle in her eyes—eyes that seemed to smile even when her heart ached*. Now readers can visualize her, making their own determination as to her beauty and character.

Rules of thumb often help as you build your story. For example, many authors, agents and editors consider the word 'was' as well as other forms of the "to be" verbs counterproductive to great writing. A rule of thumb we suggest you attempt to follow is to use these passive verbs no more than double the number of pages in your novel. That means, don't use the word "was" more than twice per page, on average. In some cases this won't be possible, other times, a simple restructuring of a sentence takes it from passive to active.

To help you spot style, grammar, spelling, and content issues, look for a local writer's critique group. They are one of the greatest sources of information on content editing, and most are free or have only small annual fees. If none are available in your local area, you could start one yourself. If that isn't a viable option, there are also online critique groups. Both types of groups can have some serious drawbacks you need to be aware of. A critique group should not just sit and applaud your work, as this does nothing to help you improve. Nor should the group change your words. They might make suggestions of possible word changes and explain why they prefer their own, leaving YOU to decide if it is a better fit. Letting a group or even a solitary writer "improve" your words, erases your "voice." A great critique group is one you are comfortable amongst, offering constructive criticism. All members gain knowledge of the craft and improve together. Take suggestions under advisement, but retain your creative license, changing only when you agree with the suggestions. After all, most of the fellow writers have not yet made the best-seller list themselves. However, there are some groups that become raging successes, such as TARA, the Tampa Area Romance Authors, a chapter of Romance Writers of America. Best-selling authors attend almost every meeting. Their input and advice to fellow members has created one of the most prolific groups of successful authors in the world. When best-sellers offer their advice, it behooves you to listen.

99

It behooves the writer to avoid archaic
expressions.
(I really enjoy using behooves.)
One should not shift from third person to
second person when you write.
Write assertively, I think.
I've told you a million times not to
exaggerate.
Avoid clichés like the plague.
Don't verbify your nouns.
Hyperbole is the worst mistake you can
make.
Be sure to use the correct word accept in
certain cases.
Each pronoun should match their subject.
Don't be repetitively redundant or
repetitious. Avoid rephrasing, which is, in
other words, paraphrasing or rewording of a
statement, sort of like repeating it.

When choosing among two, make the best
choice. Between three or more, pick the
better one.
You will die horribly if you are
overdramatic.
Miami, Florida's 2,561 politicians agree that
all statistics should be verified.
We could care less about expressions that
mean the opposite of what they say.
Vary sentence length. Conformity is boring.
Try to not split infinitives.
I once read that splitting modifiers was
wrong in the library.
Ambiguity is more or less undesirable.

       And last but not least……

It is generally recommended that the use of
the passive be minimized.

Chapter Eight: To Market, to Market

Aggressive marketing is essential for the success of your masterpiece. This statement is true no matter which publishing path you choose: traditional, self-published, or subsidy. Marketing is the work that takes place after the book is written, edited, and published. Russ Marano of "Hi-Tek Newsletter" said, "Being an author is 5% writing and 95% promotion."

We don't want to give you the impression that marketing is hard work, but it is a completely different task from writing. Most authors have little or no experience in marketing. To the novice, learning yet another new task may feel totally overwhelming. After learning how to publish, one is now faced with yet another massive chore. Learning brain surgery might be considered easier. Truthfully, many marketers look at writing a book much the same way. Many hire ghostwriters to write their books because it is a task they do not want to learn.

Marketing is about the money—more precisely, making it. If you are saying, "show me the money," we suggest quickly becoming proficient.

"Writing is the only profession where no one considers you ridiculous if you earn no money."

- Jules Renard (1864 - 1910)

There are a number of online web sites that provide bare-bone outlines for marketing campaigns at low or no cost. Of course, a full education in marketing takes time and money. A number of courses are available online or at your local college for a quick study. Another possibility is culling your friends or even members of your critique group. Some may have experience marketing their work.

Keep in mind, the marketing suggestions here are not a substitute for a marketing education and deep research. Books on marketing and promotion abound, and the subject certainly can't be covered properly in a single chapter, but we'll provide a few ideas.

First, what exactly is marketing? *Webster's New Universal Unabridged Dictionary, 2003*, defines marketing as *the total of activities involved in the transfer of goods from producer or seller to customer or buyer, including advertising, distribution, shipping, storing, and selling.*

Put simply, now that you've finished the tasks of writing and editing, you have to market your book. If readers aren't aware of your book's existence, they won't buy it, no matter how magnificent or poignant it is. You could offer the cure for cancer and sell fewer than a hundred copies without any marketing. If the public doesn't know the cure for cancer is available, how would they know to ask for it, or even where to find it online? As you can see, letting people know your book exists may be one of the most difficult tasks you've ever faced.

Research has shown that the majority of writers tend to be introverts. This personality trait is counterproductive to marketing. Most writers prefer to avoid the limelight. Now, as a marketer, you MUST sell yourself—or at least your book. You have to create a strategy that grabs the general public. The industry term for a great strategy is *marketing platform*.

What is a marketing platform?

The entire concept has morphed into something completely different than it was just a few short years ago. I spoke to an agent in California about this book. He said it looked wonderful and he believed it has a high probability of selling thousands of copies. However, he said, "You don't have a platform. You are not a famous celebrity, you don't have a television show or radio program to promote your book on the airwaves, and I don't represent anyone who is not a well-known person in their field." So he considered fame and being a top expert in a field to be a "platform." I did not have the right credentials, even with a great book that will save readers thousands of dollars.

Over the last year I have seen "marketing platform" described in many ways. Ultimately the best definition is that it is a measure of the scope of your influence. The well-known writer has influence. You need to create a "platform" as a way to reach and influence more people into buying your book. You have to clearly prove your credibility, your expertise, to readers. A substantial platform includes a web presence, seminars and speaking engagements, your established media contacts, and your publications. What makes you the best person to write this book? The stronger your platform, the better your visibility and the better your chances for increased sales. Your goal is to build a platform to reach as many readers as possible.

Now, let's move on to the specifics of marketing your book. None of these methods guarantee results, but they all enhance your chances of success.

Reviews. Most people have read a book review in a newspaper or magazine. We understand that a rave review can reap tremendous sales. Send a copy of your book to the reviewers of your local newspapers and those located anywhere you have set up a signing or are well known. Reviews are free. You will need to send the reviewers a free book and pay for shipping, but you NEVER pay for a review. Cross your fingers and hope the reviewer has time to read your book and likes it enough to issue a positive comment. Every week dozens of books cross their desks. Yours must stand out.

Don't waste your time or money sending your book to national reviewers. Many of the reviewers from larger newspapers like the New York Times will look first at the imprint (the publisher that put the book out). If the book didn't come from a traditional publisher, they won't even bother to look inside. Many claim they simply toss the book in the trash without even opening the cover. Reviewers also expect a hardcover copy of your book. Most packages from subsidy publishers don't include hardbacks, so you will need to special order these yourself.

I do want to mention that over the last two years, national reviewers (most notably, Publisher's Weekly) have begun reviewing books that make the best-seller list at Amazon and Barnes & Noble. This is a positive change for new authors.

Most reviewers are well educated in the English language, the newest trends in writing, and the *Chicago*

Manual of Style. In other words, if you didn't get a professional edit, expect a few derogatory reviews along the path.

Advertisements. Authors sometimes consider taking out an ad in newspapers or magazines. This is costly and gauging the results is difficult. It can be risky; a great expense could net you only one or two sales. Know your market and target your audience. If you've written a children's book, advertise in magazines or newspapers mothers read. An ad in *Sports Illustrated* will cost you a small fortune but few athletes will be interested in "Little Miss Sassy Frass Has New Red Shoes." If you feel you must buy advertising, place the ads where readers interested in your subject are likely to see them.

An expensive advertising technique you might consider, depending on your subject matter, is producing an infomercial for cable television. Many spots are moderately priced and, if you have nonfiction, can be a great marketing tool. It's amazing how many people watch television during the wee hours of the night.

Advertisements are simple. You show your cover, add your back jacket blurb and a few endorsements, and leave a hook. What's a hook? Ask an open-ended question that raises great curiosity. "The bullet holes in the limo that carried JFK came from a different direction. Who *really* killed America's favorite president?"

Hooks create curiosity and people want to know more, so they pick up your book. In fact, if you do it right, they may feel they have to buy a copy in order to discover the answer. Writing that kind of ad copy can be difficult, and you may wish to enlist the aid of a professional copywriter.

Interviews. Radio and television interviews can reach the largest audiences. But first accept this important advice—forget about Oprah. Few writers attain those lofty heights. If you weren't published by a large traditional publisher, your chances are further diminished. Most of us have to be satisfied with local radio and television stations. So how do you contact them?

You can call or walk into their office. Most talk shows are on the lookout for quick spots to fill airtime between the big topics. Again, aim for your audience. You certainly don't want to announce a children book at ten o'clock at night on the all-sports-all-the-time station.

The simplest way to connect with many of the schedulers is through the *Radio and Television Interview Report*. Go to www.rtir.com and check out this magazine/catalogue specifically aimed at the radio and television CEO or scheduling person. These people are responsible for making appointments for interviews. They read the magazine/catalogue and decide who they want to interview, based on their listeners and upcoming daily topics.

If you are listed in the magazine/catalogue, you might get a call from a radio station in another state and they'll interview you over the phone. Before you know it, sales for your book go up and you get a small piece of the notoriety you seek. Interviews should not cost you money. Occasionally promoters will offer to make a video or CD for you to send out to stations. As always, check out all venues before making a decision that costs money. And never assume that anything guarantees sales of your book. Marketing must be aimed specifically and accurately at your audience.

There is also a new kid in town—online radio. Radioearnetwork.com has over 200 talk radio stations, a listening audience of 10 million, and is heard in 142 countries. These stations are often looking for interviews. One show is the *Authors Connection*, a one-hour show interviewing two authors every Thursday.

A local cable station in Sarasota hosts a weekly segment on Blab TV called the Open *Book* dedicated to interviews with local authors. Leave no stone unturned in your quest for publicity.

Book Signings. Setting up a book signing is as easy as talking to the manager of a local bookstore. Every bookstore within traveling distance is a target. If you are planning to travel, for any reason, call ahead to bookstores along your route and at your destination. Some of the managers of the big box stores will say no. Others may place you in an out-of-the-way spot. However, independent bookstores are generally friendlier and welcome events that draw people in. Susan Klaus, author of *The Golden Harpy*, advised she does better signings in the fantasy/sci-fi section than when she placed at the front of the store. Readers of her genre come looking for a fantasy and she has a built-in audience.

Successful book signings are advertised well in advance. Speak to the bookstore manager and ask if they do any advance notification to the newspapers of their upcoming book signings. Work with them. Send out press releases to all the local papers with enough advance time for placement in the paper. A press release is nothing more than a short announcement stating who, what, where, when, and why. Call the local radio stations. Put up posters with the date of the signing in the bookstore where you'll be, as well as anywhere else you are allowed to post. When people know about you and your book, they'll be more likely to show up and ask for an autographed copy.

Niche Marketing. Many of us have a niche. A niche is simply a group of people who have the same interests or goals. If you write a book about a dog, dog lovers are more likely to enjoy it than cat lovers. *Bark* will be a better choice to contact than *Cat Fancy* for obvious reasons.

Occasionally thinking outside of the box will garner you an unexpected market. Terry Griffin, an author we interviewed is self-published. The title of his first book included the name of a local island, Longboat Key. About a month after the release of his book, a local gift shop asked if they could carry the book. And Mr. Griffin discovered niche marketing. The gift shop has sold out, over and over. Tourists and visitors alike are intrigued reading about all the local hangouts, eateries, and clubs. He asked a number of places on the island if they would carry *Longboat Blues*, including restaurants, gift shops, and boutiques. Most allowed him to set up a small display in exchange for a commission. He sold thousands of his novels. His sales figures drew the interest of a small "boutique" traditional publisher. Ocean View Publishing signed him for his third book, and Mr. Griffin and Ocean View just released his sixth book in the Matt Royalty series.

You need to think of unusual ways to reach your niche. For instance, what if you write about skydiving? Would you know where to go? Do skydivers have a magazine? Do they have other similar hobbies, and can you market there as well? What about the airports where they charter their planes? Have your book on display there. Check with charter firms and sky diving operations around the country. Do skydivers wear special gear? How about the extreme sports clubs? Maybe you can expand to sky-boarders, parasailing groups, and even bikers. Try hang-gliding clubs. Ask your skydiving buddies about their other interests. Send a copy of your book to any of the skydiving and extreme sports magazines for a review. Focus on your target audience.

This is your book and you want to sell it. Don't waste your money in areas that don't produce results, consider all your alternatives.

Think outside the box.

Chapter Nine: Distribution —
It Costs WHAT???

What exactly is a distributor? What do they do, and are they really necessary?

Almost all products have an avenue between the producer and the retail outlet where the product is sold. For example, most farmers don't have the time to sell their crop themselves, nor do they have access to the retail consumer. So they send their product to markets—through a distributor. The product may pass through a number of levels before it reaches the end consumer, each level ratcheting up the cost. So it is with books.

Book distributors have established a network all across the country, delivering books to retail outlets. They are responsible for listing your book in their online and printed catalogues where bookstores look to make their purchasing decisions. They list your book, have a telephone order line, store copies for immediate shipment, and ship to retailers and booksellers. They also handle returns.

WHAT!—returns? "Whatchu talking about, Willis?" The system of returns was established in the Great Depression to help keep booksellers in business. It's rather like a huge consignment program. If your book doesn't sell, it is returned. When creating your marketing plan, accept the fact that you WILL have returns. It is the nature of the business. Some will be damaged and unusable. You may sell them on e-bay as used or seconds, thereby softening the loss. Document the loss and apply it against your taxes.

Most subsidy companies have established relationships with the two largest and necessary distributors, Baker & Taylor and Ingram. If you are self-published, go to the Baker & Taylor website: http://www.btol.com and click on suppliers, then supplier information, then books, and last, establish a relationship. Fill out the form and sign up. The only way for a self-publisher to work with Ingram is to sign up through their sister corporation, Lightning Source. This is actually a boon, as Lightning Source, for a minimal fee, can print on demand and ship your books directly to the customer. Most retailers order from Ingram, so if it's not in their catalogue, your book doesn't exist.

There are smaller distributors available to self-publishers as well. Most are regional, so research which one best fits your requirements. They usually demand exclusivity. You may try to contact them to negotiate terms and percentages.

Book Clearing House   Client Distribution

Services (CDS)

Independent Publishers Group (IPG)   Midpoint Trade

Books

National Book Network (NPN)   Publishers Group

West (PGW)

Small Press Distribution

These smaller distributors often supply your book to Ingram and Baker & Taylor but verify before signing. They also charge a higher percentage in order to make some money, as Ingram and Baker & Taylor will still require their full percentage.

Another smaller category of distributors exists at the local level. They are called "jobbers" and deal with local or neighborhood publications. City or county history books, things to do and see, regional cookbooks, and lighthouse or local ghost stories do well when placed with jobbers. They often are affiliated with local libraries. Jobbers take a smaller cut of the MSRP than the small and large distributors. They rarely store any of your books, instead informing you of how many copies are needed, picking them up, and delivering the books to the retail outlet.

Last, but certainly not least, don't forget to sign up with Amazon.com and BarnesandNobel.com. They also take the standard 55% cut, but if you expect to make sales, you need to be available for online orders as well as in the brick-and-mortar stores. Amazon is quickly monopolizing the market in book sales. It is a green choice in more ways than one. Consumers do not need to waste gas going to the bookstore, they can order eBooks rather than tree books, authors earn a higher royalty percentage, and the U.S. Postal Service needs the work.

Chapter Ten: e-Publishing

> The only constant is change, continuing change,
> inevitable change, that is the dominant factor in
> society today. No sensible decision can be made
> any longer without taking into account not only the
> world as it is, but the world as it will be.
> — Isaac Asimov

Times they are a-changing!

Two short years ago, we both considered the traditional publishers the only way to go and recommended that our fiction writers keep hounding the AAR agents until they found a representative. While traditional publishers will remain with us for at least another decade, ePublishing has already decreased their market share and is expected to surge ahead of them in less than three short years. e-Books represent a wonderful cultural shift to the future and an unprecedented opportunity for unpublished authors.

Half of the population lives over 100 miles from a library. Yet eBooks are just a click away. In addition, research indicates the owners of iPads, Kindles, and Nooks purchase on average over three times as many books as tree-book readers.

A Short History:

In 2002 Random House and Harper Collins recognized the coming changes and began to sell digital versions of their books in English.

Over the past decade, most of the traditional publishers have tried to include owning the digital rights in their contract offers. Should you happen to land a contract, don't give away your digital rights beyond the time the book is in print. If you regain the digital rights after the book is out of print, you can think of it as a retirement account. Imagine, ten years and ten books later, your fan base has increased. A new reader discovers you and decides he wants to read your earlier work. The printed copies are no longer available. He downloads the eBook. Will you reap the 70% royalty or will your traditional publisher?

In 2007 Amazon introduced the first Kindle Reader for $399. Just five years ago! In 2010 they dropped the price to $199. and in 2011 they dropped it to a mere $79. Sometimes patience or procrastination pays. In 2011 they introduced the Kindle Fire, a color reader with many additional features.

During this same period Barnes & Noble introduced the Nook, Borders the KOBO, and other electronic firms cranked out a multitude of inexpensive eReaders.

After the unexpected growth of eBooks since 2007, *Publisher's Weekly* recently announced that in 2010 eBooks accounted for 8.5% of all book sales, and by 2015—just three years from now—they forecast eBook sales will total over 50% of the market. Other pundits believe it will be far sooner based on the growth in 2011 alone.

Two thoughts to consider when making your decision

1) Self-publishing, whether digitally or in tree-books, places the control of your book completely in your hands.
2) eBooks never go "out of print."

Decision made! Let's ePublish.

A few words before you ePublish. Do NOT publish crap. Use an editor. If you fail to follow this step, not only will your book suffer, you earn a bad reputation, gather negative reviews, and hurt the entire industry of eBooks. No one is good enough not to need an editor. Go back and read the chapter on editing. Your book should look professional: have a professional cover and correctly formatted pages.

Formatting:

The most difficult aspect of ePublishing on any of the sites is formatting. The sites make it sound easy, but I ran into obstacles on both Lulu and Kindle Direct. I became impatient and frustrated and drew my co-writer into the fray. He quickly realized the steps I'd inadvertently missed and in a matter of minutes fixed them. I am not stupid and have been using Word for years. The problem was that during the actual writing I was not formatting for publishing. The pages we type on are 8 x 11—trade paperbacks are 6 x 9. The need for adjustment won't go away.

Many of the sites offer help with the formatting for an additional fee. If you know someone who can assist you, give them a shot. If you discover the art of formatting leaves you frustrated and befuddled, hire a professional.

Outsourcing the formatting can take anywhere from 24 hours to six weeks depending on your formatter's workload. Prices vary widely as well, ranging from $50. to $500. Proper formatting is one of the largest costs of subsidy publishers. The same holds true for self-publishing.

If you wish to utilize the services of my co-writer, he can be contacted at www.PersonalCovers.webs.com. Putting the job in the hands of a professional…priceless!

Product Description:

No matter which company you choose to ePublish, you must have a product description that is aimed directly to your reading audience. This task is similar to the queries necessary for landing an agent. You need a hook for your first sentence, something that creates a thirst for more information about your book. Next you will need a short, concise interesting description of the plot or theme so your reader knows what to expect, and then you need a couple good reviews you have garnished from a few of your preliminary readers.

Study other book descriptions to pinpoint what works and what doesn't. What draws your attention? Build on the concepts that enhance a reader's desire to continue on.

When you have written your description, rewrite it at least ten times, honing and polishing until it shines. Then ask fellow writers to check it as well.

Author Bio:

You will need an author bio. In tree-books this is generally inside the book or book cover. When ePublishing it is included directly below the product description or a link is included to an author's page, depending on your ePublishing site.

If your book is nonfiction, you should include your professional expertise that qualifies you to write this book. If you have other books—mention them. Not only does it enhance and confirm that you are a professional writer, it also lets the reader know what other work you have published that they may want to read.

For fiction writers, mentioning your other books will produce more sales as your fan base grows.

This section should also include any related websites, Facebook, or other links to you and your book and should be written in third person.

Covers:

eBook covers are equally as important as a tree book cover. A great cover looks like a movie poster, with strong, bright colors. Remember, some readers will be viewing the book on their phones and drab, dark covers don't do well in miniature.

If you are an artist and know exactly what you want on your cover, congratulations. You will save some money. Most writers are not proficient at designing quality covers. Cover designers prices may vary from a couple hundred dollars to over a thousand.

If you have a general idea of what you want, let your chosen designer know. Send them your book description so they have an idea of what type of cover is best for your book. Based on the information you provide, they will send you a few sample covers to consider. Work with them, letting them know what you like and what you don't like and hone it until it meets your expectations. Choosing your own cover is a luxury that traditionally published authors don't have.

Depending on who you chose, how much input you provide, and how much work the designer already has, an original cover design can take from a week to three months to complete.

To find a cover designer, check your local art community, high school or college art classes, online at many writer's sites, or in the back of writing magazines. If you have seen a few covers you really like, ask the author who designed them. Most are willing to promote good cover artists. Our book cover was designed by the co-author, Al Musitano, who has designed a number of covers for authors. Samples can be seen on his website at www.PersonalCovers.webs.com

Should you know what you want, let your chosen designer know. They should offer a few choices for you to choose from, and then you'll fine tune the final copy together.

If in a week, a month, or even a year, you decide you want a different cover…with the magic of ePublishing you can change it.

Pricing:

As you near the finish line of ePublishing, you need to decide on a price for your book. Readers expect to pay less for an eBook. Compare other books in your genre and price your book accordingly. It is better to sell a hundred books at 99 cents ($.70 to you) than ten books at 4.99 ($35.00) for a few reasons. Not only is your overall profit higher, but the more books you sell, the higher your Amazon rating rises, and you may even make the best-seller list in your genre, reaping even more attention and more sales.

Amanda Hocking, the newest and brightest self-publishing legend, priced her young adult paranormal novelettes at 99 cents and her novels at $2.99. In less than a year, she sold over a million books and St. Martins Press offered her a two-million-dollar contract for two more books. Ms. Hocking recommends a strong social networking presence, focusing on reading blogs like goodreads.com, Amazon's kindleboards, and readingblog.com. The use of Twitter, Facebook, and other social sites also increased her sales.

Her readers did not mind paying under three dollars a book, but if they'd been priced at $5.00 or more, we likely would never have heard her name. Price matters!

Another reason for her growing sales is that she writes series. Fiction series sell well in ePublishing if the characters are good and the author develops a fan base.

If after a week or two, you want to alter your price, Voila! You can change it instantly at any of the online bookstores. Change it and see if sales increase. It is all part of the magic of ePublishing.

We were also told by one Kindle author that after a month he'd only sold 15 books. He lowered the price to zero for one day and 2000 readers downloaded. When the price went back up, he sold 200 books. Amazon has a special category for "free" books. It brings them to the notice of thrifty readers and increases your rating. If it is good, the readers will tell others, thereby gaining you sales. If your book is a bore, it won't work. He highly recommends trying this sales tool.

ISBN:

Most eBook publishing sites do not require an ISBN, but we recommend you assign one. An ISBN will differentiate two books with the same title, and while rare it prevents anyone else from claiming your book as theirs. If you publish on Amazon, they will supply you with an ISBN for free if they are listed as the publishing company. We noticed a number of the other eBook sites are now offering this benefit as well.

Just a note to clarify an issue regarding titles. Titles cannot be copyrighted. Many books share the same title.

When you decide on a title, check on Amazon and see how many others are listed. If you look up *Tick Tock*, you will find three authors on the first page alone. Dean Koontz, James Patterson, and J Robert Kennedy have all used the same title. Each has a vastly different ISBN.

Marketing:

A website is necessary. If you have more than one book, each should have its own page and be linked to you as the author. It also helps to have a blog with a link to the book, and the newest marketing tool for your book is YouTube. Film an interview or have a trailer created, link to it from your website, or embed the video right onto your website.

Coming Soon:

With the advent of Kindle Fire and other tablets capable of multimedia uses, art and music may soon be a part of your e-Book.

Children's books are the first to reap the benefits of this step forward. Self-publishing color illustrations were costly until the advent of color eReaders. Even more importantly, children take to e-Books like ducks to water. Three-year-olds happily turn pages and interact on tablets, phones, and readers. These advancements encourage reading among our children.

I recently published a book of Art, Poetry, and Lyrics. The Tower of Babel displays color art and photographs on almost every page. The artist, Karen Klosky, can share her art with fans around the world. She included the lyrics to two songs she has written as well. At this time we were unable to embed the melody onto the appropriate pages, but Amazon has the technology and will soon offer this feature as well. (For an in depth view on publishing through Amazon's Kindle Direct, be sure to read Chapter 12.)

The eruption of e-books has already decimated the subsidy/vanity publishers. During our past two years researching for this book, dozens have gone out of business, leaving only the few who can afford advertisements in the writing magazines to continue. Many others have shifted gear and become book brokers, companies that assist you with all the other facets of preparing your book for publication for a fee.

Traditional publishing is scrambling to work with ePublishing. Over the past year there was a battle between the traditional bookstores and Amazon. Amazon won, Borders was slain, and B&N suffered massive casualties. The traditional publishers started a fight, won a skirmish, but quickly backed down when they realized the long-term futility. If they do not find a way to work with Amazon, they too will be left behind on the path of imagination.

Even though Amazon's CreateSpace and Lulu are POD publishers, we placed them in this section rather than with the other subsidy publishers because we have actually published through them and wanted to provide our personal experience with both companies.

Chapter Eleven: And Then Came Amazon

No matter which side of the battlefield you may be rooting for, Amazon has won. The publishing industry is undergoing a complete upheaval. Over the last five years, the industry has changed more than it has in the last five hundred years.

The speedy shift from traditional publishers to Amazon went far beyond anyone's expectations—possibly even Amazon's.

So where do writers fit into this new world?

Three years ago we both were adamantly against self-publishing or ePublishing for our group members and for ourselves. We worked to improve our skills, sending out query letters, critiquing, and polishing our work in the belief that one of the traditional publishers would recognize our brilliance and open our path to fame and fortune.

We won writing awards, we sold short stories and essays that were published, and yet our books were rejected. Novel after novel, nonfiction after memoir, we were rejected. Conference visits gained us momentary confidence as agents advised us our books sounded great, go ahead and send them. Then we waited. And waited. A few agents told us this book was fabulous but we didn't have a "platform." After explaining that we are both leaders in the local writing communities and have been writing for years, they explained what they considered "platform."

"You aren't famous. You don't have a radio show like Delilah, or fan clubs like Brittany, or a reality show like Paris. You aren't a political celebrity. You aren't Dr. Phil or personal friends with Oprah. Basically, you aren't famous. Not even a little bit. If we sign you, we will have to actually work at marketing."

My reply, "So if I go out and kill my child, or sleep with a teenager, and I'm found 'not guilty,' even if I can't spell and can't write, you will represent me?"

"Absolutely!"

This is the reason so many writers turned to subsidy/vanity publishing and self-publishing over the last few decades. It has become harder and harder to break through to the traditional publishers. Their editors no longer edit, they spend their time working with management to squeeze the last sale out of the celebrity novels. They are selling to the lowest common denominator. They will not accept an unagented manuscript. Editing is now left to authors and agents. Agents don't handle unknown authors. Stalemate.

Seminars, conferences, speaking engagements, we have attended them all. And the successful authors have told us becoming a best-seller is usually a good book plus "sheer dumb luck." "Timing is everything." "Even Dickens or Hemingway would not be published today." "You have to know somebody." New agents occasionally sign a new author, but most newbies are recommended by one of the authors already with the agency.

The advent of ePublishing on Amazon changed everything. If timing is important, than the time is now. The complaint often heard by the defenders of the traditional publishers is "Who will curate the work? The good books will be lost under a mountain of trashy, poorly written books? How will a reader know what is good?"

Amazon has an answer. Technology provided them the edge to level the playing field, to become the gatekeepers, the curators. If you have ever purchased anything from Amazon (you know you have), they record your purchase and the computer files the information into its brain. It offers you choices, "Customers who looked at this item also purchased this item?" or "You purchased a gothic vampire novel and a new author has just published a book in this genre." When an author's book is posted on Amazon (they sell 85% of the e-Book market), the computer sifts through the product description and places notices in the personal files of every customer who has purchased something with many similarities. It does not matter if they are a best-selling author. It doesn't even matter if the book is good. It is something that customer might like. The reader has the opportunity to open the page, read a chapter, read the reviews, and decide if it raises their desire to read more and purchase the book.

Ultimately, the customer now decides if the book is good or trash by choosing to read a few pages. Previously, the job performed by agents and editors. Yes, thousands of poorly written books will be published. But they won't sell well and will disappear into cyberspace. Some good books may even slip into oblivion. But many of the books that have good plots, great characters, and are well written will find a home and an audience. Books that agents and editors have ignored because the writers weren't proven sellers can now be enjoyed. Amazon has given them a chance.

A little history of Amazon impresses most of us. They incorporated in 1995 and sold their first product online. Fifteen years from scratch to becoming the largest worldwide online seller of ....everything. Even if you hate them, you have to acknowledge their innovation and adaptability.

But wait....There's more!

(I love those middle of the night infomercial claims.) Amazon is not a company that rests on its successes. They push forward, exploring new horizons. So, first they sold books, then they provided self-publishing options through CreateSpace, their POD division, and Kindle Direct Publishing, their e-Book division. Now they are actually publishing some authors themselves.

In May 2009 they launched Encore, their flagship for titles that are either out-of-print or self-published books where they feel there is great potential.In May 2010 they launched their next imprint, Crossing. This division publishes books they've translated into English from other languages.

In May 2011 they launched two new imprints, Montlake Romance, for romance novels and Thomas & Mercer for mysteries and suspense.

Speeding up the process now in place, they launched a science fiction/fantasy/horror imprint in October 2011 named 47 North. Two months later, in December

2011, they purchased the entire collection of Marshall Cavendish Children's Books and have named it MCCB.

I'm sure by the time our annual update is released in 2013, Amazon will have more innovations and treats for writers and readers alike.

Chapter Twelve: Kindle Direct Publishing (KDP)

Amazon is the leader now and in the foreseeable future in the e-book market. Eighty percent of eBooks are sold through Amazon and their 70% royalty rate beats all other publishers, bar none.

To ePublish on Amazon you will need to set up an account. Since you purchased this book, there is over an 80 percent chance that you already have one. If you don't, go to: www.amazon.com and register. You will be required to fill in your name, address, and social security number as well as your bank information for your royalty checks. After your account is set up, go to: https://kdp.amazon.com/self-publishing/help?

On the left-hand side of the page there are lists. Under "Prepare Your Book," click on Getting Started. Kindle walks you through the process step by step. Try not to allow your excitement to overwhelm you, causing you to jump ahead and start in the "Publish Your Book" section. Save yourself some headaches and make sure your book is formatted properly for Kindle, your cover is ready, and all the other steps are known before you jump into "Publish Your Book." We know you are in a hurry and have probably heard "Even a caveman could do it in five minutes." Relax. It isn't easy if you haven't done it before. Once you publish the first book, it gets easier. Unless you decide to try a completely new format, but that is a whole different discussion.

First, if you manage to get through the entire process without asking Amazon to format or design a cover, publishing is FREE. You won't have to pay a penny. Even better, when the book is downloaded, you will receive 70% royalties. At this time, Amazon truly can claim the highest royalties paid. After they close out the competition, they may change their tune, but that would open a wedge for other companies to gain market share. Unlike traditional publishers, Amazon seems to understand that without authors, they don't have a product.

AFTER my first KDP publishing project, I discovered a whole world of free videos to watch that cover every aspect of publishing to Kindle Direct. You can find them on www.YouTube.com . Just search for Publish to Kindle and choose a few to watch. You have to love today's technology.

I mentioned previously that we will issue annual updated editions to this guide because of the rapidly changing world of ePublishing. One example of the rapid changes is that KDP now has a video tutorial right on the website. It is only six minutes long, and while it does not really help with the formatting, I'm sure they will soon cover formatting on their video as well.

Watching the YouTube videos, I felt some instructors spoke far too quickly and I fell behind. Yes, I know I can hit Pause, but why not just speak a little slower? I am not going to recommend any one video in particular, as the point of this book is letting YOU choose which path (or in this case which video) is best for you. Check out a couple videos before attempting to publish your first eBook. A few of the videos do an excellent job explaining the formatting process, and a few address creating your cover, and others cover marketing and distribution.

According to the information they supply on formatting, Kindle claims to accept .doc, .docx, .pdf, .epub, .txt, .rtf, .mobi, or .prc. Then they qualify the claim by stating that not all formats export well. This is an understatement. No matter which format you have, save it as an html. Use the html file for your Kindle upload.

The site also suggests you review their "Simplified Guide to Building a Kindle Book." Seriously? I get chills remembering Christmas Eve's assembling a toy or bicycle with instructions written by a Chinese worker with little understanding of English. The Simplified Guide met that expectation. (Sorry, Amazon.) For example: Tables: A new feature in KF8 is tables. After returning to the beginning and scouring the page, I learned that KF8 is short for Kindle Format 8. I still don't have any understanding of the instructions, but since I don't have a table, I ignored this step.

They further advise that if you have bullet points, special fonts, or headers and footers, their format does not transfer them correctly. Another problem? In order to prepare your manuscript for Kindle, NO TAB spacing for your indents. Tabs do not convert to Kindle. I suspect that eventually Amazon will offer a software program especially for writing Amazon eBooks. No formatting necessary when completed.

Uh Oh! Table of Contents. They advise that page numbers don't apply to ebooks since the content is resizable for the reader's comfort. They recommend an active Table of Contents for easy navigation.

No offense but WTF is an active Table of Contents? Sorry. I'm taking one of those deep breaths. In – Out, In – Out. The instructions should be simpler to understand, but they probably had a trusted whiz kid (PC expert) write them. They offer further information through a link. Another deep breath. I click on it. It takes me to …Microsoft Support.

Hmmm. The words appear to be in English. But they do not make sense. I have used Microsoft Word for years and never heard of an "active" Table of Contents. According to the instructions, Word allows you to create a TOC without using styles and by allowing you to make a single word or group of words in a particular body of text and add that information to the TOC. Got that? Me neither. Thanks, Microsoft, for…nothing.

Okay—I give up. Maybe it's time to hire a professional formatter. Luckily, my co-writer is very good at understanding the language of computer techs, so I am giving him the reins on this task. If the Table of Contents in this book works, he is the hero.

A nice feature in the steps is a reminder to add front pages: Title page, Dedications, Forwards, and Prefixes.

Now—you have your book properly formatted for Kindle in html. You have your cover, both front and back in jpeg format, you have written and honed your product description, your reviews, blurbs, your bio, and all front matter and are all ready to go. You have done your research and have settled on a competitive price for your book.

Let's do it!

Sign in to your account. Go to the Bookshelf page of your account and click on "Add a New Title." Then follow the step by step instructions. Most are easy to understand and answer.

Last year Amazon let you place your book in up to five categories, they have now dropped it to two. Choose wisely. This step is extremely important. The right choice will increase your sales, the wrong one will bury your book. I will explain. If you have written a suspense thriller with a female sleuth and choose female detective/ suspense. BZZZZ. You lose. Amazon has "Bestseller Lists" in many of the categories. An unknown author can't compete in this particular category. It is filled all the time with familiar names: Tami Hoag, Catherine Coulter, Patricia Cornwell, Janet Evanovich, JD Robb, Lisa Gardner, Kathy Reichs, Linda Howard, Kay Hooper, Brenda Novak, Tess Gerritsen, Lisa Jackson, or Lisa Scottoline. I apologize to any other FAMOUS best-selling authors in this genre who I inadvertently left out (the list is very long), but my point is, no unknown author, no matter how great her characters are, no matter how tight and suspenseful her plot is, no matter how beautiful her writing, no unknown author can compete in this genre/category. Heck, I suppose there are weeks when even these authors can't hold onto a spot here. The field is full, and it is full with really great writers.

So what is another theme in your book? Brenda Novak usually writes about women in peril due to domestic abuse. Aha! A social issue. Or maybe your protagonist is from the future like Eve Dallas in JD Robb's novels. You could opt for science fiction or fantasy. Go to possible categories your book could fit into and look at the best seller list on Amazon. Choose a category that isn't filled with famous authors in the top ten slots. If you choose wisely, you may make the top ten list, and once you make this list, your sales will increase. Another way to make the list is to market your book BEFORE the release on all your social networks. When you release it, send out notices to one third of your contacts and ask them to buy the book. The next week, ask another third, and in the third week send out the request to the remaining third. This may keep you on the best-seller list for three weeks. Every time a new reader goes to the category, they see your book in the top ten and many will check it out, gaining you new fans and increasing your sales. This method does depend on the size of your....friends list. If you only have fifty friends, best-seller status may not occur.

Now you have chosen your two categories.

Upload your html formatted book and cover, and continue through the steps.

There are some miscellaneous questions to answer that may seem unusual. There is an option regarding DRM, Digital Rights Management. If you chose this option, Amazon will set a code into your eBook. The code is intended to stop "hackers" from stealing your book. Many writers do not have DRM because it will not stop people from stealing your book. Any hacker can break the code in a matter of minutes. As with the music market, the best way to prevent piracy is to price your product affordably.

People will buy a book, a song, or a product if they believe it is fairly priced. You are also offered a choice to make your book available worldwide. Choose the option. In some cases writers find their work does better in other parts of the world than in their own country. You are offered two royalty rates. If you price your book between $2.99 and $9.99, choose the 70% option. Generally the books under $2.99 are novelettes, essays, and short stories. They only receive 30% royalties at this time. However, if you have a series and want to entice fans and establish a readership, you might want to go for the lower percentage on your first book in the series, so price the book for 99 cents and hook your fans. Price all future books in the series at $2.99. The readers understand, and if you have established a character they care about, they will buy each book when it is released.

You are also asked if customers can sample your book. For a new author, you should answer yes. Most readers will not purchase an unknown author's book without checking out a few pages in order to decide if they are interested enough and you write well enough to warrant their expenditure.

There is also an option to place your book in Kindle owners Lending Library. We have not utilized this service, but one of our author services providers, Ron Dryer of Voice Projects, has. Here is what he had to say. "I put my book in their program for three months, and although I didn't make much in royalties, the book was downloaded more than 3,000 times, presumably by readers who wouldn't have seen it otherwise. It's another arrow in the author's quiver."

You are ready to publish. Go ahead, click on the Publish button.

Generally in twelve hours or less your book is available for sale. If you see something you don't like, the magic of ePublishing is that you can change it. If the cover doesn't seem to be working or maybe the price seems too high, you can change it instantly. All you need to do is sign in, go to the Bookshelf page, and scroll through the Action bar.

You can track sales on a daily basis through the Reports section of your Bookshelf. And if you get completely stuck, you can send KDP/Amazon an email detailing your problem. They generally answer you within 24 business hours. I have also heard that joining some of the discussions and chats through the "community" tab can generate interest with people who are interested in your genre. Don't overdo it. After all, you should now be gearing up to market your book and start writing another.

After your book has been purchased, ask everyone you know who has read it (and likes it) to write a review on Amazon. Most buyers read reviews before purchasing a book.

Chapter Thirteen: CreateSpace

CreateSpace, Amazon's POD publishing branch, began operating in 2002 as CustomFlix Labs. They provided inexpensive DVD production. Two years earlier, in 2000, a group of writers formed BookSurge to self-publish at an affordable price, retain content rights, and increase profits. In 2005 Amazon purchased both companies, renamed CustomFlix CreateSpace and merged BookSurge into CreateSpace in 2009.

The only POD publisher at the time providing low-cost self-publishing was Lulu.
Amazon built up their new publishing company and thrived. When they introduced a full global online distribution package to CreateSpace, they shot ahead of all the competition. Their Pro Plan provides access to Extended Global distribution and reduces your manufacturing cost, enabling you to buy the book for less and increase your royalty. They provide all these benefits for $39.00. After the first year, it costs only $5.00 annually to retain these benefits. This is half the cost of Lulu's distribution package, which was the best distribution deal until Amazon undercut them.
CreateSpace enables a writer to upload their completed book following the step-by-step instructions. It has its little obstacles, just as we encountered on other sites, most involving the formatting.

One of the first steps you will need to take is your ISBN option. If you want the book published with/by CreateSpace as the publisher, it is free. You may also choose to be listed as the publisher with a custom ISBN for $10.00. With this choice the book is ONLY available for sale through Amazon. You may choose a Universal ISBN, which will keep your distribution and publishing options open for $99. Or the final choice is to import your own ISBN and enter the imprint (publisher's name) associated with the ISBN purchase.

Before going on to the next decision, I will remind you: Amazon is expected to sell more than half of ALL the U.S. book business across all formats by the end of 2012. In 2007 when they launched Kindle, they held a mere 15%. Your choice of ISBN should hinge on your marketing plan. If you eventually want the book distributed through Lightning Source, you should choose either Universal or Bring Your Own.

The next step will be to choose your interior. Color or black and white? Unlike ePublishing, color graphics, illustrations, and photographs substantially increase the cost of manufacturing your book, generally putting the retail price out of reach for most readers. Your best option for a book with color is ePublishing.

Next, choose your book size. CreateSpace recommends the trade paperback size of 6 x 9. Other sizes are available but increase the cost of the book.

Then we reach my nemesis. Time to format. As we mentioned in other chapters, formatting can be difficult. Before you upload your book file, you need to resize your Word file to accommodate the size of your book. After adjusting the page size, go through your manuscript online, page by page, and verify your chapters all start at the top of the page and you don't have extraneous blank pages.

Just a reminder, if you wrote your manuscript in double space, go back and decrease the spacing to 1.15 or 1.5. This enables readers to view it better than single spacing. Using 1.5 shortens the book length by 25%, 1.15 by over 40%. Once you are satisfied with the formatting in Word, upload your book to CreateSpace. Their program will detect your page count and give you an estimated per book cost to publish.

CreateSpace provides an option of handling the formatting process for $299.00. If you don't have a friend or professional to assist you with the process, do a little research and see if you can find a reputable, less expensive formatting professional. You may also contact my writing partner at PersonalCovers.webs.com for low-cost formatting.

Your cover is the next step. I ran into serious trouble again. I was tasked with performing these online self publishing sites because I am a novice and do not know a lot about graphics, formatting, and other publishing programs. I already had the front and back jpegs for my cover. I did not want to use a template. Period. I paid for the cover and was extremely frustrated trying to upload it to CreateSpace.

Again, you have multiple choices, three of them. My problem arose when, after looking at the three options, I inadvertently chose the wrong one. Because the first option mentioned importing your text and they provide the template, I believed I needed to choose the PDF cover option. I was perplexed as to how to turn my two jpegs into the correct size of a pdf. I made an attempt. CreateSpace rejected it. Back to the drawing board. Over and over I worked to rearrange my cover and turn it into a single back-cover/spine/front-cover pdf.

By the way, I do not own Adobe Photoshop. I mention this because my next step was to read the community boards and see how others were managing this perplexing task. Many mentioned using Photoshop with ease to create the pdf required file. The others who managed to overcome the problems were unable to advise me as to the correct stops. Over and over something was wrong, something was missing. I finally contacted CreateSpace via email. I mentioned to them that due to the difficulty level, I suspected they were forcing users to purchase their services. I also mentioned that I planned to show users how to publish on CreateSpace. I received a very polite email back that said they were unable to help anyone specifically and suggested I contact their professional services. Whooooeeee. Unacceptable for a writer who plans to publish not only our own work but also that of others as well. So I called in my expert sidekick. He read their directions and also found them baffling and unusable.

Please, when becoming your own publisher, stick with it. After two weeks, I finally discovered the correct answer. Take note, it is important. The first option, "Cover Creator" has two templates hidden among the others that are specifically for those who have their own jpeg covers. You import your jpeg into the proper area, Amazon knows the word count and creates the spine, you import the second jpeg and voila. You have a cover. I did run into another small glitch. My dpi was too low for high quality. Amazon requires 300 dpi. A number of photo programs are able to correct this problem. I used GIMP, my expert cover designer used PictureIt.

The three choices for a cover on CreateSpace:

1) You can use Amazon's "Cover Creator" program which enables you to import your logo, photos, or text. It automatically formats and sizes the cover based on your book's size and page count. This option provides templates AND also options for uploading your jpeg pictures into their template.

2) You can upload a print-ready PDF cover. Amazon provides information on all the requirements and calculations needed to fit the cover to the book based on the page count. I found this option to be almost impossible, even after chatting with numerous users on the CreateSpace community board.

3) CreateSpace will work with you to design and create your own cover for $299.00

Throughout the process, Amazon provides video tutorials and article links to assist with each step at the bottom of the site page. However, if you run into a problem and email them, they may not answer the questions appropriately. I'm almost (okay, I am convinced) that they hoped I'd NEED their professional help in order to charge me a little extra money.

With the exception of formatting and the cover upload, the CreateSpace publishing process is easy to follow through their step-by-step guide. We highly recommend purchasing the EDC upgrade. EDC, an acronym for Expanded Distribution Channel, makes your book available to most online retailers, bookstores, and libraries that purchase books from large wholesalers. If you are not listed and available through these wholesalers, some retailers are unable to purchase your book even with a special request. There are three distribution outlets when you opt to use their EDC.

1) CreateSpace Direct: your book will be available to certified resellers through their wholesale website.

2) Bookstores and Online Retailers, your book will be available to most major online and brick-and-mortar retailers

3) Libraries and Academic Institutions, your book will be available to U.S. libraries and colleges.

At a mere $39.00, this package offers as much as any other publisher at a fraction of the cost.

We chose CreateSpace to publish this book, as well as making it available through KDP. Their product is comparable or superior to most other POD companies, their price per book is lower than most alternate options, and they are associated with the largest bookseller in the world.

If you need further information on the process, Amazon has a number of FREE book downloads to help you overcome the many obstacles that will crop up. I never said it was easy. It just becomes easier with each book.

Chapter Fourteen: PubIt!

PubIt! is the eBook publisher for Barnes & Noble. Publishing eBooks is free, and the format is actually even easier to use than KDP. (Another possibility exists, having published eBooks on a few other sites, I may be getting comfortable with the process, so maybe it just feels easier.) PubIt took me only thirty minutes to reach the "submit and sell" button, and I did not need my co-writers help. I believe this is due to the fact that he already formatted the book for a POD publisher. As Barnes & Nobel hold 15% of the market and Pubit! Books are not available on Amazon, it would behoove you to cover your bases by having your book published on both sites. It costs you nothing but a few minutes of your time, and neither site forces you to commit to only their book store, although Amazon offers special benefits to writers/publishers who are willing to commit to a 90-day exclusive.

To begin, go to the Barnes & Nobel website, www.barnesandnoble.com. If you already have an account, just sign in. If you don't, sign up to open an account.

The next step was the most difficult for me, and hopefully Barnes & Nobel will make it easier over the coming year. I could not find a link to the PubIt! website anywhere on their home page. To begin your publication process, just go to www.pubit.com. IF you need to log in, the log in area is in the upper right corner.

Have your formatted eBook, your cover jpeg, and your bank and credit card information available. Pubit needs your banking and tax information in order to pay you your royalties and to send your 1099 earnings statement every year.

They ask a series of questions that need answers you most likely have already completed elsewhere. You need a description of the book, an author's bio, some keywords, and you need to decide on a price for your eBook.

Their pricing policies are similar to Amazon; however, their royalties are slightly different. Books priced from $2.99 to $9.99 pay a royalty of 65%. Five percent lower than Amazon's KDP. But, the royalty paid on book below $2.99 or above $9.99 is 10% more than Amazon's KDP. You earn 40% on these lower and higher-priced tomes. Hmmm. Can eBooks be called tomes? I suppose it depends on your interpretation of weighty. eBooks don't weigh much, but we are wordsmiths and additional meanings of weighty include "important and momentous." Of course, your book is important, if not to the world, at least to you and those who agree with your stance or enjoy your characters. Or maybe it exerts influence or power onto those reading it. Novelist John D. MacDonald was well known for using fiction to offer his perspective on social and environmental issues. Many readers found themselves swayed by the insightful ponderings of Travis and Meyer. Check out books for sale on PubIt! and price yours competitively.

It took you countless hours to write your book, but it is no longer necessary to wait years to see it published. The outlets are varied and the costs are now minimal. Times they are a changing!

Chapter Fifteen: Lulu

The first book I published was on Lulu, "The Unraveling of Aggie Layman." What a learning curve. It took me weeks to navigate through formatting, cover design, pricing, ISBN research, types of distribution available, and so much more. I almost gave up in frustration a few times. It took the help of my co-writer and publishing partner to overcome many of the obstacles.

I made some mistakes, and unlike eBooks, Lulu can't be easily changed. The site never mentioned front matter; things like dedications, forwards, and acknowledgements, so I neglected to include them.

For a first attempt, it was "okay' but I hope every book we publish in the future looks far more professional. I have learned so much about publishing on multiple sites, and I am starting to feel comfortable with the process.

I chose Lulu for our first publishing attempt because for the last three years I'd heard them extolled as the least expensive option for POD books. And if you chose global distribution, you could contract with Lightning Source to POD publish for far less and take advantage of Lightning Sources affiliation with Ingram, the largest book distributor in the world.

They no longer hold the distinction of being the least expensive POD publisher. Amazon's CreateSpace now offers the same service and their global distribution package is half the cost. Either choice costs less than $100.00, and both companies have provided authors with an alternative to endless rejections and moldering pages left in the back of the filing cabinets, never read. Readers and writers owe a debt of gratitude to all the companies that have made publishing affordable for both the writers and their readers.

Publishing starts out easier on Lulu than the other sites. To publish a POD (Print on Demand) book on Lulu, go to their site at www.lulu.com . Then click on the big button that is labeled "Publish." Lulu provides far more choices than most other POD publishers. The higher end the choice, the more money the book's sale price will be.

Your first decision will be the type of binding you want for your book. Most books utilize the "perfect" binding. The saddle stitch works best for presentation booklets for seminars and conferences. The coil bound is a great option for cookbooks, music books, or children's books, where you prefer to have the pages lie flat, whether lying open on a counter or on a stand for easy reading. They also offer hard cover books, called casewrap. For a few pennies more you can add a dust jacket. For most sales you will not desire hard cover as the cost is prohibitive, BUT…if you want to order a small quantity in hardcover to disperse to reviewers, it makes sense. Until recently, reviewers would not even look at a book if it did not warrant the expense of a hard cover. The past year many reviewers altered their demand for hard cover due to the explosion of "good" books being self-published in trade paperback or ePublished. However, let me offer a word of warning. If your book isn't creating a buzz, don't waste your time or money sending free copies to a national reviewer. If they hear about it through Publisher's Weekly or by word of mouth, most reviewers will first check the "inside the book" section on Amazon. If the writing piques their interest, they will manage to get a copy themselves.

Whew. We made the decision on the cover. All set?

Hit the brakes! What's this, we have to decide on the size of the book? Well, what is standard? Paperbacks, the type you buy at Wal-Mart, the grocery store, or the drug store, generally are sized at 4 x 6 ¾. Hard cover books tend to be all different sizes, making it difficult on our shelves at home. Lulu gives you fourteen different size options to cover most any type of book. like most publishers, they suggest using the standard trade paperback size of 6 x 9. If you are doing a brochure or sales manual, the standard 8-½ x 11 with saddle stitch might be best, but the most cost effective option is the trade paperback at 6 x 9. Glad that's over. Now we can publish, right?

Not yet, my fellow author. Now we choose the paper type. Here they offer three choices. Lulu's standard is what you are used to when reading most books. The publisher grade is rather thin and tears easily and the premium is the heavy shiny paper used in "coffee table" books. Unless you need the publisher grade or premium for a specific reason, choosing the Lulu standard is generally the best option. While it does not cost you anything to publish, each higher-end option increases the price of the book, in many cases making it unaffordable for your audience. Okay, you know there are more decisions, right?

I won't disappoint you. It is time to decide on your cover. Do you already have a concept in mind? Are you overwhelmed with all the decisions and ready to grasp at the first template that looks colorful? Do you have an artist in the family, or maybe a close friend who is great with computer graphics? This is where your creative genius can shine. The cover can make or break a book. The best book may never be noticed because it sits on a shelf with a drab cover, while a mediocre book may tempt and entice the reader to pick it up, hook them with the blurb on the back, and find a new home on the reader's bedside table. You will need to design the front and the back, including the blurb and any reviews or endorsements you have gathered. The range of possibilities is endless. If all else fails, Lulu has a design team you can hire to create your cover, or you can go online and connect with one of the thousands of book cover designers, some famous, some unknown. I will remind you that my co-writer designed our cover as well as many others, and you can contact him through his website at www.PersonalCovers.webs.com .

Next choice, your ISBN. Do you want Lulu to publish the book? They will provide you with a free ISBN if they are listed as the publisher of record. If you want the distinction for yourself, you will need to buy your own. Lulu again walks you through the options and has links directly to Bowkers if you prefer to purchase your own. Be aware that ISBNs can only be applied to certain sizes of books, so if you plan to use one, be sure your book is an eligible size.

Lulu has video tutorials to help you, but they are overly simplistic and don't cover many of the obstacles I encountered with my first book. So you have made your choices. Is that your final answer?

Did you decide on a title? Some authors know from the start, others continue to hope that something will come to them, something that stands out and really covers the plot or theme of the book. If you really aren't sure, ask your editor or friends who have read the book.

Now that you have made all your publishing decisions, it is time to get started with their publishing app.

Formatting, as I have stated previously, is not the easiest task. It is an art. First, I hope you used Word while writing. Better yet, I hope you have used a recent edition. You must open your Word book file and custom-size the book to fit 6 x 9 pages. Uh-oh! Isn't that going to mess up my pages? My chapter endings? Some of my breaks? You betcha. After resizing, you will need to go through your file page by page. If at some point you used the enter key to get to the next page to start a chapter, it will leave a huge gap. At the end of each chapter make sure you hit, "insert page break." If you used any special symbols, they usually don't convert. Tables and illustrations must be inserted through the Word insert tab, not as a copy and paste. I hope I haven't confused you. Follow the steps Lulu provides and pay close attention to the wording of each instruction. At one point I was expecting the uploaded file to have the tab I needed when they had actually told me to go back to my original Word file, fix it there, and re-upload it. When you think you have it right, upload it and preview the book. I found a number of errors each time and had to keep going back to fix them, uploading over the previous copy every time. There is no time limit, so if it becomes too much…walk away, take a break. It's not easy, but it isn't rocket science either. If you really can't do it, and can't find someone to do it, you can choose to let Lulu do it for you with prices starting at

$299. For a plain text only book. Or you can hire an online formatter. There are more and more formatting artists online every week. If you don't overwhelm him with work, my co-writer also offers this service on his website for far less than Lulu at PersonalCovers.webs.com

When you are done, and satisfied with all steps of the publishing project and your final result—the book—hit save and publish. Lulu will send you one free book to verify that it is the final product you want. When you have verified this information, notify Lulu and they will offer the book via the distribution system you choose. Again there are options. Lulu offers the book without charging you for distribution on their website. They also offer author discounts, so you can order as many books as you need for your private sales. And for various prices, they offer extended and global distribution packages.

Lulu does not offer a phone contact for customer service, but if you encounter a problem you can't solve, you can email them and receive an answer in a day or two.

Chapter Sixteen: Smashwords

All the following information is directly from the
Smashwords website. We can't argue with FREE, and
suggest you check it out as long as you are semi-computer
literate. If you have read the previous chapters, you will
discover much of this is repetitive information, but we
chose not to exclude any information. We have not yet
used Smashwords, but Ron Dryer, the owner of Voice
Projects provided some words of wisdom. "Authors should
be advised to use Smashwords for all the EPUB formats,
but use KDP for Kindle. The reason is—Smashwords'
meat-grinder does OK if you target EPUB from the start,
but they no longer give you the option to upload an AZW
directly. The same upload to both makes mincemeat out of
Kindle because they necessarily use lowest common-
denominator formatting techniques. Just my $0.02 worth."

So….directly from Smashwords:

"Your eBook, your way

" Welcome to Smashwords! Smashwords is an ebook
publishing and distribution platform for ebook authors,
publishers, agents and readers. We offer multi-format,
DRM-free ebooks, ready for immediate sampling and
purchase, and readable on any e-reading device.

"Smashwords is ideal for publishing novels, short fiction,
poetry, personal memoirs, monographs, non-fiction,

research reports, essays, or other written forms that haven't even been invented yet.

"It's free to publish and distribute with Smashwords.

"What is Smashwords?
Smashwords publishes and distributes ebooks. Authors and publishers retain full control over how their works are published, sampled, priced, and sold. If an author wants to charge one dollar or ten thousand dollars, or give it away for free, they have that freedom. **Smashwords was launched in May 2008,** and in this time we've become the leading ebook publishing platforms for indie authors and publishers, with over 95,000 ebooks published.

"Who publishes on Smashwords?
Over 30,000 serious writers and hundreds of small independent publishers publish and distribute with Smashwords. Many Smashwords authors have been previously published in print through mainstream publishers, or have had their works published in well-respected literary journals. Starting March, 2009, Smashwords introduced new publishing options for publishers who want to publish and centrally manage two or more authors.

"What is an ebook, and how do I read these books?
Ebooks are digital books. They're similar to print books, but you read them on screens. The ebooks on Smashwords can be read online using our online readers, or they can be downloaded to other reading devices such as the iPhone,

iPod Touch, Amazon Kindle, Sony Reader or Barnes & Noble Nook, or to other eReading devices. Smashwords offers generous sampling options so readers can try before they buy.

"Why would authors and publishers give part of their book away as a free sample?

"More and more publishers realize they're competing against free already, and they're competing against the millions of alternative entertainment or learning options out there. The most valuable thing they're competing for is the reader's time and attention. Smart publishers realize if a reader invests the time necessary to read 100 pages of a 300 page book, they're much more inclined to purchase the book to know how it ends. Some authors choose to give their entire book away for free because it's more important to them they reach an audience, or they may want to leverage the notoriety from the book to monetize their fame in other ways.

"How does Smashwords compensate authors and publishers?

A primary mission at Smashwords is to help make publishing more rewarding for the world's indie authors and publishers, and more affordable to the world's readers. **Authors and publishers earn 85% or more of the net proceeds from the sale of their works. Net proceeds to author = (sales price minus PayPal payment processing fees)*.85 for sales at Smashwords.com, our retail operation. Authors receive 70.5% for affiliate sales. Smashwords distributes books to most of the major**

retailers, including the Apple iBookstore, Barnes & Noble, Sony, Kobo and the Diesel eBook Store. Sales originated by retailers earn authors/publishers 60% of the list price. Our generous earnings shares mean if an author has a book they might otherwise publish via a traditional commercial publishers as a $8.00 mass market paperback with a 40 cent royalty, they could publish the same book at Smashwords as an ebook and earn up to $6.45, or 16 times more. Or, they could price their ebook on Smashwords for $4.00 and make nearly 8 times the per unit amount of selling a traditionally published print book. The economics are equally advantageous for publishers.

"What marketing tools does Smashwords offer authors and publishers?
Smashwords offers multiple free marketing tools to help authors and publishers connect with readers. We offer distribution to major online ebook retailers such as Barnes & Noble, Sony, Apple iPad iBookstore, Kobo (and Borders) and the Diesel eBook Store, and to all major smart phone platforms via app providers such as Stanza, Aldiko, Kobo and Word-Player. We also offer free author pages with bios, headshots and lists of works; the industry's broadest range of sampling options; embedded YouTube videos for video book trailers and virtual author events; reviews from readers; ebook downloads in multiple ebook formats; a coupon code generator for custom promotions; and more tools in the works. For a great summary of what Smashwords does to market your book, along with over two dozen marketing ideas you can implement at no cost, download our free Smashwords Book Marketing Guide.

"Will I sell a lot of books on Smashwords?
Probably not. How's that for an honest answer? Some Smashwords authors don't sell a single book. Some authors sell thousands of dollars worth of books per year. Authors should publish their books on Smashwords not because they'll make a lot of sales today, but as a long term investment in their writing career, and at the same time they should also self-publish in print. eBook authors face the same marketing challenges all authors have always faced. By publishing digitally on Smashwords, however, authors and publishers can expand their potential readership by leveraging the power of viral marketing to reach more potential readers with less effort.

"Will Smashwords market my book for me?
Although thousands of readers march through our virtual doors every day, the bulk of your sales will come as a direct result of your own marketing and promotion efforts. We provide you free tools to help you do this, but it'll be your hard work that makes sales happen. For authors who want to maximize their sales opportunities on Smashwords, we created The Smashwords Book Marketing Guide. The Guide starts with an overview of how Smashwords helps you sell your book, and then provides a series of tips for how authors can take their book marketing to the next level.

"How does Smashwords change the economics of authorship?
Smashwords turns traditional authorship, publishing and pricing models upside down. With 85% of the net purchase

price going to the author/publisher, author/publishers can charge readers significantly less for their works than would otherwise be possible through traditional print channels, while making greater per-unit profit on each book. When costs to the reader drop, there is a fundamental change to the demand side of the equation. This creates a virtuous cycle of more per-unit profit for the author/publisher, lower prices for consumers, and greater demand and consumption for written works. It's a win-win-win for publishers, authors and readers.

"Does Smashwords require exclusive publishing contracts? All author contracts with Smashwords are non-exclusive. We are the distributor. You (the author or publisher) are the publisher, and retain all ownership rights to your works, and are still free to publish your work elsewhere if you choose. Authors and publishers can remove their works from Smashwords at any time (although they cannot take back works that have already been purchased or sampled by readers).

"If I publish first with Smashwords, will my "First Publishing Rights" become less valuable to a publisher? "If your ultimate dream is to be published by a mainstream publisher, this is possible, but not necessarily inevitable. Traditional commercial publishers have warmed to independently published authors, especially if those authors sell a lot of books and thereby prove that a large commercial market exists for their books. If you do well as a self-published author, you will increase the value of your book because you will have proven the market for it. Your decision needs to be a personal decision. Most Smashwords authors believe it's better to get their work out there now for readers to start discovering than to allow their books to languish in obscurity as they wait for a publisher to publish it. Some Smashwords authors have decided they don't want to work with a mainstream publisher.

"If Smashwords publishes all authors and publishers, how do you maintain quality?
Our mission is to give every author and publisher a chance to find their audience. At Smashwords every author or publisher has a right to publish, and it's up to readers to decide what's worth reading. Because we publish everyone, it means we publish brilliant up-and-coming writers who haven't yet been discovered, and we'll also publish authors of lesser quality. The great authors will bubble up to the top and build audiences and the lesser authors will drop out of sight.

"What does it cost to publish on Smashwords?
It's free to publish on Smashwords. There are no hidden fees. We earn our revenue by taking a commission on all net sales. The cut is 15% of the net for sales at Smashwords.com or on Stanza, 15% or more of the net proceeds from our retail partners, and 18.5% for sales that are originated by affiliate marketers. If your book is purchased via one of the major online retailers we distribute to, your earnings are 60% of the suggested list price you determine. Our distribution commission is only 10% of the list price for sales through retailers.

"Can Authors Publish Partially Written Books to Gather Feedback?

No. Smashwords is a place for complete, finished books that are ready to be published. Numerous other writer's web sites offer communities where authors can critique each other's partially written works. Smashwords is a platform for complete, finished, and original works.

"Can I publish public domain books on Smashwords?

No. You must be the original author of the work, or the exclusive electronic publisher or distributor of the work. The only exception to this rule is if you are the author of the public domain book.

"What other types of books will Smashwords *not* publish?

Smashwords will not publish works that advocate criminal activity. We do not publish books that appear elsewhere on the Internet under other people's names, or books that come from private label subscription services that give an entrepreneur the right to distribute the ebooks or content under their own name (please don't throw your money away on these scam services!). We're also wary of many Internet marketing-related books that promise the reader simple "systems" for making money on the Internet, especially if the books advocate sneaky systems designed to trick search engines. If your book is nothing but an advertisement, we will delete the book and your account. Bottom line: for it to appear on Smashwords is must be legal and original, and you must either be the original author or the exclusive publisher.

"I've been offered a book deal with a big mainstream print publisher. Should I take it?

This is really a personal call, and depends on the terms of book deal. For most authors, if a publisher offers you a six figure advance (and this is rare for any author), you'd be foolish not to accept it. However, if they're only offering you a couple thousand dollars, and they don't allow you to retain digital publishing rights, then, well—it's a personal decision. And if you do sell the rights to your book, make sure rights revert back to you if the publisher takes your book out of print or fails to deliver agreed-upon sales, marketing and distribution support. Better yet, if you have the ability to do so, consider retaining digital rights for yourself (so you can continue publishing on Smashwords) and sell the print rights. A good literary agent can help you navigate these negotiations.

"I'm a book reviewer and want to review a Smashwords book. How do I obtain a free review copy?

"If you're a reviewer for a newspaper, magazine or blog, please email Mark Coker at first initial second initial at you know where dot com and please provide a hyperlink to your most recent review and let us know which author and book you want to review. We will coordinate it for you.

"How does Smashwords work with traditional book publishers and university presses?

Smashwords welcomes large and independent presses alike to list DRM-free ebooks of all their titles with us. Starting May, 2009, Smashwords introduced expanded support for publishers. Publishers can now publish multiple authors and their books, and centrally manage all aspects of the accounts from a single console.

"Why should a publisher work with Smashwords? Smashwords makes it easy for you to publish and distribute your catalog. When a publisher sells an ebook through Smashwords, they receive up to 85% of the net sales price (they receive 70.5% for affiliate sales). Publishers receive only about 40-50% of the price of a print book sold through a bookstore or online retailer. That small number from traditional print book channels can drop to 20% or less once unsold inventory returns are factored in. With Smashwords, publishers have no inventory, no shipping expenses and no returns. Like authors, publishers can increase sales volume and profits by selling their books for lower prices.

"Does Smashwords publish only self-published authors whose works are not owned by a publisher? Smashwords publishes everyone's content, provided the author or publisher is legally entitled to publish with us, and provided the work satisfies our strict standards for originality. We welcome the opportunity to publish self-published authors, unpublished authors, authors of out-of-print books for whom the rights have reverted, and authors under contract with big-name publishers. If you own the digital publishing rights to your works, we want to publish you.

"What is Smashwords' position on digital rights management (DRM)?

We think DRM is counterproductive because it treats lawful customers like criminals. Consumers value non-DRMed content and there's a growing body of evidence that digital content producers who have abandoned DRM are enjoying greater sales. Many buyers of ebooks resent DRM because it limits their ability to fully own and enjoy their digital book. At Smashwords, we only publish DRM-free works. By the same token, we strictly discourage illegal pirating of an author's works.

"Do I need to copyright my work prior to publishing with Smashwords?
If you are the author - the creator - of an original work, then most laws automatically give you copyright to the work. Although most authors don't choose to do so (because it's difficult to justify the expense), if you want to go the extra mile, you can hire a lawyer to formally register your copyrights with the federal government.

"Can I publish my book in print as well?
Since you own your book, you can publish your book anywhere you choose. Print publishing is more complicated, expensive and time-consuming than ebook publishing. For this reason, some indie authors skip print entirely. If you do decide to publish in print, consider starting out with a free print on demand service rather than filling your garage with a large and expensive print run of unsold books.

"Why did you create Smashwords?
Smashwords was inspired by my own unsuccessful multi-

year attempt to get my novel published. In 2002, my wife, Lesleyann, and I co-wrote a novel called Boob Tube, a roman a clef set within the daytime television soap opera industry (Lesleyann is a writer for the Huffington Post and a former reporter for Soap Opera Weekly Magazine). We were fortunate to have multiple top tier literary agents compete for our representation, and in the end we selected one of the most respected firms in New York City. Our agent contacted all the top publishers of commercial women's fiction, and each rejected us. We took their feedback to heart (the book was too long, too complex, characters needed better development) and completed a major revision. We then shared the manuscript with multiple test readers. Soap fans and those who enjoy celebrity gossip loved it, and even non-soap fans enjoyed it. Confident we had a winner on our hands, our agent again pitched the book to publishers. All of them rejected it. Some publishers told our agent they didn't believe soap opera fans read books! I found it frustrating that the whims of a publisher could stand between our book and those who would want to read it. I ultimately came to the conclusion that the publishing industry is ill equipped to serve all authors.

"Why can't the publishing industry serve all authors?
"First, I should state I am a big admirer of the publishing industry. A good agent, editor and publisher can add a lot of value to your work. The pre-publication support provided by a publisher is invaluable, especially in terms of getting your book edited, packaged and carried by bookstores. However, beyond getting their books carried by

bookstores, publishers are unable to provide all authors the publicity and post-publication support they need. First time authors often find themselves disappointed by the lack of publicity support. I can't completely fault the industry for this because publishers can't afford to lavish tens of thousands of dollars in publicity support and advertising on every author. As the publishing industry navigates the rough waters facing all media companies, it's likely over the next few years we'll see fewer publishers publishing fewer authors, and we'll also see many brick and mortar bookstores closed. With fewer physical bookshelves to showcase books, it will become increasingly important for authors and publishers to replace those shelves with digital shelves.

"What challenges does the traditional publishing industry face, and how do these challenges impact authors?
"The publishing industry, like most media, is undergoing some wrenching but necessary change. Overall book industry sales, according to recent data from the AAP, have stagnated or declined. Many publishers have reduced the number of new acquisitions and have laid off employees. Bookstores, too, are facing massive consolidation. It's likely in the years ahead, we'll see fewer bookstores carrying fewer titles. There are several reasons for the challenges faced by publishing:

- Publishing is expensive: Books are expensive to produce, distribute and promote. Book publishers are structurally limited in the number of new titles they can publish each year, because each book requires editing, artwork, promotional flaps, production, sales support, inventorying and shipping.

- Books are expensive: If a $25 or $30 book is expensive to the average American, imagine how expensive that book is to literate people in developing countries?
- Publishers have difficulty predicting demand for a book: Despite hundreds of years of experience, consumers are fickle and it's difficult for publishers to predict which books will sell, and which won't. As a result, they can't predict the proper size of their print runs, and often saddle their warehouses and bookstores with expensive unsold inventory.
- Publishing is a "hit" business: Publishers lose money on many books they publish and try to make up the difference by having a few bestseller hits.
- Shelf space is limited: Bookstores are physically limited in the number of titles they can carry. Most Borders or Barnes & Noble superstores cannot stock more than 100,000 books at any one time. Amazon, by comparison, stocks approximately 2.5 million titles. The major bookstores are also struggling to remain profitable, and we'll likely see many bookstore closings in the years ahead.
- Bookstores have short attention spans: New titles are allowed only a couple weeks to find their audience and sell well before the books are returned to the publisher for full refund.
- New titles must compete against midlist: New titles are not only competing against each other, but also

against established midlist books - published titles
that continue to sell moderately well, year in and
year out (often classics and former bestsellers).

- Tiny earnings: Most authors receive royalties of
  only 5-10% of the retail price of their written works.
  The other 90-95% goes to bookstores, distributors,
  publishers, printers, agents and discounts.
- Publishers don't promote most books: Many first
  time authors receive little to no post-publication
  publicity support from their publishers. Many
  authors recognize they have to do the promotion
  themselves. They have to do their own PR; call
  bookstores to arrange signings; and personally hand
  sell books to local bookstores.
- Limited geographic distribution: Book publishing
  today is still geographically constrained. Most
  works are never published outside their own
  country, or in languages other than the native
  tongue of their author. In the United States, most
  published works will never receive distribution
  outside the US. Authors outside the US have little
  chance of finding an audience outside their own
  country.
- There's no "long tail" in print book publishing: To
  enter the midlist, books must be able to meet a
  certain threshold of sales, often several thousand
  copies per year, year in and year out, with little to
  no promotion from the bookstores or the publishers.
  What about the millions of previously written and
  out of print works which could be selling 50, 100,

or 1,000 copies each year, if only they were available for their audience to discover?

- Readers are left unserved: All of these challenges faced by the publishing industry harm not only authors, but readers as well. Readers are effectively denied the freedom to discover new voices in the written word.

"What is the business model for Smashwords?
Although Smashwords was founded to achieve a strong social purpose, we also recognize we must produce a profit so we can continue to carry out our mission. Smashwords generates income through commissions from the sales of written works and in the future, affiliate fees earned from our partners, and later, possibly through premium membership options. Guiding all of our business decisions will be an overarching mission to serve the needs of the authors, publishers and readers who participate in our community.

"What's next for Smashwords?
We've been in business for just over four years, growing quickly, but we still feel like we're just getting started. We're constantly improving the service, and we have hundreds of ideas for how we can further help improve the digital publishing experience for authors, readers and publishers. We listen closely to our members, whose valuable feedback guides our daily development. Stay tuned and tell a friend!

Smashwords Distributes your ebook to the Apple iBookstore, Barnes & Noble, Sony Reader Store, Kobo and the Diesel eBook Store

Earn 60% of List Price from Major Ebook Retailers and 85% Net at Smashwords.com

"Smashwords Highlights**:**

- World's largest indie ebook distributor
- 80,000+ titles published by 30,000+ authors and publishers
- 85% net back to the author/publisher/agent
- Distribution to Apple (31 countries), Barnes & Noble, Sony, Kobo, Diesel, others
- Consolidated sales reporting
- Centralized metadata management
- <u>FREE</u> ISBNs
- <u>FREE</u> ebook conversion to nine formats
- <u>FREE</u> unlimited updates to book and metadata
- <u>FREE</u> exclusive marketing and selling tools such as our Smashwords Coupon Manager!

Getting Started is Easy as 1-2-3:

1. <u>Sign up</u> for your free account at www.smashwords.com. Your confirmation email will summarize your next steps.

2. Format your manuscript as a Microsoft Word .doc file per the guidelines in the Smashwords Style Guide, or, if you don't have the time or patience to do it yourself, send an email to list@smashwords.com to request "Mark's List" of low-cost Smashwords ebook formatters and cover designers.

3. Click Publish and follow the simple steps to upload your book and cover image.

Ebook Distribution Made Fast, FREE and Easy

"We invite you to join our 30,000+ authors and publishers from every corner of the globe who publish and distribute over 80,000 original ebooks with Smashwords!

"Smashwords makes it fast, free and easy to publish, distribute and sell your ebooks to a worldwide audience at the largest ebook retailers. At Smashwords, there are no setup fees, no packages to buy, and no cost to update or revise your book. We also provide free ISBNs.

"Smashwords is an authorized ebook distributor for most major online ebook retailers, including the Apple iPad iBookstore (Smashwords is a certified Global Apple Aggregator distributing to iBookstores in 31 countries), Barnes & Noble, Sony, Kobo (our books also go to Borders and Samsung, powered by Kobo), the Diesel eBook Store and EbookEros (Romance & erotica only, operated by

Diesel). Our books are also distributed into the native catalogs of top mobile e-reading apps such as Stanza on the iPhone and iPad (used by 4 million+ people) and Aldiko (over 2 million users) and Word-Player on Android devices. Your book is also available for immediate sale at Smashwords.com, our retail operation. Smashwords books are also promoted via a growing network of Smashwords affiliates.

"To publish at Smashwords, you must be the original author or the exclusive digital publisher, distributor or literary agent. Smashwords does not publish public domain or Private Label Rights books.

Smashwords for Authors

"Smashwords is the world's leading ebook distributor for indie authors. Our free service helps you publish, distribute and sell your masterpiece at major ebook retailers such as the Apple iBookstore (now reaching 31 countries!), Barnes & Noble, Kobo, Sony and the Diesel eBook Store. Because we produce multi-format conversions, your book is readable on any e-reading device, including the Amazon Kindle, the Apple iPhone/iPod Touch/iPad the Sony Reader, the Barnes & Noble nook, your personal computer, Android devices, and others. As a Smashwords author, you gain access to free, do-it-yourself sales and marketing tools to help you promote your book. You receive 85 percent of the net sales proceeds from your titles (70.5% for affiliate sales), and 60% of the list price for all sales through our major retailers.

Smashwords for Publishers

"If you're the exclusive publisher of two or more different authors, and you want to list and control your authors' titles on Smashwords, then upgrade your account for free to Publisher status. This allows you to list and publish all your authors and their titles as multi-format, DRM-free ebooks. Each publisher is provided a custom-branded online bookstore, and the ability to list an unlimited number of ebook titles from an unlimited number of authors. Publishers receive 85 percent or more of the net sales proceeds from their titles (70.5% for affiliate sales), and gain access to numerous free promotion and selling tools offered by Smashwords, including our popular Smashwords Coupon Generator which makes it easy to run custom coupon promotions across online social networks, blogs and web sites. If you don't publish two or more authors, there's no reason to upgrade your account.

Subsidy Publishers

A – Z

Due to the hundreds, if not thousands, of new startup subsidy/author services companies now available, we were unable to locate all of them. We will be offering annual updates in the future to remain as current as possible with the services offered and their comparative costs. Please feel free to email us any information on subsidy companies we have inadvertently omitted at DGould497@aol.com so we can include them in future publications.

Introduction to Subsidy Publishers

The future is bearing down on us like a runaway train, and our best choice is to hop aboard and enjoy the ride. Gone are the days when the creative talent in publishing received 8% of the sales dollar while the publishers, printers, jobbers, bookstores, and supermarkets split the other 92%. Finally, the chains have been cast off and the authors are free to pursue their muse where they will.

The companies included in the following section are by no means all inclusive, but they cover far more choices than any other guide put together. We plan to issue annual updates each year removing the companies that go out of business and adding the new companies available. If you personally know of subsidy, independent, or author services companies that are not on the list, please forward the information to us via DGould497@aol.com and we will include verified information in the updates.

The following list includes not just subsidy publishers and printers, but many various author services like audio tapes, editing services, cover art, and formatting services as well.

We also do not guarantee that the listed companies will not alter their prices or services. Some may go out of business. From the time we started researching until we finished our editing process over twenty companies closed down, and I discovered at least a dozen new companies. The shifting sands are eternally in motion, occasionally a dust storm barrels through like Amazon and completely changes the landscape, but writers will continue to write and publish because it is what we do and who we are.

Chapter Seventeen: 48 Hour Books

Offset printing
Go to www.48hrbooks.com
(48 Hour Books has a cost calculator onsite to determine
the price per book based on how many copies you require.
The greater the quantity, the lower the per book cost.
As an example we used a 100 page, black and white print,
trade paperback, standard paper grade.)
10 copies...............$14.55 per book
20 copies...............$ 8.55 per book
50 copies...............$ 4.95 per book
100 copies............ $ 3.75 per book,
they offer 25 free books with orders of 100, effectively
lowering the price to 3.00 per book.

(Shipping is additional. Enter your zip code and the
calculator also includes shipping costs. Shipping time is
NOT included in the 48 hour turnaround time they
promote. They claim to print most books from the time
you approve the final file within 48 hours. Shipping UPS
most books are delivered 2 to 5 days after printing. If you
are in a hurry, they have faster, albeit costlier shipping
options.

The site also offers formatting for $75.00, an option
that takes the pain out of formatting, and they design covers
from their templates for an additional $100.00. You won't
have the most unique cover design, but it's a cover.

If you run into any problems or have questions, 48
Hour Books will answer their phones Monday through
Friday from 8:30 a.m. – 5:00 p.m. EST or you can send
them an email. They will reply as fast as possible, usually
within an hour if it is during their normal operating hours.)

Chapter Eighteen: A Cappela Publishing

Book Broker

Previously a subsidy publisher, A Cappella has switched gears and now offers tools for writers. They have books and online classes to help you improve your writing skills, they offer editing, coaching, and evaluations as well as information on locating an agent, a traditional publisher, or self publishing.

After you are published, opportunities are offered for marketing.

Chapter Nineteen: Aachanon

POD publisher

Aachanon promotes itself as an Author Services Company. They provide help with POD printing.

They have three packages of help:

"We offer three levels of service to the self-publishing author—the book publishing packages: *Budget, Basic,* and *Basic Plus.*"

Budget

The Budget package is one of the most economical ways you can use to get your book into print. It is limited in its features, no more than 10 black and white illustrations or photographs in the text, but is of the same quality as the books offered at the more expensive levels.

If you are able to submit a spell-checked and copy-edited manuscript, with pre scanned graphics, and are planning a book in a standard size, for family histories, poetry, business reports, manuals, personal sales, teaching or seminar material — anything that does not require too many illustrations or commercial distribution through bookstores, this may be what you need.

Budget Package:

• Soft-cover, smooth, 90-lb. cover paper, 50-lb. text paper. Maximum of 300 pages.

• Book pages in sizes, 5" x 8", (standard soft-cover book size).

• Standard color cover design, (preformatted), with two graphics, (author provided). Standard page layout with black text and up to 10 black and white illustrations or photographs (author provided). All illustrations and photographs must be pre scanned.
• The finished book is mailed to you for approval. You can check the layout and positioning of any illustrations, proofread the text and make corrections (no rewrites or additions). Then return the book to us for final correction and printing.

• Three free books.

• Price: $195.

Basic

The Basic package is a practical level for many authors. More flexible than the Budget package, it is for the author who may want to choose a cover design and interior layout more in harmony with his aesthetic desire. The package also offers the author the opportunity to add color pictures to the pages of his book and a glossy cover. With the addition of an ISBN number and price code (author provided—see ISBN page), the author will be able to sell his book on Amazon.com and through bookstores.

The package allows up to 350 pages, with up to 15 photographs or illustrations (Color or black and white) on the text pages, gloss (laminated) cover. It offers a quality product to the author with experience in writing, copy editing and proof reading, or authors who have already arranged for the copy editing and proof reading of their writing by a competent editor.

The Basic package is for a professional-grade book. It is recommended for authors who want book wholesalers to carry their book, and to sell their book through bookstores. It is also a good package for those who write for organizations, manuals, reports, etc., and for writers who wish to publish teaching or seminar materials. You can sell the books personally, advertise them on E-Bay, or your Internet web site, sell them through flea markets, direct mail, or simply give copies to family and friends.

Basic Package:

• Soft-cover or spiral-bound, gloss (laminated) cover for added thickness, strength, protection and superior look. 50-lb. text paper. Maximum of 350 pages.

• Book page sizes 5 x 8" (standard soft cover book size), 6" x 9", 8 x 10" (soft-cover or spiral-bound), and 8.5" x 11", (spiral-bound only).

• Custom color cover design, with up to five color images, (author provided), that follows your vision for the book; and a custom interior layout in black text with up to 15 photographs or illustrations, in color or black and white (author provided). The graphics may be either pre scanned, or copies of the photographs or illustrations mailed to us for scanning. If mailed, they should be no larger than 81/2" x 11".

• Our designers will design the cover or emulate the appearance of an existing book cover or interior page layout that you like. (You must send us copies of a few pages to show us what style you wish us to copy.)

• Proof pages of the typeset book are mailed to you for approval. You can check the layout and positioning of the cover copy and graphics, the text copy and any illustrations. You may also proofread the copy yourself and mark corrections on the proof pages (no rewrites or additions), then return the book to us for final correction and printing.

• Printing of the International Standard Book Number (ISBN) and price grid on back cover. (ISBN code grid supplied by author.)

• Five free books.

• Price: $295.

Basic Plus

The Basic Plus package is the most popular one for the new or relatively inexperienced author. It adds professional copy editing and proofreading to the elements of the Basic package. These editorial features are strongly recommended, especially for the author who may be in need of editorial help in the structure and readability of his work; is grammatically "rusty," and in need of professional help for the proof reading of his copy.

If you choose this package, you get all the features of the Basic package plus:

Up to eight hours of copy editing (this is usually enough for most manuscripts that are submitted). Our experienced copy editor will mark (in pen) your hard copy for correction, concerning punctuation, grammar, word usage and sentence structure. You will then have the option to accept or reject her suggested corrections before sending the final manuscript copy to Aachanon. Additional copy editing, if necessary, is charged at the rate of $15 per hour.

Proofreading of the typeset copy.

The Basic Plus package is the right one for you if you desire a professional-grade book, with professional copy editing and proofreading services.

Basic Plus Package:

• All the features of the Basic Package plus:

• Copy Editing —Up to eight hours of editing by an experienced editor. A reading, and marking of your manuscript, in pen, to check punctuation, grammar, word usage and sentence structure. The marked up copy of your manuscript is returned to you for your consideration. You can make acceptable changes and then submit your edited copy for bookmaking.

• Proof Reading — an editorial check of the typeset text for typographical errors, spelling, hyphenation, and layout problems. Two readings are made, the first comparing the text to the submitted copy, the second checking the pages for spelling, hyphenation, and layout difficulties.

• Five free books.

• Price: $595.

Chapter Twenty: Aardvark Global Publishing
POD

Also operating as Ecko Publishing, they are based in Sandy, Utah. Founded by independent authors with the primary intention of helping other independent authors get the publishing services they need in the simplest and most inexpensive way possible while never compromising quality or customer service.

Company Statement: "We know how challenging it can be to get professional quality and inexpensive publishing services - not to mention how complicated it can be for new authors. As a result of our own experiences, we came together to form a company dedicated to helping authors publish their book products while keeping control of their work, as well as, maintaining the ability to market, distribute and sell their book products to bookstores and many other unlimited sources."

List of Services offered:

Editing: $5.00 per page.

Formatting: Basic Package: $279.00
Custom Package: $399.00 (allows for up to 35 graphic image inserts and 3 revisions)

Cover Design: $229.00   (starting at)
All covers are custom made based on your ideas and the book theme. Up to three changes allowed, covers front, back and spine.

ISBN: Author's Package $69.00

Aardvark or Ecko Publishing listed publishers. Author retains all rights

Book is listed on Google and Bookscapes, Your own website connected to Google

Book eligible to be listed on Amazon, at Bookstores, etc.

Self Publishers Package: $139.00

You or your publishing company is registered with Bowkers

All other items remain the same.

Copyright: $119.00 filing fee for listing with the U.S. Copy Right Office.

Printing:

Quantity Printing Cost Per Book

Qty Ordered	25-99	100-249	250-499	500-999
Non Members	$4.68	$4.45	$4.21	$3.98
Premiere Members	$4.14	$3.93	$3.73	$3.52
Platinum Members	$4.14	$3.93	$3.73	$3.52

For quantities over 1000, please call or email for custom quote.

Print on Demand $4.14 per book. To be eligible for Print-on-Demand Distribution, you must be an ECKO House Platinum Distribution Member. This allows us to get your book into the major distribution channels and books are printed on demand as they are ordered from retailers worldwide.

Distribution Packages:

1. **Basic ISBN Package** - Single ISBN Number with Barcode - $59.00

2. **Independent ISBN Package** - Single ISBN with Barcode; you are listed as the publisher (takes 3 business days) - $127.00

3. **Premiere ISBN Distribution Package** - Includes ISBN, Barcode, Copyrighting, Amazon and much more! $249.00

4. **Platinum ISBN Distribution Package** - Includes ISBN, Barcode, everything in the Premiere Package plus Worldwide Distribution! $447.00

Marketing: Everything you need to promote your book - $289.00

    100 full color postcards 4" x 6"
    100 full color bookmarks 2" x 8"
    25 full color Posters 12" x 18" on
    100# Matte or Laminated Cover Stock

Chapter Twenty-One: Arbor Books

A full-service book publisher specializing in ghostwriting, editing, cover design, typesetting, printing and marketing. They are a well-known company and provide all author services.

(Arbor Books does not offer prices until you provide all your information on what services you are interested in purchasing, including your home number. However, when price isn't mentioned, I tend to lean toward the saying, "If you have to ask, you can't afford it."

They did offer the information that they can convert your book to an audio book with prices starting at $7500. Not many companies offer this service and the audio market is growing and in need of submissions.)

Ghostwriting & Self Publishing Services

"Arbor Books offers a wide range of ghostwriting and self publishing for our customers. Whether you would like the assistance of a ghostwriter to get your book just right or need a skilled marketing team, we can help."

Cover Design

"Our captivating covers all but guarantee sales. And you get spectacular full-color covers at no extra cost!"

Editorial

"We provide the editorial services you need, whether you want ghostwriters to work on your manuscript or need help with researching, editing, rewriting, and proofreading."

Typesetting

"Our publishing company does it all: digital layout, scanning text and photos, indexing, footnoting, photo restoration enhancement and more."

Endorsements

"Endorsements sell books! We'll provide you with all the endorsements you'll need—or help you get the ones you want!"

Printing

"Our self publishing company offers a wide selection of book sizes, binding choices and paper stock; full color or black and white; hardcover or paperback. Print as few as 25 copies or as many as one million copies."

Registrations

"ABI can obtain your copyright, Library of Congress Catalog Number (LCCN) for sales to libraries, and International Standard Book Number (ISBN) and bar code—necessary for sales to bookstores."

Marketing

"ABI can handle all your marketing needs! ABI has numerous contacts with reviewers, distributors, book chains and TV and radio producers, as well as a database of over 250,000 media outlets and nearly 10,000 agents and publishers. In addition to being sold through bookstores, libraries, seminars and the Internet, your book can be used as a premium, incentive, gift or giveaway."

E-Book

"In addition to the 'store-bought' version of the book, convert your book into an e-book or electronic book and place it with Internet bookstores including Amazon, Barnes & Noble, Borders, Bibliophile and others."

Audiobook

"We can convert your book into audio format—either tape cassettes, CDs or DVDs—so that you can take advantage of the $2 billion audiobook market. Prices start at $7,500."

Book Fulfillment

"We can place your book with a fulfillment house to take all your orders and do your mailings."

Branding

"ABI can design logos, business cards, letterhead stationary, etc."

Logos, Bookmarks, Posters, Flyers

"We can create postcards, bookmarks, posters, flyers, ads in books, etc. Plus, we can print them in any size or quantity you want!"

Chapter Twenty-Two: Ardith Publishing

Ardith is a full service self publishing company that provides book editing, design, marketing, publicity, distribution, and printing services to authors in Canada and the U.S. All prices are in American and Canadian dollars—same price.

Ardith's Self Publishing Package – *only $399!*

"Have you ever wondered how to get published? With Ardith's Self Publishing Package, book publishing has never been easier. Our package is designed so that you can easily publish a professional book.

If you have a completed manuscript and want to use one of our templates to produce a four-color cover and the interior page layout for the book, this package is for you. With this service, you provide the manuscript to us in a Word document and choose a predesigned book cover and inside page layout. We'll format the cover and pages to your specifications and supply you with a proof for your approval. At this point, your book is ready to print."

Book Design, Publishing, and Distribution at Your Fingertips

"The package includes the following from our self publishing services:

- Paperback or hardcover formatting
- Choice of predesigned page and cover layouts
- Your own Ardith representative to assist you in the book design and publishing process

- Registration with Books in Print database providing worldwide availability
- Assignment of ISBN (International Standard Book Number)

Only $399.00

THE FINE PRINT: Additional charges apply for printing books and shipping and handling of books.

Complex manuscripts such as illustrated children's books, cookbooks, poetry, or textbooks usually require custom services. See our list of **self publishing services** for more information."

Editorial Services:

Manuscript evaluation

(150 pages, $12/additional 10 pages)	$200
Copyediting	3¢ per word
Substantive editing	4¢ per word
Translation or translation checking	quote upon request
Ghostwriting	$250 for sample $40 per hour
Research and fact-checking	$40 per hour
Proofreading	2¢ per word
Indexing	15¢ per word

Design Services:

Interior book layout	$4 per page
Custom book design	$75 per hour

Production Services:

Book printing		Pricing calculator @ site
Page Proof		$100
Ebook conversion		$100

Marketing services:

Press release writing		$150
Press release campaign	100 media outlets	$350
	500 media outlets	$500
	1,000 media outlets	$750
	5,000 media outlets	$1,500
Email campaign		$200
Web marketing campaign		$300
Electronic media kit		$100
Author website		$200
Personal publicist		$90 per hour

Promotional materials:

Promotion Pack		$600
Posters	5 posters	$150
	25 posters	$250
	50 posters	$500
Bookmarks	100 bookmarks	$150
	200 bookmarks	$250
	300 bookmarks	$350
Postcards	500 postcards	$300

	1,000 postcards	$400
	2,000 postcards	$650
Business cards	500 cards	$150
	1,000 cards	$225
	2,000 cards	$350

Distribution Service:

Notification of trade	$300
Book distribution	$100 per year, paying 40% royalties on net sales

Chapter Twenty-Three: Author Solutions

Author Solutions is the parent company of a multitude of
subsidy publishing companies, many well-known. Their
imprints are:

Author Solutions:

iUniverse™
1663 Liberty Drive
Bloomington, IN 47403
(800) AUTHORS
(288-4677)

Wordclay ™
1663 Liberty Drive
Bloomington, IN 47403
(877) 655-1720

AuthorHouse™
1663 Liberty Drive
Bloomington, IN 47403
(888) 519-5121

Xlibris™
1663 Liberty Drive
Bloomington, IN 47403
(888) 795-4274

AuthorHive ™
1663 Liberty Drive
Bloomington, IN 47403
(888) 232-4444

Trafford Publishing™
1663 Liberty Drive
Bloomington, IN 47403
(888) 232-4444

Palibrio™
1663 Liberty Drive
Bloomington, IN 47403
(877) 407-5847
Inkubook™
9045 River Road, Suite 400
Indianapolis, IN 46240
(877) 886-7034

Chapter Twenty-Four
AuthorHouse

1663 Liberty Drive
Bloomington, IN 47403
888.519.5121
www.authorhouse.com

Paperback and Hardback – Starting at $598

1) $598-Essential (paperback) includes the
following:
One-on-One Author Support
When you publish with
AuthorHouse, we schedule a
conference call with you to review
the initial cover and galley proof.
Custom Full-Color Cover
Your cover designer will create a
unique cover that reflects your vision
for the book and helps make it more
marketable.
Custom Interior Design
At AuthorHouse, your book interior
is custom-designed.
ISBN Assignment
AuthorHouse will provide a unique
International Standard Book Number
at no extra charge so booksellers can
find and order your book.
Electronic Proof
As your design team completes work
on your book, you will receive

electronic proof copies of your
galley (book interior) and cover.
Online Distribution
When your book is finished, it's
available for order at thousands of
online booksellers, including
Amazon.com, BarnesandNoble.com,
and through the AuthorHouse online
book store.
Professional Marketing Consultation
Our marketing consultants will work
with you to choose the best plan for
your goals.
Bookstore Availability
With a unique ISBN, your book will
be available at more than 25,000
retail outlets worldwide.
Complimentary Author Copy
Once you've signed off on your
completed galley and cover proofs,
we'll send you the first printed copy
of your book.
Image Insertion
If you'd like images to appear in your
book, we can work with you to place
them.
2) $948-Premium (paperback) includes all
Essential plus:
E-Book
Get your book published and
distributed in a popular electronic
format.
Book Buyers Review
When book buyers access their
ordering database, your
chapter preview will appear with

your book's ordering information to aid buyers in making a purchasing decision.
10 Complimentary Paperbacks

3) $1298-Premium (hardback & paperback) includes all previous plus:

Personalized Back Cover
Make your book stand out by adding your photo and promotional text on the back cover.

10 Complimentary Paperbacks and 10 Complimentary Hardbacks

Children's & Color Book – Starting at $549

1) $549-Essential (up to 48 pages) includes the following:

One-on-One Author Support
When you publish with AuthorHouse, we schedule a conference call with you to review the initial cover and galley proof.

Custom Full-Color Cover
Your cover designer will create a unique cover that reflects your vision for the book and helps make it more marketable.

Custom Interior Design
At AuthorHouse, your book interior is custom-designed.

ISBN Assignment
AuthorHouse will provide a unique International Standard Book Number

at no extra charge so booksellers can find and order your book.

Electronic Proof

As your design team completes work on your book, you will receive electronic proof copies of your galley (book interior) and cover.

Online Distribution

When your book is finished, it's available for order at thousands of online booksellers, including Amazon.com, BarnesandNoble.com, and through the AuthorHouse online book store.

Professional Marketing Consultation

Our marketing consultants will work with you to choose the best plan for your goals.

Bookstore Availability

With a unique ISBN, your book will be available at more than 25,000 retail outlets worldwide.

Complimentary Author Copy

Once you've signed off on your completed galley and cover proofs, we'll send you the first printed copy of your book.

Image Insertion (50 included)

If you'd like images to appear in your book, we can work with you to place them.

2) $849-Premium (up to 480 pages) includes Essential plus:

Book Buyers Review

When book buyers access their ordering database, your

chapter preview will appear with
your book's ordering information to
aid buyers in making a purchasing
decision.
Personalized Back Cover
Make your book stand out by adding
your photo and promotional text on
the back cover.
10 Complimentary Paperbacks

Poetry Book Publishing – Starting at $399

1) $399-Essential Poetry (up to 100 pages) offers
   everything listed here:

   One-on-One Author Support
   When you publish with
   AuthorHouse, we schedule a
   conference call with you to review
   the initial cover and galley proof.
   Custom Full-Color Cover
   Your cover designer will create a
   unique cover that reflects your vision
   for the book and helps make it more
   marketable.
   Custom Interior Design
   At AuthorHouse, your book interior
   is custom-designed.
   ISBN Assignment
   AuthorHouse will provide a unique
   International Standard Book Number
   at no extra charge so booksellers can
   find and order your book.
   Electronic Proof

As your design team completes work on your book, you will receive electronic proof copies of your galley (book interior) and cover.

Online Distribution

When your book is finished, it's available for order at thousands of online booksellers, including Amazon.com, BarnesandNoble.com, and through the AuthorHouse online book store.

Professional Marketing Consultation

Our marketing consultants will work with you to choose the best plan for your goals.

Bookstore Availability

With a unique ISBN, your book will be available at more than 25,000 retail outlets worldwide.

Complimentary Author Copy

Once you've signed off on your completed galley and cover proofs, we'll send you the first printed copy of your book.

2) $598-Premium Poetry (up to 200 pages) also includes:

Book Buyers Review

When book buyers access their ordering database, your chapter preview will appear with your book's ordering information to aid buyers in making a purchasing decision.

5 Complimentary Paperbacks

3) $998-Premium Hardcover Poetry (up to 300 pages) offers additionally:

    E-Book

        Get your book published and distributed in a popular electronic format.

    Personalized Back Cover

        Make your book stand out by adding your photo and promotional text on the back cover.

    5 Complimentary Paperbacks and 5 Complimentary Hardbacks

Authorhouse offers line editing at 2.9 cents a word and generally takes about two to three weeks. They can custom design your cover for an additional $499. Manuscript Preparation at $2.00 per page, which includes:

Removing headers, footers, page numbering, etc.
Inserting page breaks appropriately
Correcting soft and hard returns
Correcting line and paragraph formatting
(To avoid these fees please adhere to the manuscript submission guidelines. They will accept your edit and your original cover design, thereby saving you a lot of money.)

Minimum Price for Standard Paperback Books Sold on the AuthorHouse Online Bookstore	5% Royalty	20% Royalty	30% Royalty	50% Royalty
Size and No. Pages				
6x9 softcover, 125 pages	$8.30	$9.80	$11.20	$15.70
6x9 softcover, 250 pages	$9.90	$11.70	$13.40	$18.70
6x9 softcover, 400 pages	$11.60	$13.80	$15.70	$22.00

Minimum Price for Standard Paperback Books Sold through a Retail Store

Size and No. Pages	5% Royalty	10% Royalty	15% Royalty
6x9 softcover, 125 pages	$10.99	$12.49	$16.49
6x9 softcover, 250 pages	$14.49	$15.99	$21.49
6x9 softcover, 400 pages	$17.99	$19.99	$26.99

"At AuthorHouse, we calculate royalties from the suggested retail price of your book; we never charge for any additional printing costs, administrative fees, or retailer discounts. You'll regularly receive royalties from sales through AuthorHouse and retail outlets."

Chapter Twenty-Five: **Aventine Press**

"Aventine Press provides the author who has decided to invest in his or her own work, the tools to bring it to fruition quickly, expertly and economically. Our services encompass everything you'll need, start to finish, in the book publishing process while making it an easy, step-by-step experience. It's both an extremely practical and efficient method for today's author to get into print with the best possible results.

By choosing Aventine Press as your book publisher, you join a rapidly growing and innovative group of self-publishing author-entrepreneurs who elect to take control of their own project. You retain all rights to your work and determine the content, style and marketing of your book.

We offer professional publishing services that include the formatting of your book for publication; interior page layout, book cover design, indexing and advanced marketing tools like website design. These services are individually priced, and you can choose to use them or not at your own discretion or level of publishing experience.

>   **Author Discount:** Most self-publishing authors purchase numerous copies of their own book for marketing giveaways, reviews, to sell or to distribute to friends and family. Our authors pay only the actual printing and shipping cost plus 10% - with no quantity restrictions and no minimum purchase requirements and also receive printing discounts with orders of 25 or more copies.

>   Authors may purchase copies of their own title in quantities of 25 to 150 copies to qualify for a 10%

discount, quantities of 151 to 550 copies to qualify for a discount of 25% or quantities of 1,100 copies and up for a discount of 35%.

Author Royalties: Our royalties are paid biannually and are substantially larger than the royalties paid by most book publishers. We pay you 80% of the payments we actually receive from sales of printed copies of your book. (This is after subtracting book production cost)

Trade Discounts: Some book publishing companies offer booksellers minimal discounts on titles already overpriced for the marketplace, a practice that can doom your book to obscurity. Aventine Press will price your book right and attract booksellers with generous discounts up to 55% off the cover price. (This will lower your royalty but hopefully increase sales)

Highest Quality: No self publishing company offers you a higher quality print-on-demand product or faster service and fulfillment. Our trade paperbacks and hardcovers are printed to order usually within 72 hours and are printed on premium quality, acid-free, book-grade cream and white paper stock *(must be 108 pages or more)*. Paperback covers are printed on a bright white 80# cover stock.

Our Basic Service Package Includes:

Your choice of cover design; use our professional custom covers (as low as $295.00), our cover templates ($175.00) or supply your own design.

Your choice of styles from our Interior Templates.

International Standard Book Number (ISBN).

Inclusion of author photo and cover photos.

Inclusion of author biography.

Electronic proofs.

UPC bar-code.

Indexing, up to 25 keywords free. (On request)

Two free trade paperback copies of your book.

Listing of your book with online booksellers.

Your completed book (final proof) plus cover art on CD.

Quarterly royalty payments and accounting.

Submission to Ingram's Ipage Registration and Database Listing

Basic Service Package Fee: $399.00

Add-On Services:

Because we work with authors of varying self publishing experience and needs, we offer additional services for you to achieve the personalized look and feel you want for your book. These services and fees are in addition to our Basic Service Package:

Custom Cover Design: $295.00

Statistics show that eighty percent of what goes into selling a book is the cover design. A professional cover designer will create your cover for you with your input. Please take note of the book covers you'll find through-out our web site, we have a reputation for producing quality covers that grab attention and **sell more books!**

Hardcover Edition of Your Book : $295.00
(Includes separate ISBN and sales reports)

Your book and cover will be formatted to be produced in a hardcover version, complete with full color dust jacket and durable cloth-style (patriot blue or slate gray) cover with gold foil stamped title on spine.

Interior Images : $5.00 / *per image*

If you choose to add interior pictures or illustrations to your book, there is a $5.00 per image processing fee. Interior images and graphics will be printed in grayscale (black & white).

Image Scanning : $7.00 / *per image*

Professional image scans of your photo's or artwork for use in your book's interior. We can accommodate photo's or artwork up to 8.5 X 11 inches in size.

Alteration Fee: $50.00 / *per hour* , **$75.00** / *per hour for web*

If you decide to make editorial changes (author's alterations) or cover design changes to your submission during the production process, we may find it necessary to charge you an alteration fee to defray the additional expense. An alteration fee will also be charged for web changes if we find it necessary. We define an alteration as an authors change to text or template while your book is in production. These fees will be charged to your credit card (a credit card number must be provided in the event that you request changes with the applied fees).

Aventine can be contacted during business hours by phone or email anytime and an answer should be forthcoming within 24 hours M – F."

Chapter Twenty-Six: **AuthorHive**

An **Author Solutions** affiliate providing marketing services

(It should not be a surprise that this new service came via Author Solutions. No prices are mentioned anywhere on the site. Marketing is expensive no matter what you are attempting to sell or promote so I expect they have hefty price tags. On the other hand...most authors are not remotely aware of how to market their book and an excellent marketing plan could put a good book by an unknown author on the best seller list. Is it worth the cost? Only if you can afford it.)

"Let AuthorHive take the hassle and confusion out of the business of book marketing. We can do a little—or a lot—depending on your needs and your budget, in the areas that matter most when you need to create BUZZ for your book."

Campaigns

"Without AuthorHive, you likely have to settle for a piecemeal approach to market your book. Publicist A to handle press releases. Freelancer B to design a Web site. Producer C to create a promotional video. And so on.

AuthorHive simplifies the whole process of book marketing and promotion. We're a one-stop solution that brings all of your marketing needs under one roof. And we're backed by the resources and proven expertise of Author Solutions, one of the fastest growing indie book publishing and marketing companies in the world."

Publicity Marketing

"AuthorHive publicists have helped thousands of writers get the word out about their book. Our expertise in publicity services gives us the unique resources to give your book an effective promotional platform. Choose from a package of services that could include the following:

- Book Review
- Press Release
- Press Kit
- Publicist

Multimedia Marketing

"Multimedia—the artful combination of video and audio—has changed the face of book promotion. A video can make an immediate emotional connection with the viewer in a way that a written review or press release cannot. But you don't need a Hollywood production budget to promote your book through the medium of video. Not when you have AuthorHive."

Choose from among these visual tools:

- Author Video Interview
- Video Book Trailer
- Hollywood Movie Trailer

Online Marketing

"AuthorHive has all the expertise you need when it comes to Online Marketing. We're your one-stop destination for any promotional element needed to put the worldwide reach of the Web to work for you. AuthorHive Online Marketing Services include:

- Author Web Site
- Social Media
- Search Results
- E-mail Marketing

Event Marketing

"Personal appearances are an excellent way to generate sales and increase public awareness and visibility for your book. AuthorHive expertise can help make those appearances happen, putting you face-to-face with fans and publishing industry insiders at the venues that matter, including:

- Book Signings
- Book Galleries

Call for more information: 866-697-5289

Chapter Twenty-Seven:
Beckham Publications Group

A joint venture assistance to publishing...an exciting new alternative for writers who believe in their writing...are willing to invest in it...and want control over it.

- You call the shots
- You receive more attention
- Smaller print runs mean lower costs
- You get full support including marketing and distribution
- Profit potential is greater than the usual seven to 10 percent royalty of the traditional houses

THE BECKHAM PUBLICATIONS GROUP JOINT VENTURE APPROACH TO SUBSIDY PUBLISHING:
A Real Difference

"When you enter a joint venture arrangement with Beckham Publications, you'll get the attention you need and deserve...professional editorial support...state-of-the art book production...expert marketing advice...niche distribution marketing. Plus we have a solid track record of publicity successes. We've been covered in *Newsweek*, *USA Today*, *Mademoiselle*, *Black Enterprise*, *The Washington Post*, *Chronicle of Higher Education*, *Publishers Weekly*, *Ebony*, *Emerge*, and others."

JOINT VENTURE ASSISTANCE TO SUBSIDY PUBLISHING –

"A joint venture occurs when two parties decide to invest in a project and share in the profits generated. In publishing, the investing partners are you, the author, and the publisher.

Typically, you pay us a fee for a three-fold arrangement.

• First, we design the cover, edit, typeset, print and bind, and deliver a quantity of books for you to resell.
• Secondly, we print copies at our expense, sell to retail markets and pay you a royalty on each copy sold.
• Thirdly, we reprint additional copies at your request for you to resell.

In addition, you can contract us for extra promotional materials including order takers and press releases.

You, as a partner in the project, have a great deal to say about the cover design, editing and even marketing strategy. Joint venture publishing has so many advantages. Today's world of publishing is dominated by larger commercial houses that shun works which don't have mass appeal. Further, larger houses take 12 to 18 months to produce a book, and control all aspects including whether it will ever be reprinted. Traditional houses are not even accepting manuscripts unless submitted by a literary agent. Writers of new, provocative, or of limited interest material don't have much of a chance.

However, your joint venture book can be produced in half the usual time commercial publishers take. And in this age of specialization, many more outlets other than the routine mass market centers are available for your book—including your own network of friends and colleagues."

WHAT DO WE DO?

"Beckham comes as a partner offering editorial, production, marketing and distribution capabilities to complete that "publish your own book" project. Obviously, each project has a different set of needs. Every title will require entirely different levels of support in each area. Some will need considerable editorial assistance and others will need very little. What Beckham determines as its fee is based on these factors. Basically, then, our efforts fall within one or several of these areas: editorial, production, marketing and distribution."

• Editorial

"The author of a good book must give adequate attention to its theme, style and structure. Our editorial philosophy is based on the importance of these three elements. Accordingly, we do what is necessary to assure that the finished product, the published book, is written in the most readable and appropriate style, is well-organized and smoothly structured. Some manuscripts require simple proofreading; others, line-by-line editing. Still others may need extensive re-writing. Our editors are prepared to correct textual matters like grammar, punctuation and spelling, as well as make changes to improve the manuscript overall."

• Production

"Everything must work together. The physical appearance of your book must reflect its thematic uniqueness--its set of ideas that makes it different from any other title. Production is the process of putting the book together physically. It includes text design, jacket design, typesetting, printing and binding. Each detail like title page design and chapter headings receives individual attention. We design and layout pages, position chapter headings, titles, folio numbers, table of contents and an index. We layout pictures, graphs, and illustrations, placing them in proper position. You review your manuscript before final approval is given to the printer. We fill out necessary forms and pay for your Library of Congress copyright.

We give you one of our pre-assigned International Standard Book Numbers as part of the system for numbering and identifying books in print. We supply a bar code, used by libraries and resale stores to monitor inventory and to reorder. (This makes Beckham the PUBLISHER, not you.)"

• Marketing

"Many have said that writing the book is just the beginning. Now it has to be sold. Beckham offers a number of marketing packages that will bring the book to the attention of your primary readers, the larger audience beyond them, libraries, reviewers and other distributors. Our basic package can be customized to include additional services.

In this package, we first prepare and mail news releases (capitalizing on the unique selling angle we devise for your self-publication) to reach local or specialized radio and television stations, newspapers, magazines, reviewers, librarians and wholesalers. Then we mail direct response flyers announcing your book to names supplied by you. Each contains an order coupon to be used to purchase copies of your book directly from Beckham.

We can also supply you with 500 direct mail pieces for your own use.

Do not expect to receive reviews in national media; your book probably doesn't have so large an audience. But be prepared to receive some local and specialized exposure like news items, feature stories and radio and television interviews. Publicity generated through these efforts can help stimulate interest in your book."

• Distribution

"Most of our joint venture publications will not attract a large reading audience. Therefore it is unlikely that it will attract the interest of the big chain buyers. But they will be aware of your book, so you will certainly have a fair shot at being distributed nationally in addition to making the expected sales to your narrowly defined target market. And remember that our web site is seen by readers all over the globe. Between 1998 and 1999, books sold online tripled their market share from 1.9 percent to 5.4 percent. Nobody expects that trend to slow down.

Authors who travel in wide circles and enjoy a large following will be able to market their books exclusively to their already established audience. Some pastors of large churches, college professors and workshop presenters have an excellent opportunity to market their own books, recoup their investment, and enjoy handsome profits."

JOINT VENTURE ASSISTANCE TO SELF
PUBLISHING: What Does It Cost?

"Each book is different. Our fees are determined by how much editorial and production work must be done, by the trim size, illustrations, charts, number of pages and words, and number of books printed. After these variables have been evaluated, we can provide you with an estimate.

Still, we cannot quote exact prices until we examine the entire manuscript. Our terms are at least 50 percent with order, the balance due upon approval of final page proofs for printing. Shipping is billed with final invoice."

HOW TO GET STARTED

"Fill out the estimate request form today, and email us requests@beckhamhouse.com sample pages so that we can send your quote. Or if you feel confident about Beckham and want to save time, include your manuscript with the request form and we'll send a binding quote and agreement letter. We prefer to work by email."

Chapter Twenty-Eight: Black Forest Press
A Christian Subsidy Publisher

BFP has been in business for 17 years. They are a subsidy
printer of Christian books. If your book does not conform
to Christian principles they will turn you away.

They do not provide any costs on site, you must send them
the manuscript before they advise you of the possible costs.

Below are some of the FAQ's gathered from their site.

"Black Forest Press© (BFP) is a Christian book publisher.
We are considered to be a 'one-stop-shop' subsidy-
publisher of book manuscripts submitted to us for
publishing."

What is the cost of publishing my book?
"BFP is more than happy to discuss the cost of publishing
your book with you in conversation, over the telephone.
Once we have seen your manuscript and can determine
what needs to be done to it prior to being printed for
publication, and knowing certain things like, is the book
simply a black and white text, or an all color book, BFP is
then able to begin a cost work-up on your book. We also
need to know how many books will be printed, and will the
book be a POD book or an offset print run. What size will
the book be? Will it be a hardback cover, saddle stitched or
a perfect bind. The number of pages after formatting must
be determined. Are there pictures? If so, how many? How
many special scans will be needed for those extra items you
want included in your book? These are some of the items
BFP and you, the author, will have to decide upon before
we can give you an accurate quote. Anything less would be

guesswork and we would be doing you a disservice instead of providing you with an accurate figure."

Do I still need to advertise my book?
"Self-published books usually don't become good sellers without having some money and personal time invested in them for promotion. Get ready to promote yourself along with your book. Get ready to spend time and money to put your book in front of those who need to see it in order to buy it. An author cannot simply sit and wait for book sales to materialize."

Will I still retain 100% control and profits from my book?
"BFP gives every author 100% control of his or her book and 100% profit from that book."

To contact Black Forest Press: www.blackforestpress.com

Black Forest Press©
Belle Arden Run Estate
496 Mountain View Drive
Mosheim, TN 37818-3524
Telephone: (423) 212-1208
E-mail: authorinfo@blackforestpress.net

Chapter Twenty-Nine:
BookMasters Group

With nearly 40 years of experience, BookMasters handles every step of the publishing process — from initial documentation and developmental editing to text and cover design, book printing, warehousing, fulfillment, and distribution. When it comes to print production, BookMasters takes pride in managing every detail so you can focus on the business of publishing. Because of our state-of-the-art capabilities and great passion for providing exceptional service, publishers get exactly what they want: more choices and fewer hassles.

Printing Options
"Our book printing capabilities include high-quality, sheet fed and web offset and digital, one-to-four-color text at both our Ohio and BMI Asia printing facilities. We provide economical solutions for your printing needs by utilizing a wide variety of quality house stocks. Common trim sizes range from 4.75 x 7 to 9 x 12. Using the most popular coatings for your cover or dust jacket creates a professional finishing touch.

Our binding capabilities include perfect binding, case binding, saddle stitch, GBC comb, plastic coil, Lay-Flat, and trim-four/drill-three for loose leaf."

Content
"BookMasters Content Services is one of the leading pre-publishing service organizations offering publishers total content management solutions. Whether it be project management, editorial, or our sophisticated conversion services, the publishing teams at BookMasters

are equipped to deliver all types of services and solutions for our clients' print, online and e-publishing medias."

Distribution

"BookMasters Distribution Services is the new name for the distribution arm of BookMasters, a $100m owner-operated publishing services company that was established in 1972. The integrity and expertise of BookMasters' existing infrastructure provide a strong platform for BookMasters Distribution to set new industry standards in full-service distribution.

Our state of the art production and warehouse facility is strategically located in central Ohio. It features a 24/7 customer service team, 24 hour order turnaround, a client base that includes Pearson and Thomson, and a wholly-owned $100m sister company that is a tier one supplier of toys and sporting goods to Walmart and Target.

BookMasters Distribution boasts a group of leading industry professionals dedicated to providing the best possible services for publishers at the best price. We have a team of top flight sales and marketing professionals, who are well-networked with key buyers in the chains, independents and special markets.

Our vision is for BookMasters Distribution to be a flexible, secure and effective partner for independent publishers looking to maximize profits in a challenging marketplace

BookMasters does not provide generic costs. You must request price quotes based on what you want. They will work up the quote and respond. This must be done separately for each option: Printing, Content, and Distribution. They can be found at www.BookMasters.com."

Chapter Thirty:Book Printing Revolution

An affiliate of Hillcrest Publishing
 Short Run Offset Printer
Minimum 200 books

Nearly Limitless Printing Options

"While our instant quote page provides pricing for the most
common soft-and-hardbound, black-and-white interior
book printing needs, we can accommodate nearly any book
printing need you may have. Our exclusive book printing
partner has one of the largest and most advanced book
printing facilities in North America, with constantly
updated equipment and advanced personnel training.
Unbeatable Prices

"Our book printing pricing is unmatched in the Industry.
We beat the competition, in almost all cases, by at least 10
– 15%, all while getting your book printing from one of the
most advanced, respected book printers in America. We've
shopped the competition, and we know we can always give
you the best price. You will typically save hundreds, even
thousands of dollars!"

How to Get Started

After visiting their book printing quote page, you can
proceed directly to the book printing order page by logging

in with your sign-in name (your e-mail address) and your password. From there, you'll be instructed on how to upload your book, given full details in the Terms and Conditions page, and asked for payment and shipping information. You can contact them with any questions, initiate a live chat, or call the staff for help and information. Call at 1 866-797-4314 or 612 455-4301, email at info@bookprintingrevolution.com , or mail at Book Printing Revolution, 212 3rd Ave. North, Suite 290, Minneapolis, MN 55401.

Standard Costs

Using the standard book sample: 6 x 9 trade paperback
100 pages Black & White
Costs to print:

Quantity ordered	Price per unit	Cost of order
200	$5.47	$1094.00
400	$4.59	$1836.00
600	$3.81	$2286.00

Chapter Thirty One: BookPros
No longer in operations

Chapter Thirty-Two:
Book Publishing.com

A Jenkins Group Affiliate

For more than 20 years Jenkins Group, Inc. has been a leading publishing services firm assisting individuals and corporations with custom published book projects and post publication services. For the first time ever, we are now offering our professional services to the entire industry.

Here you will find a comprehensive and unique menu of premium services that serve your needs no matter where you are in the process of creating or marketing your book. Our services are designed to create and market the very best books through our unprecedented level of customer service and attention to detail. When you need help, we have the answers to get you through.

Our custom solutions fit a variety of budgets and publishing timelines. We work in all genres of book publishing including business, fiction, non-fiction, children's and corporate anniversary among others.

From ghostwriting, manuscript development, editing, illustration, cover design and proofreading to printing, binding and the shipping of your book our comprehensive menu of services covers any and every aspect of the publishing world.

(The websites are visually pleasant but I went from page to page, becoming frustrated at the game of cat and mouse. A few pages gave general estimates, such as Ghost Writing costing between $10,000 and $60,000 grand. But in most case the visitor learns how professional the Jenkins Group is and is advised to call or email them for more information.

In this digital age can't we get instant digital answers anytime, anywhere?)

If you are interested in learning more about any of the Jenkins Group's many services please visit their website at www.bookpublishing.com.

Chapter Thirty-Three: BookSurge
is now CreateSpace,
a division of AMAZON

"BookSurge and CreateSpace, have united on the CreateSpace platform, now offering you more publishing options than ever before. Whether you have ready-to-print PDF book files or a manuscript in need of professional editing and book design support, we can help you effectively publish, market and sell your book. Access us at www.CreateSpace.com"

(For more information on CreateSpace, please refer to Chapter 13, our personal experience using CreateSpace. We provide an in depth look at the process, the obstacles, and the costs.)

Chapter Thirty-Four : Books Just Books

An Offset Printer

An affiliate of RJ Communications
An affiliate of Selfpublishing.com

RJ Communications, the predecessor of **BooksJustBooks.com** and SelfPublishing.com was started in 1994 as one of the Internet's first commercial printing services, specializing in book printing for major New York City publishers. While there are thousands of commercial printers who can print books, there are very few true book printers. Owners Ron Pramschufer and Dana Cole together have over 60 years of book printing and book publishing experience and the printing and publishing experience extends throughout the entire company. Online instant book printing pricing was introduced in 1996. Since then, the company has overseen the printing of thousands of different titles totaling well over 100 million copies. The **BooksJustBooks.com** network of book printers enables book printing buyers to print in offset book manufacturing facilities located in Minnesota, Michigan, New Hampshire, North Carolina and California. Digital facilities are located within a Zone 4 UPS shipment to virtually any state within the continental US.

Because this is offset printing, not POD, there is a minimum order of 100 books. You supply the digital formatted manuscript, jpeg cover, and a check for the number of books you want. They supply them at low costs.

Our standard sample of a book of 100 pages, black and white, 6 x 9, color soft cover has a unit cost of $3.86. With a minimum order of 100 books you would need $386.12 plus shipping and handling and don't forget the storage.

Chapter Thirty-Five: BRIO

Brio
888-333-7979
www.briobooks.com

BRIO is full service and full of spirit. We are excited about helping our clients reach their publishing goals. BRIO provides publishing services to independent authors. We work with clients nationwide to provide professional editing, design, illustration, printing, promotion, warehousing, and fulfillment services.

At BRIO we believe that authors should enjoy and appreciate the publishing experience. Authors should expect high quality services and products, within a reasonable time frame, and at competitive prices. BRIO strives to exceed the expectations of independent authors. Our goal is to simplify the publishing process so you are involved and informed and can make the best decisions for your book, and have fun doing so. No matter what stage you are at in publishing your book, we invite you to call and speak with one of our experts for a free consultation

BRIO publishing services are for authors who need more than printing alone. We will consult with you about your book and make recommendations to create a professionally finished product.

Suggested services may include editing, cover design, illustrating, interior layout, printing, formulating a promotional plan for yourself and your book, storing your books, and fulfilling orders. We create customized solutions, not packages that include services you don't need. We will find the answer for you within your budget.

Chapter Thirty-Six:
Camp Pope Publishing

What is Camp Pope Publishing?

"Camp Pope Publishing is me, Clark Kenyon. I am a publishing services provider. I am not a commercial publisher and do not accept unsolicited manuscripts. But I am here to help you get your book into print by providing the services you need, from editing, design and layout, to complete printing and binding.

"I have been editing, designing, and typesetting books since 1991, for my own company, Press of the Camp Pope Bookshop, and for other organizations and individuals. The printing and binding part of the business I contract out to either offset or digital (Print on Demand) book manufacturers.

"The nature of contract book publishing is that you pay all the costs. You then receive all copies of the book to sell or distribute as you please. You are the copyright holder and retain the rights to your book, and you set the retail price. Although I don't get into the marketing of your book, I can provide distribution services worldwide through Ingram, Baker and Taylor, Amazon and others if you choose to have your book published Print on Demand. And, if you wish, I will design and maintain a website with a unique URL based on your name or the name of your book for the direct sale of your book from my online store. Either of these distribution models will require you to allow up to a 55% discount off the retail price of your book.

"The costs to you of evaluating, editing, typesetting, printing, and binding your book (and any other services you may require) will be clearly laid out in a non-exclusive, non-transferable contract before any of these costs are incurred."

Publishing

In the past several years, digital book printing and the Print on Demand (POD) production model have become very popular, especially for the printing of small quantities. Digital book manufacturers keep a PDF file of your book on a server, then when they receive orders for your book, send that file to the printer. In a matter of minutes the book is printed and bound and ready to be shipped to the customer. We now have something called the Espresso Book Machine (EBM), basically an ATM for books, where a book is automatically printed, bound and trimmed while you wait. Currently there are 30 EBMs installed around the world. As streamlined and cost effective as POD is, offset printing and binding are still superior in terms of quality and the choices of formats available to you. POD is limited to just a few trim sizes, two (and sometimes only one) choices for paper color, and, although hardcover books, even with dust jackets, are available via POD, the choices here are even more limited. Halftone reproduction in black and white can vary widely from one printing to the next. With POD, one needs to keep cover design modest. POD reproduces gradients poorly, it can't do high ink coverage. On the other hand, color interior books, while more expensive than black and white, are more affordable via POD. (Four-color interior from offset is very expensive domestically; most publishers use Asian manufacturers to print 4-color interior books by offset).

Marketing and Distribution Plan

"I can offer you a limited marketing arrangement which would be to both our advantages. If you so desire, I will create a webpage for your book with a unique URL containing the title of the book (or as close as we can get to the title). This will be an add-on domain to camppope.com, but it will appear on the web as a separate website. Visitors to the website can read some advertising copy (which you can write or you can pay me to write) and order the book directly from Camp Pope Publishing through my secure shopping cart. The design of the site will be simple and straightforward and subject to your approval (you may design the site, which will then be subject to my approval). I will require a 40%-50% discount on your books to sell via this website. For example, you set the retail price of your book at $20.00 and your book costs $4 to print (which includes the 10% CPP service charge). Your profit would be $16, less my 50% discount, so your final profit per book sold via the website would be $8.00. Payment will be made to you monthly and only after a balance of $50 has been attained, or at least twice a year, when statements of account will be submitted to you. If your book has been manufactured POD, you will not have to provide me with inventory; I can order it directly from the printer. If you have gone the offset route, I will order inventory from you at a 40%-50% discount, and no further payment will be made to you.

"If a separate website for your book seems like too much, I can sell your book from my website for which I would require the same 40-50% discount. This is a very simple arrangement which requires only your approval. Naturally, if your book is for private distribution to family, you're not obliged to make it available for sale to the general public.

"If you want to go POD and would like to have your book available on Amazon.com, I recommend we have your book printed by Amazon's POD service, Createspace. If we make your book available for distribution through Ingram (and its POD printer Lightning Source, Inc.) it will show up on Amazon, but without the perks that Createspace users enjoy, such as your own eStore page where Amazon promotes and sells your book, plus easy integration into Amazon's retail program and free software for converting your physical book to an eBook available to owners of Amazon Kindle eBook readers.

"I would recommend for your POD book, that we go with Lightning Source, Inc. For a nominal yearly charge your book will be made available worldwide through Ingram, Barnes & Noble, Baker & Taylor and other book distributors. You would be expected to allow up to a 55% discount (you can specify less, as little as 20%, if you don't think bookstores would be likely to want to stock your book) and accept returns, but it's an inexpensive way of getting your title into the distribution pipeline. Books printed by Lightning Source are also available via the Espresso Book Machine."

(Amazing! Up front, owning what they are. The only thing
not exceptional about this site is the fact that you must fill
out a short questionnaire to receive a price quote.)

Chapter Thirty-Seven: CreateSpace

The Print on Demand branch of Amazon.

Please see Chapter Thirteen for complete information.

Chapter Thirty-Eight: Creation House
Offset Printer/Christian Subsidy Publisher

"Mission Statement: To provide a level of excellence in books and services that represents the Kingdom of God and proclaims Jesus to the world.

Creation House, a division of Charisma Media, publishes Christian books with a high standard of quality. We specialize in a variety of genres and provide professional production, editing, and marketing for our authors.

Today, our 40 years of successful publishing have equipped us to offer Christian authors unique advantages in affordable, customized publishing. Major publishing houses are increasingly selective about works from new or unknown authors, so getting even very well-written manuscripts published is usually quite difficult. That's why we offer co-publishing as an alternative.

We use the term co-publishing to describe a hybrid between self-publishing and conventional royalty publishing, utilizing the best of both worlds. In co-publishing, we partner with you, the author, to develop a quality book according to your specifications, producing a finished product suitable for the bookselling marketplace. Included in our contracts are the marketing, sales, and distribution tools needed to give your book a chance to succeed. Your co-published book becomes a Charisma Media product that bears the Creation House imprint and becomes part of our publishing legacy.

This is made possible by your willingness to purchase your own significant quantity of books at a deep discount from the first press run. We in turn purchase an amount of books to sell through the trade and pay you a royalty for each book we sell.

- First, submit your manuscript/book for review by filling out our book proposal form.
- If your book is accepted and meets our company's publishing guidelines, we will send you an acceptance letter that includes customized printing costs based on the information you provided in the proposal form.
- Once the print proposal is finalized you may then request a Creation House publishing contract. If you agree to the contract, you will sign two copies and return them to us with your first payment. When we receive the signed contracts and payment we will sign the contracts and return one copy for your records.
- After the contracts are finalized we start the production of your book. This includes editing, copyediting, and typesetting. At the same time, we begin the marketing process with a review of your title and subtitle, professional cover design, and by preparing your book information for our sales team.
- After the production process and cover process are complete and you have sent us your final payment and signed approval form, we will then send your book to the printer.
- The full co-publishing process, from the time we receive the signed contracts to when the books are shipped from the printer, takes about 12 weeks with no delays."

(No prices available without a submission. Even though they are a Christian site, remember the warning flags from Chapter Six.)

Chapter Thirty-Nine: CrossBooks

Cross Books
1663 Liberty Drive
Suite 200
Bloomington, IN 47403
(866) 879-0502
customerservice@crossbooks.com

The Basic Package ($699.00) includes a review of the theological basis in your novel. You also receive a classic cover design, a custom interior, and an ISBN. Besides getting 5 copies of your printed book, you are also awarded huge volume discounts on your purchases of your book.

The Select Package ($1399.00) offers all the above with 10 free books. There is also channel distribution to 25,000 retailers worldwide, listings on Amazon, Barnes & Noble, and Borders online. You also get listed on Google/Amazon book search programs, a Library of Congress Control Number, copyright registration, and a marketing content composition.

In the Pro Select Package ($2799.00) you get everything listed above along with 25 free books. CrossBooks also includes an editorial review, booksellers return program, book signing kit, and a press release composition.

Chapter Forty: Cypress House
Print Brokers

"Cypress House does not do the actual printing, they send it to the printer they feel fits your project. They apply for the copyright and ISBN, (Making them the publisher, not you-- remember self publishing is when you purchase the ISBN and your name or publishers name is on the book and you retain ALL rights).

Their editing services include manuscript evaluation, editing, rewriting, and ghost writing. They assist with cover art, believing the back of the book blurb closes the sale on more books but that it should tie in to the front cover art. They provide 'interior book design' offering you different fonts and formats, letting you choose which style you like best and they prepare (format) your manuscript for the printers.

Their marketing and promotion is a combination of mailing lists, media lists, and Web design for your marketing, as well as distribution packages.

They do not offer a generic calculator, instead preferring you send them your manuscript and they will access your needs and offer you a quote. They do imply that the book may cost thousands. As previously stated, any time prices are not discussed upfront, apply with caution. If you decide you are not interested in them, ask them to remove you from their marketing list.

The costs below are based on a book that is 5 1/2 x 8, perfect bound, standard paper, laminated paperback cover between 150 - 175 pages.

After a contract has been signed to publish your book, a project coordinator will be assigned to oversee the process. The first hour of phone and mail consultation is provided without charge; additional consultation time, if desired, is billed at $75 per hour with staff ($150 per hour with the president or senior editor)."

Evaluation and Editing

"If you haven't prepared a marketing plan or had your book professionally critiqued, we offer a thorough and professional evaluation for $250 (under 100,000 words; $350 for books over 100,000 words). We'll provide a detailed, multi-page analysis of your book's content, structure, and sales potential that can save you time and money while pinpointing problem areas. If we think that your book needs editing, we'll supply a free sample edit of a page or two along with a bid to edit the rest. If this appeals to you, please send your manuscript and payment (along with return postage), allowing 4-6 weeks for our report. You may send your manuscript on disk; we'll print out a hard copy for an additional charge of $.15 per page and return the printout with the evaluation."

Pre-Press

"If your book is not camera-ready (see camera-ready requirements), we will provide page samples, professional page and book design, light editing, 1200/2540 dpi typesetting, and make-up to camera-ready (includes author's proofing copy): $1000 to $1500.

For those new to printing, camera ready is when every page of your manuscript is typeset and formatted on a page exactly as it will appear in the printed book, which means true quotes rather than inch marks, true em and en dashes rather than hyphens, running headers and footers (with odd-numbered pages on the right side and even-numbered pages on the left), crop marks to indicate trim size, and type resolution and density optimized

Preliminary cover sketches cost $75 each. Finished full-color cover design ranges in price from $400 to $1500, depending on complexity and medium. We can scan your photos or artwork or provide high quality interior illustrations, maps, charts, indexing, etc. We can train you to complete necessary publishing forms or file them for you. The forms relevant to your project and other publishing practices will be discussed in personal consultation with you."

Paperback Printing Prices
1000 copies: $2500 - $3000 (that's 2.50 – 3.00 per book, rather avg. per printing standards.)
2000 copies: $3200 - $3500
3000 copies: $4000 - $4500

Casebound Printing Prices
1000 copies: $4500 - $5500
2000 copies: $7000 - $8000
3000 copies: $9000 - $10,000

(Per the following statement, shipping is included in the price above, which makes this a fair deal.)

"Printing prices include finalizing print specifications; packaging and shipping all materials with detailed instructions; ongoing communication with the printer to maintain a timely production schedule; reviewing cover key and text (blueline) proofs; printing, binding, and overseeing any changes made pursuant to proofing or as a result of last-minute revisions; tracking the shipment of finished books from the printer to a designated storage facility, distributor or wholesalers; and representing your interests in the unlikely event of printing, binding or shipping problems.

Complete book publishing costs are the sum of pre-press, printing, shipping and freight charges. If books are to be promoted to the trade, a marketing and promotion budget should be allocated. We recommend you spend as much to promote your book as you do in printing it.

Here are some of the promotional services we offer. We can:
* Promote and sell your book in our catalog (30,000 copies distributed annually) and at our web site
* Write press releases and reviews
* Create press kits and produce posters, flyers, order forms, book displays, etc.
* Prepare pre-publication review copies
* Mail books and promotional materials to reviewers and follow-up with personal phone calls
* Obtain permissions and secure blurbs
* Conduct database research and prepare bulk mail (up to 40,000 pieces)
* Contract with distributors to carry your book
* Represent your book at conferences and trade shows
* Handle subsidiary and foreign rights, including audio, video, book club, and film rights
* Schedule radio and television interviews and book signing tours
* Coordinate advertising, premium, and direct mail campaigns
* Arrange press conferences and book parties
* Warehouse your books, insuring them against loss
* Conduct telemarketing and toll-free order taking

Chapter Forty-One: Diggypod

(Cute name for this printer and author services site. They are NOT a publisher so you will have to obtain your own ISBN and copyright if desired.)

"DiggyPOD offers short-run book printing services for self publishers. We are committed to giving you online printing services with straight forward prices, fast turnaround times, great service, and excellent quality. Our job is to make you look good.

All of our book prices include a full color cover, printed on 10pt C1S with Gloss Film Lamination on one side. On the inside, the text is black and can be printed on either 50# or 60# white smooth offset, or a 60# natural offset. Full Color Book Printing services are also provided. All books are perfectly bound and trimmed to industry standards

We have created a Custom PDF Print Driver to help you convert files quickly and easily. Our custom driver was created to take your book from the program that it was originally created in, and convert it to a PDF file ready for uploading. We want to make your book printing process easy."

They also provide numerous videos to help you master each step of the process. Diggypod offers a generic cost calculator based on choosing cover, pages, and size, and quantity. They have a minimum order of 25 books.

(Based on providing them with a properly formatted disk or attachment, and not needing a cover design or other assistance, a print run of 100 books comprised of 100 pages 6 x 9 size, perfect bound, standard paper cost 3.09 per book. If you only order 25 books, their minimum order, the cost per book more than doubles rising to 6.97 per book.

They offer formatting templates and inexpensive cover design (under $100.00). Two of their biggest assets are the fact that they have live people to answer the phones and answer your questions, and they have some pretty good explanatory videos to explain each step of the process.

They have a comparison chart to help you see in which areas they beat the competition. However, the charts change categories for each comparison. It is rather like comparing apple prices to orange prices. We wouldn't put much stock in these comparisons anymore than we consider all the claims about highest royalties paid.)

(Diggypod appears to be exactly what they say. A company that assists you with most author services and offset printing for a low price. They aren't free, they do need to be compensated for their work. This is the way I wish most sites worked. Lay it all out there.

Reading over the reviews, most were pleased with their final product. We found one complaint that advised they charged an additional unexpected $25.00 fee for a third file reading fee. I don't know how well they explain additional charges, but the author was pleased with the overall book, just not the fee he wasn't told about beforehand.)

They can be contacted at www.diggypod.com or call 877-944-7844 Hours 9-5 EST.

Chapter Forty-Two: DogEar Publishing

DogEar publishing is a full service author's service,
offering far more than most Subsidy publishers.
(Their prices in some areas are extremely high, but in other
categories are very fair. Choose what you like, omit
services you can do for yourself or find at a comparative
service level for less cash elsewhere.)
POD printing cost estimates are based on an order quantity
of 1000. The price goes up considerably with smaller runs.
If you are ordering over 2000, they use an offset printer,
drastically reducing the cost per unit. Contact DogEar for
quantity price quotes.
Cost estimate
6 x 9 trade paperback/color cover
Base rate $1.28 per unit + $0.02/pg x 100 pages ($2.00)
= total price cost per book is $3.28

They have four Self Publishing Packages.

All packages include:

Paperback or Hardcover format
Completely unique, custom interior and cover design
Up to 30 interior images
5 free paperback books or 5 hardcover (1 color),
5 color paperback (dependent upon format and page count),
Your own **Author Representative** who provides support
throughout the publishing process,
Book and author web page within the Dog Ear web site,
Registration with **all major online booksellers and
national distributors,**

Registration with Books in Print database providing worldwide availability,
Assignment of International Standard Book Number (ISBN),
Library of Congress control number and US Copyright information on the copyright page,
Inclusion in Google Book Search program,
Availability in one digital format (Google Editions.)

1) Basic..........................$1099.00

    Custom Designs
    Full Distribution
    POD availability

2) Professional..................$1699.00

    Aggressive Marketing Campaign that includes:
    Media Release created by our copywriting staff and released to 250 targeted media outlets
    Full-color print marketing materials
        1,000 business cards
        100 postcards
        10 full-size posters
        Custom SEO Web site
        Optimized for Google, Yahoo, MSN and more

3) Professional Plus..................$2199.00

    All the professional package assets plus:

    Up to 50 interior images
    Consultation with a DogEar Publishing

design professional
Media Release created by our copywriting
staff and released to **500** targeted media
outlets
eBook distribution to Google
Author Store Shopping Cart
To process orders and payments,
dramatically increasing the profitability of
your book.

4) Masterpiece......................$3499.00

All the Professional Plus package assets
plus:

Professional Copy Edit
Marketing Consultation
Media Release created by our copywriting
staff and released to **1,000** targeted media
outlets
Full-color print marketing materials
2,000 business cards
250 postcards
10 full-size posters
Custom SEO Web site including WordPress
Blog Feature
Optimized for Google, Yahoo, MSN and
more!
eBook Distribution to Google and Kindle
PPC Marketing Campaign (Pay per click)
Including up to 250 search terms and 5 ad
categories to direct search engine visitors to
your store front or site.
Inclusion in Google Book Search program

DogEar also offers extensive editing options.

Manuscript evaluation $250.00

Proof Reading .015 word Avg book of 80,000 words = 1200.00

Copy Edit .02 word Avg book of 80,000 words = 1600.00

Literary Edit .022 word Avg book of 80,000 words = 1760.

Development edit (also known as coaching) Avg book 80,000 = 3200.

Ghostwriting estimated upon consultation

They offer a proof reader after the proof copy is completed, an "indexer to assist with nonfiction books and book cover copywriting

A few features offered are a cut above those many other author services provide:

1) Video book trailers starting at $799.00
2) Audio Books call for price options as there are many factors that affect the price, such as who is hired to read to the length of the book.
3) Email campaigns start at $195.00
4) Author Websites $395. to $695.
5) Targeted press release campaigns:

     100 Media Outlets - $299.00
     500 Media Outlets - $499.00
     1,000 Media Outlets - $599.00
     5,000 Media Outlets - $1,299.00
     10,000 Media Outlets - $1,999.00

6) Search Engine Marketing, also known as pay per click.

7) Provide Business Cards, Postcards, book Marks, posters

8) They will ePublish your book and place it on Amazon, Barnes & Nobel and Apple's iBookstore for $399.00

> (This is rather excessive since it is free to ePublish on all three sites. It is your call, but I suggest saving the money by doing this yourself and apply the money to one of their marketing services.)

Chapter Forty-Three: Dorrance Publishing

(Dorrance Publishing has been subsidy publishing since 1920. They make no bones about what they do. They do not try to convince you they are traditional or a partner. They charge a fee to provide you a service.)

The only problems we found with their methods were that they charge far more than most other companies we came across and they do not provide even a hint of their sky-high charges until after you submit your manuscript. Then you are inundated with information for months or even years in your mailbox, through your email, even phone calls trying to convince you they are the way to go (a common practice with most subsidy publishers).

While researching I did find an author who diligently promoted them, but he also stated that he has sold over 4000 books and still has not earned his initial cost. Most writers don't sell 200 books, therefore most writers will never break even.

However, he lauded their service and stated they did everything they said they would do. They do not try to convince anyone they are a traditional company. Above board, high costs, but they believe they are worth it since they perform a quality service. Can't beat the logic. This is exactly what we stated we wanted companies to do. Admit what you are and what you provide, be ethical. Some people can afford to pay ten thousand for a quality print run of the book they wrote.

From some of the statements I researched, I believe storage and shipment of the books is included in the price you pay. I also believe it includes editing. But since they have no prices listed on the website, the only way to find out their prices is to provide them with your manuscript.

If you are not looking to earn a profit from your book, can afford high costs, but want a quality product, Dorrance may be your answer. They have live people to answer your questions, they have been in business over 90 years, and they are not trying to trick you.

Can you find a less expensive option? Heck, yes! But as we have said from the start, not everyone is looking to self-publish, not everyone can, and many people are willing to pay for a quality product. If the person contracting their services is rich, owns yachts and fur coats, and Ferrari's, they might be a match.

(There is a publishing company right for everyone.)

Chapter Forty-Four   Dragon Pencil

Dragon Pencil subsidy publishes children's books.

A family business located in Savannah, Georgia, began long, long ago. Jerry made his living illustrating children's books as a freelance artist. As time went on, he met lots of great people who freelanced in other areas of publishing such as editing, design, and printing. After marrying his amazing wife, Samantha, the pair decided to build a business to support their family. And so, Dragonpencil was born. Together with all the great people Jerry encountered over the years, they forged a company with the goal of helping authors publish great children's books.

Board Book Packages:

DP has packages for board books, also called baby books, concept books, and toddler books. They are tough and durable, able to stand up to the abuse babies and toddlers give them.

Conventional Package for a board book: $1245

includes:

    Pre-design
    Editing

A project manager assigned
Quality book design
Cover design
ISBN
LCCN
BISAC (book identification?)
Fulfillment Services ***
Long and brief summary
Illustration discount
Offset printing discount
Additional discounted services

*** Fulfillment Services—"In order to provide the industry with books, we must have books in our Minnesota warehouse. From there we pick, pack, and ship all orders both retail and wholesale. Any real shipping costs, not paid by your customers, are passed on to you. There are other minimal fees for processing orders and returns. Fulfillment fees are minimal; 1 cent per book per month for storage and insurance. There is a minimum storage fee of $15 per month. There is also a half cent per book per month fee for insurance. For example if you have 2000 books in fulfillment, you would pay a total of $30 per month in fees. If you had 100 books in fulfillment, you would pay $15.50 in fees." (This price seems rather excessive, after all it is $360.00 a year and remains in effect until all your books have sold, if they all sell. Be sure to consider it when figuring your cost per book.)

Non-traditional Package for a Board book $590.00

Pre-design
Project Manager
Quality book design
Cover design
Illustration discount

Offset printing discount
Additional discounted services

Picture Book Packages:
Picture Books are also called children's books, story books, and bedtime books.

Deluxe Modern Package $987.00

    Pre-design
    A project manager assigned
    Quality book design
    Cover design
    ISBN
    POD setup
    BISAC (book identification?)
    Long and brief summary
    Illustration discount
    Additional discounted services

Conventional Package $1395.00

    Pre-design
    Editing
    A project manager assigned
    Quality book design
    Cover design
    ISBN
    LCCN
    BISAC (book identification?)
    Fulfillment Services ***
    Long and brief summary
    Illustration discount
    Offset printing discount
    Additional discounted services

Digital Publisher Picture Book $791.00
   Pre-design
   A project manager assigned
   Quality book design
   Cover design
   ISBN
   BISAC (book identification?)
   Fulfillment Services ***
   Long and brief summary
   Illustration discount
   eBook set up
   Additional discounted services

Non-traditional Publishing package $620.00
   Pre-design
   A project manager assigned
   Quality book design
   Cover design
   Illustration discount
   Offset printing discount
   Additional discounted services

Easy Reader Packages
Easy readers are also called early readers or illustrated story books.

Deluxe Modern Easy Reader Package: $1101.00

   Pre-design
   A project manager assigned
   Illustration discount
   Quality book design
   Cover design
   ISBN
   BISAC (book identification?)

Fulfillment Services ***
Long and brief summary
eBook set up
POD set up
Additional discounted services

Conventional Package $1395.00
   Pre-design
   Editing
   A project manager assigned
   Quality book design
   Cover design
   ISBN
   LCCN
   BISAC (book identification?)
   Fulfillment Services ***
   Long and brief summary
   Illustration discount
   Offset printing discount
   Additional discounted services

Digital Package $901.00
   Pre-design
   A project manager assigned
   Illustration discount
   Quality book design
   Cover design
   ISBN
   BISAC (book identification?)
   Long and brief summary
   eBook set up
   Additional discounted services

Chapter Books:

Chapter Books are also called early readers or illustrated story books.

Deluxe Modern Package $1287.00
   Pre-design
   A project manager assigned
   Illustration discount
   Quality book design
   Cover design
   ISBN
   BISAC (book identification?)
   Long and brief summary
   eBook set up
   POD set up
   Additional discounted services

 Conventional Package $3395.00
   Pre-design
   Editing
   A project manager assigned
   Quality book design
   Cover design
   ISBN
   LCCN
   BISAC (book identification?)
   Fulfillment Services ***
   Long and brief summary
   Illustration discount
   Offset printing discount
   Additional discounted services

Digital Package $991.00
   Pre-design
   A project manager assigned

Illustration discount
Quality book design
Cover design
ISBN
BISAC (book identification?)
Long and brief summary
eBook set up
Additional discounted services

Non-traditional Package $820.00
   Pre-design
   A project manager assigned
   Quality book design
   Cover design
   Illustration discount
   Offset printing discount
   Additional discounted services

~~~~~~~~~~~~~~~~~~~~~~~~~~~~~~~~

Illustrators rates are listed online

They run between $125.00 and $300.00 per page depending upon which artist you choose.

Cover Design ala carte
Cover illustration $795.00
Cover Design $625.00

There are other services Dragon Pencil provides, see their website for a more in depth look: www.dragonpencil.com. We love their logo.

Chapter Forty-Five: E-Booktime

E-Booktime offers authors the ability to quickly and easily have their book published as a print on demand paperback or hardback and as an eBook for Amazon's Kindle and Barnes & Noble's Nook. If you are not familiar with print on demand, it is a process where the printer can create a single copy as a customer places his order. No mass purchases required, no shipping fees to pay, no storage necessary.

Paperback and eBook publishing for $395.00

Hardback and eBook publishing for $695.00

The cost of a 'tree book' is based on the number of pages and other variables such as color, size, and paper quality. All eBooks have a required minimum price of $5.95. E-Booktime is the subsidy publisher of record and they pay you royalties on each sale.

Royalties on paperbacks pay 30% if sold through the E-Booktime website and 15% when sold through any other retailer.
 Royalties on hardcover sales are 25% when purchased from the E-Booktimes store and 10% when purchased elsewhere.
 Authors may purchase a quantity of the books at a discount but no royalties are paid on the discounted sales.
 eBooks royalty pays a 50% although if you price your book higher than the required minimum it will increase your royalty amount.

Covers:

They have 32 free templates for your cover. While the site does not specify that they are a Christian publisher, all their covers have a Heavenly scene or a cross. They advise you can provide your own custom cover.

If you want:
A copyright $125.00
Interior pages with pictures, illustrations, or other graphics (Black and white only) - $5.00 per page
Library of Congress Control number - $50.00
Copy Edit -1 cent per word

E-Booktime is one of the few services that agrees to accept a manually "typed" manuscript if it is legible. They prefer manuscripts in a computer file, however, they'll scan a typed manuscript for publishing as long as the print is computer readable – pages are not damaged or marked up, font is not cursive or complex. Scanning service fee is $100.00 for 125 manuscript pages or less. Add $1.00 per page for each additional page. This file will be a jpeg not a document file.

E-Booktime has an A+ rating with the BBB.

Chapter Forty-Six: Friesen Press

"Friesen Press is a division of Friesen's Corporation, an award-winning North American book printer. We've been in the book business since 1923, and over the decades we have developed close relationships with many of North America's traditional publishers. By capitalizing on these relationships, we can now bring you this breakthrough in self-publishing to help you get closer than ever to your publishing dream."

(It is still subsidy publishing. A rose by any other name....)

All Frieson Publishing Packages include the following:
Author Rights

- Non-exclusive contracts
- Author retains 100% of copyright
- Author retains 100% of creative control

Book Layout Customized to Your Needs

- Professional custom layout of inside pages
- Professional full-color front and back cover layout
- First proofing round included at no charge

Attractive Discounts for Author Copies

- 55% off suggested retail price for author copies
- Further discounts for volume purchases
- Order fulfillment service (print, pack, and ship anywhere in the world)

World-Wide Trade Distribution

- Online book sales through Amazon.com

- Worldwide distribution through the Ingram Book Company
- Book available for ordering at over 25,000 bookstores worldwide

Generous Royalty Structure

- Wholesalers: up to 10% of the book cover price
- FriesenPress online bookstore: up to 55% of the book cover price

Fiction

Fiction Niche Package $599.00
all the above features plus:
    Amazon.com Look Inside
    5 Paperback copies of your book

Fiction Mass Marketing Essentials
Package $989.00
all the above features plus:
    eBook standard distribution
    Google Books/Barnes & Noble See Inside
    Amazon.com Look Inside
    Print Media Training Module
    1 hour of one-on-one Book Promotion Coaching
    10 Paperback copies of your book
    50 Postcards, 50 Bookmarks, and 50 Business cards displaying your book cover and ordering information
    5 Posters displaying your book cover in full color
    First 5 interior image insertions
    First 5 footnotes & endnotes and first 5 layout complexities
    Additional revision round

Fiction Mass Market Best Seller Package
$1,499.00
all the above plus:

eBook Premium Distribution—incl. Kindle, iPad,
iPhone, iPod Touch and BlackBerry
Hardcover Edition
Google Books/Barnes & Noble See Inside
Amazon.com Look Inside
Print Media Training Module
Book Promotion Plan
3 hours of one-on-one Book Promotion Coaching
15 Paperback copies of your book
5 Hardcover copies of your book
100 Postcards, 100 bookmarks, and 100 business
cards displaying your book cover and
        ordering information
Ten Posters displaying your book cover in full color
First 10 interior image insertions
First 10 footnotes & endnotes and first 10 layout
complexities
Sales monitoring by traditional publishers
Additional revision round

Fiction Mass Market Best Seller All inclusive
package $2499.00
all the above plus:

     Professional copyediting up to 70,000 words

Nonfiction
Nonfiction Niche Package $699.00
all the standard package plus:

     Amazon.com Look Inside
     5 Paperback copies of your book
     First 10 image insertions free of charge
     First table insertion, first 10 footnotes or endnotes and
     first 10 layout complexities no charge

Nonfiction Mass Market Essentials
$1129.00
all the above plus:

     eBook standard distribution
     Google Books/Barnes & Noble See inside the book
     option
     Amazon.com Look Inside the book option
     Print Media Training Module
     1 hour of one-on-one Book Promotion Coaching
     10 Paperback copies of your book
     50 Postcards, 50 Bookmarks, and 50 Business cards
     displaying your book cover and ordering
     information
     5 Posters displaying your book cover in full color
     First 20 interior image insertions
     First 2 table insertions, first 15 footnotes or
     endnotes, and first 15 layout complexities
     Additional revision round

Nonfiction Mass Market Best Seller
package $1169.00
all the above plus:

> eBook Premium Distribution—incl. Kindle, iPad, iPhone, iPod Touch and BlackBerry
> Hardcover Edition
> Google Books/Barnes & Noble See Inside
> Amazon.com Look Inside
> Radio & TV Media Training Module
> Print Media Training Module
> Book Promotion Plan
> 3 hours of one-on-one Book Promotion Coaching
> 15 Paperback copies of your book
> 5 Hardcover copies of your book
> 100 Postcards, 100 bookmarks, and 100 business cards displaying your book cover and ordering information
> 10 Posters displaying your book cover in full color
> First 30 interior image insertions
> First 3 table insertions, first 20 footnotes or endnotes, and first 20 layout complexities Sales monitoring by traditional publishers
> Additional revision round

NonFiction Mass Market Best Seller All inclusive
$2699.00
all the above plus

> Professional copyediting up to 70,000 words (All-Inclusive Bestseller package only)

Poetry Books
 Poetry Niche Package $579.00
all the standard package plus:

        Amazon.com Look Inside
        5 Paperback copies of your book

Poetry Mass Market Essentials $969.00
 all the above plus:
        eBook standard distribution
        Google Books/Barnes & Noble See Inside
        Amazon.com Look Inside
        Print Media Training Module
        1 hour of one-on-one Book Promotion Coaching
        10 Paperback copies of your book
        50 Postcards, 50 Bookmarks, and 50 Business cards
        displaying your book cover and ordering
        information
        5 Posters displaying your book cover in full color
        First 5 interior image insertions
        First 5 layout complexities
        Additional revision round

Poetry Mass Market Best Seller
$1399.00
all the above plus:
    eBook standard distribution
    Hardcover Edition
    Google Books/Barnes & Noble See Inside
    Amazon.com Look Inside
    Print Media Training Module
    Book Promotion Plan
    3 hours of one-on-one Book Promotion Coaching
    15 Paperback copies of your book
    5 Hardcover copies of your book
    100 Postcards, 100 bookmarks, and 100 business
    cards displaying your book cover and
    ordering information
    10 Posters displaying your book cover in full color
    First 10 interior image insertions (black & white
    package) or first 30 interior image
    insertions (full color package)
    First 10 layout complexities (black & white
    package) or first 15 layout complexities
    (full color package)
    Sales monitoring by traditional publishers
    Additional revision round

Color & Children's Books

Color & Children's Niche Market
Package $659.00
all standard features plus:
    Amazon.com Look Inside
    5 Paperback copies of your book
    First 12 image insertions free of charge

Color & Children's Mass Market Essentials
$999.00
all the above plus:
 eBook standard distribution
 Google Books/Barnes & Noble See Inside
 Amazon.com Look Inside
 Print Media Training Module
 1 hour of one-on-one Book Promotion Coaching
 10 Paperback copies of your book
 50 Postcards, 50 Bookmarks, and 50 Business cards
 displaying your book cover and
  ordering information
 5 Posters displaying your book cover in full color
 First 24 interior image insertions
 Additional revision round

Color & Children's Mass Market Best Seller
Package $1399.00
all the above plus

 eBook standard distribution
 Google Books/Barnes & Noble See Inside
 Amazon.com Look Inside
 Print Media Training Module
 Book Promotion Plan
 3 hours of one-on-one Book Promotion Coaching
 15 Paperback copies of your book
 100 Postcards, 100 bookmarks, and 100 business
 cards displaying your book cover and
 ordering information
 10 Posters displaying your book cover in full color
 First 48 interior image insertions
 Sales Monitoring by traditional publishers
 Additional revision round

Children's Mass Market Best Seller 6
Pack Package $2279.00
all the above plus:
  6 custom inside-page illustrations plus one custom
  cover illustration

Color & Children's Mass Market Best Seller
Package $2995.00
all the above plus:

  12 custom inside-page illustrations
  1 custom cover illustration

eBook Standard features included in all packages:

Author Rights

- Non-exclusive contracts
- Author retains 100% of copyright
- Author retains 100% of creative control

Book Layout Customized to Your Needs

- Professional custom layout of inside pages
- Professional full-color front and back cover layout
- First proofing round included at no charge

World-Wide Trade Distribution

- Online book sales through Amazon.com

Generous Royalty Structure

- Up to 30% of the book cover price

eBook Niche Package $399.00
all the above eBook features plus:
        Amazon.com Kindle Distribution
 eBook Mass Market Essentials Package
$699.00
all the above plus

        Amazon.com Kindle Distribution
        Google eBookstore Distribution
        Online Media Training Module
        1 hour of one-on-one eBook Promotion Coaching
        First 5 interior image insertions
        First 5 endnotes and first 5 layout complexities
        Additional revision round

eBook Mass Market Best Seller Package
$999.00
all the above plus:
        Amazon.com Kindle Distribution
        Google eBookstore Distribution
        Apple iBookstore Distribution
        Nook Distribution (Barnes & Noble)
        Kobo Distribution (Chapters-Indigo/Walmart/Best
         Buy)
        Online Media Training Module
        eBook Promotion Plan
        Personalized Social Media Plan
        3 hours of one-on-one eBook Promotion Coaching
        First 10 interior image insertions

First 10 endnotes and first 10 layout complexities
Sales monitoring by traditional publishers
Additional revision round

eBooks Mass Market Best Seller All-Inclusive $1999.00
all the above plus:

includes professional copyediting up to 70,000 words

Recommended Optional Services

"To help you increase the appeal and market penetration of your book, we recommend the following add-on services for our packages:

- Copyediting
- Content Editing
- Proofreading
- Author Website
- Premium Sales Campaign
- Non-Traditional Channels
- Social Media Setup
- Online Media Promotion
- Book Return Insurance

If you are interested in more information or wish to use Frieson, go to www.friesenpress.com"

Chapter Forty-Seven:
Hillcrest Publishing Group

Mill City Press: POD & Author Services
My Book Orders.com
BPR Book Group
Publish Green: ePublishing
Bascom Hill Publishing Group: a traditional publisher who expects the author to handle marketing
Book Printing Revolution: short-run and offset printing/distribution/fulfillment

Hillcrest is located in Minneapolis, Minnesota.

Can a technology company's About Us page be written without buzzwords? Yes.

Hillcrest Media Group is a technology company that happens to be a book publisher. We've patented our e-book formatting process. Our portfolio of 1200+ book publishing-related domain names rivals any in the world. And, our back-end system can manage the publishing process for thousands of authors and small publishers while simultaneously managing the dissemination of thousands of book reviews to genre-specific directories. Yeah, it's some pretty cool stuff. All created by our own in-house team of mad scientist / D&D types. Throw in a few idea people and some folks who know how to make sure the system plays nice with the customers and you have something pretty special.

In the nearly six years of our existence, we've expanded into just about every area of book publishing: printing, fulfillment, distribution, marketing, and sales. In

2013, we'll be launching Fiction.com. As Miley Cyrus would say, "It should be pretty cool."

"If you just read the sentence above, you might have the idea that we are unconventional. We are. It doesn't matter to us who or what is in the rearview mirror. Our employees are encouraged to create and execute their ideas without having to convince layers of people with window offices that their concepts are viable. Hillcrest Media Group is successful because our employees have the freedom they need to be the innovators we hired."

Chapter Forty-Eight: IBJ Book Publishing

IBJ is an affiliate of the Indianapolis Business Journal, with nearly 30 years experience backing us. They do NOT provide any costs on their website, preferring to speak with you in person to decide what services you may require and base their fees accordingly.
IBJ Book Publishing advises they specialize in helping authors achieve success." Whether you have written a novel, a historical profile, or you are a business person with aspirations of creating a 'book as your business card,' we're dedicated to offering the personal guidance you need.

We have created an easy and gratifying way to turn your unpublished work into a finished book. The next step is to partner with IBJ Book Publishing and let our experienced and talented team bring your creativity and expertise to life."

MAINTAIN CONTROL OF YOUR WORK
"Unlike traditional publishing, our authors retain 100% ownership rights to their work and they maintain complete editorial control. With a nominal investment, authors receive maximum financial benefits.

We prefer to provide one-on-one customer service. This means you meet with actual people rather than submitting everything electronically, although we can work electronically.

Our team of experts will answer your questions and walk
you through the steps to becoming a published author
including the following:

- Registration: ISBN, Bar Code, Library of Congress
  Number and Copyright
- Manuscript Status: Editing, Word Count, Sections
- Book Specifications: Trim Size, Binding, Quantity
- Basic Design – Color, Photos, Illustrations
- Time Frame
- Layout Process
- Marketing Plan
- Distribution Plan

Please visit their site for further information @
www.ibjbookpublishing.com"

Chapter Forty-Nine: Infinity Publishing

"Since 1997, we have been the leading innovator in print-on-demand book publishing. As a publisher we have worked with over 4,800 authors and published over 6,000 titles. We've published best-selling authors, celebrities, hard working professionals, and first-time authors with a story to tell. We publish all genres of books, and our long-standing service to the book publishing community has allowed us to develop strategic global partnerships with book distributors, retail stores and libraries.

Our Essential Softcover Package:
Our most affordable book-publishing solution is also our most popular. The gold standard of quality and service for one low price."

$499 - Softcover, Full Color Cover, B&W interior. Includes a Premium Custom cover design*. Advanced interior formatting*. ISBN. unlimited interior images. hardcopy galley proof*. return-ability for stores. 5 free books. standard global distribution and much more.

Add $200 for Softcover. Full Color Cover & Interior - this includes an eBook with global distribution and much more.

*Other companies charge extra for hard copy galleys and what they deem as "premium" cover design and "advanced" interior formatting. All of our books are custom created with no hidden fees or extra charges.

$199 – Extended Distribution, includes formatting and distribution through the world's largest distributors: Ingram Book Group and Baker & Taylor. Over 50,000 brick and mortar stores will have access to your book, which will also be sold at online retailers such as barnesandnoble.com, borders.com, buy.com, target.com and countless others.

Hardcover Packages:

$799 - Hardcover, black & white interior, dust jacket, eBook publishing and 10 free books (5 hardcover, 5 softcover)

$899 - Hardcover, color interior, dust jacket, eBook publishing and 10 free books (5 hardcover, 5 softcover)

eBook Packages:

$349 - eBook Design and Conversion. Includes premium formatting, color cover and interior page creation and all of our major online distribution channels including iPad, Kindle, Nook and more.

$199 - eBook Conversion. Only for books that do not require additional design or formatting. Includes all of our major online distribution channels.

$149 - eBook Conversion. When added to our essential softcover package. Includes all of our major online distribution channels.

Audio Book Packages:

$599 - The 1-Hour Audio™ book. Publish streamlined non-fiction, fiction short stories, children's or poetry books of approximately 11,000 words for 1-hour of audio. Published as a single CD product and also distributed via the iTunes Store, Audible.com and many others.

Unabridged Audio Books – the ultimate in professional presentation. Books are recorded in specially designed recording studios with a director and engineer on each session. Every second of audio is edited where mouth clicks, swirls, and other noises are replaced with clean room sound. Books are made available where audio books are sold. $599 per 10,000 words.

OneBook – The All-in-One Solution

$995 - OneBook™. This all-in-one solution for print, audio, and eBook is the perfect solution for the author looking for an affordable way maximize exposure to all types of readers in virtually all channels of distribution. Working with a single publisher makes it easy from production to royalty management.

Infinity Publishing has extensive marketing plans to fit every budget. Starting at $125.00 going all the way up to $3000.00. But that's not all!!!....Sorry, for a moment I thought I was on the television info channel. Surfing the marketing offerings by Infinity, I saw some vastly overpriced options such as setting you up with a Facebook profile and Twitter accounts for nearly three grand. These are free sites and anyone can set their own up. If they can't, then having a site will not help since they won't be able to check it regularly. The same applies to the Blog setups, and the Youtube channel. Although I never thought of having a Youtube channel before, it is still overpriced, in my humble opinion. Great ideas though! And that is what marketing is all about.

(They also tout the fact they have live people for you to speak to in order to overcome many obstacles. Remember the inexpensive sites offer virtually no one to speak to, although they do accept email inquiries, these answers are not always the correct answer to a question and you need to start the entire tedious process over again. Frustrating! So—live representatives to help is a big bonus.)

Chapter Fifty: Inkwater Press

Inkwater Press is a full-service subsidy publisher. The publication packages are designed to include all facets of the design and distribution process. Professional editing and additional publishing services can be added to any package to fit the needs of the individual author's work. Inkwater Press can custom design promotional materials for the author's book/events, create a variety of websites and provide publicity services for the author, including seeking out reviews, entering contests, or booking events and interviews.

"At Inkwater Press, our focus is on our books, our authors and our customers. We consider each manuscript submitted and we offer personalized service and professional quality to our authors. While our roots are firmly in the book world, as 21st-century publishers our vision extends beyond the printed page to eBooks, the internet, merchandising, events, film and television.
We offer author-subsidized contracts and the same personal service and professional quality to authors with promising manuscripts.
If we accept your work for publication, we strongly recommend it be professionally edited, and we work with you to create a comprehensive, tailor-made marketing plan for your book. Typically, the publishing process takes four months from the time we accept your manuscript until publication; however this timeline may fluctuate depending on each book's custom plan.
You are welcome to call to discuss your manuscript or any other questions you may have Monday through Friday, from 8 – 5 pm Pacific Time at 503-968-6777. We look forward to hearing from you."

~ ~ ~ ~ ~

(After researching their site, I was perplexed. They do not include prices for any of their services, and are only willing to discuss prices after seeing your manuscript. They have ended up on a number of boards warning about duplicitous behavior. They claim to traditionally publish 3 books a year. Three books a year! That is less than any small boutique press. It is believed to be done in an effort to sell themselves as traditional rather than subsidy publishers. As we have stated many times, own what you are. Many authors are willing to pay for legitimate services. It breeds distrust when you are not open about what you do and at what price. This does not mean that Inkwell or any other firm is doing anything illegal, they are providing a service…a legitimate service. For this guide, we are unable to offer you any standard prices for this company as they do not have any prices or estimates listed on their site.)

Chapter Fifty-One: Innovo Publishing

Innovo Publishing provides full-service publishing and marketing of your Christian book, ebook, audiobook, music and videos. From hardbacks & paperbacks to eBooks (Kindle, Nook, iPhone, iPad, Android), and CD & MP3 audio books and music titles.

They state they offer three levels of publishing, one of which is 'traditional'. Here are their three levels:

Traditional Publishing:

- Author/Artist/Agent submits title (manuscript, music or video) using Innovo's upload tool to right.
- Innovo reviews submissions for quality, style and market match.
- If selected, Innovo offers contract and acquires all title rights.
- Innovo pays advance to author/artist and pays royalties on each copy sold.
- Innovo prepares, publishes and markets title.
- Innovo assumes financial risk for project and funds entire publishing effort.

(It does not state anywhere on the site how many books they purport to publish traditionally every year. One? Ten? Twenty? Feel free to submit to them if you have a Christian book. They claim to respond in three to six weeks as to acceptance. If they offer you subsidy, compare prices and service with other sites, Christian and those with no religious affiliation.)

Co-Operative Publishing:

- Author/Artist/Agent submits title (manuscript, music or video) using Innovo's upload tool to right.
- Innovo reviews submissions for quality, style and market match.
- If selected, Innovo offers custom contract and acquires limited/time-bound exclusivity to publish.
- Author retains ownership and copyright.
- Innovo & Author split royalties.
- Innovo prepares and publishes title.
- Innovo refunds 100% of Author/Artist Publishing Package investment and *converts the contract to a Traditional Publishing* agreement when target sales outlined in contract are met.

(If target sales are not met, the author is on the hook for the entire amount required for publishing. Innovo has nothing to lose whether you make it or not. Just as with any subsidy agreement, you pay. And you do NOT own the rights to the book in this deal. They are the publisher and pay you royalties.)

Innovo's Independent Publishing:

Author/Artist/Agent submits title (manuscript, music or video) using Innovo's upload tool. Innovo reviews submissions for quality, style and market match. If selected, Innovo offers contract and Author retains all title rights.

Author/Artist receives 100% royalties on each copy sold. Author/Artist/Organization pays Innovo to prepare, publish and market title.

Innovo provides turn-key publishing services and access to the world through thousands

(Innovo's publishing rates are posted on line and appear to be reasonable. They have a 50 book minimum in order to maintain these prices but they state a 6 x 9 Trade paperback, black & White, Color cover, 150 pages is 4.65 per book. A total of $232.50 for the publishing. Innovo has more expensive packages in order to assist with many other phases of publishing which include editing, cover design, and marketing and distribution. They also publish children's books and audio books.

They have a number of services available as well; Editing, Cover design, Interior layout, ISBN and copyright registration. Marketing packages range in price from $299.00 to $1500.00. They also have marketing tie ins, plaques, pens, desktop marquees, and more.)

"All submissions, traditional or subsidized must align with Innovo's published Statement of Faith or it will not be considered. Innovo Publishing is a conservative, evangelical Christian publisher. We do not publish 'prosperity gospel' titles or similar." (If you have written a Christian book that passes their Statement of Faith, any Christian publisher would be a good match. With Christian bookstores around the country, Christian books have a built in Niche outlet. If you have written a book that can be sold in these stores, take advantage of it.)

Chapter Fifty-Two: Instant Publishers
A Short Run publishing company, minimum order 25

"InstantPublisher.com is a nationally recognized **book publishing** company that has helped turn thousands of authors' dreams into reality over the past 10-years. We offer quick, affordable service, knowledgeable customer support representatives and many different printing options to choose from featuring easy-to-follow, step-by-step instructions.

1. Fast Turnaround. Perfect bound B/W books with color cover shipped in as few as 7-10 days.

2. Affordability. InstantPublisher simply cannot be beat in the short run book printing industry.

3. Ease of Use. With our easy-to-follow website tutorials on book setup and being able to accept all file formats, even rookie authors find it easy to self-publish with InstantPublisher!

4. Options. InstantPublisher offers a multitude of options to keep the savviest authors and designers satisfied. If you don't see it listed on the website, just ask, because we can create a custom quote!

5. Customer Support. Once an InstantPublisher customer, always an InstantPublisher customer. We strive to help new authors **self publish** with InstantPublisher and make the file submission and order process as quick and painless as possible for veteran authors and designers who have very little time.

Instant Publisher is a subsidiary of Fundcraft Publishing Company, a **book publisher** for 100 years, and one of the nation's most trusted names in Fundraising cookbooks. All book printing is done in house in our Collierville, TN production facility which is centrally located for *the best* possible shipping times and rates."

(Using their cost calculator our standard 100 page 6 x 9 book with a color cover we provide is $9.71 with a minimum order of 25 books. Prices will go down if larger quantities are ordered. This does not include any editing, marketing, or distribution. They did charge $50.00 for shipping you a proof copy, but ANYONE who does not check out the proof copy before ordering is making a big mistake. You must be sure that all is in order BEFORE spending $250.00. If it is not what you expected, and you don't check out the proof copy, you don't have any recourse. You bought it.

Compared to some subsidy publishers, their prices are reasonable. They offer two marketing kits, both remarkably inexpensive. The Basic Kit is $75.00, and the Marketing Kit is $175.00. After seeing some of the other sites marketing kits, this is a fair deal.)

Chapter Fifty-Three   Ithaca Press

"At Ithaca Press you will receive professional publishing from experienced proofreaders, editors, book designers and cover designers. Your success is our success. Ithaca Press provides professional publishing, giving you high quality books of which you can be proud.

We copyright the book in your name. You retain rights to your work. We will provide worldwide marketing for your book. Your book can be offered through Books in Print, Amazon.com, and other avenues for sales. We provide many other unique marketing suggestions that will be of great interest to you.

Ithaca Press pays attention to the important details of your book. We provide experienced and professional proofreading, copyediting, professional book design and professional cover design.

Whether you are publishing your book to augment your professional practice, looking for a market for your book, or publishing your historically important memoirs, you will find that Ithaca Press will produce a book of which you can be proud."

~ ~ ~ ~

(Ithaca Press offers all the same author services of other subsidy publishers, however, for every single service, from cover design to editing to marketing, you must request a quote, making it nearly impossible to compare them to other subsidy publishers on their prices.)

Chapter Fifty-Four: iUniverse

An Author's Solution subsidiary

"Since 1999 iUniverse has helped more than 35,000 authors publish their books **professionally and affordably**. We have crafted a reputation for breaking records and blazing new trails in the self-publishing industry.

iUniverse offers all author services.

For further review of their packages, please check on their website @ www.iUniverse.com . We have provided their ala carte menu and the prices for their Select packages.

In addition to their Select packages they have:

Premier Packages	$1099.00 online $1199.00 by mail
Premier Pro Package	$1549.00 online $1649.00 by mail
Bookstore Premier Pro	$2099.00 online $2199.00
Online Premier Pro	$3149.00 $3249.00
Book Launch Pro	3149.00 3249.00

Editorial:

Manuscript Evaluation: $599.00 (included in all packages except select)

The Editorial Evaluation is a manuscript checkup that assesses your work to be sure that it has fulfilled the basic requirements of a published book. The editorial evaluator will not only provide you with a general overview of your manuscript, but also educate you through constructive comments on how to write a better book.

Copy Editing:	$0.022 per word
Line editing:	$0.029 per word
Content Edit:	$0.035 per word
Content Edit +	$0.042 per word
Development Edit	$0.064 per word
Book Doctoring	$72.00 per hour
Ghost Writing	$72.00 per hour

Indexing, proof reading, and cover copy polish are also available.

Check all the additional services on line at www.iUniverse.com"

Online self publishing book packages offer various combinations of their self publishing, editorial, and marketing services for a truly customized self-publishing experience. With iUniverse, you can choose the self publishing package that best suits your publishing goals. There are six levels of packages.

None of the packages include:

Additional editorial services are not included and must be purchased separately.

**Shipping and handling for complimentary titles not included in publishing package price.*

Select Package $599.00 online or $699.00 by mail

The **Select** Package Includes...

The following options are available as add-ons to the Select package:

- Trade Paperback Binding
- Book Design and Page Layout
- Digital Formatting and

- Web Design
- Hardcover Format (Read FAQ for requirements)

- One-on-One Author Support
- Custom Cover Design
- ISBN Assignment
- Volume Discounts for Author Book Purchases
- One Round of Author Proof Corrections
- Five Free Paperback Copies**
- Twenty-five Black & White Image Insertions
- Distribution Wholesalers
- Worldwide Distribution through Barnes & Noble.com (www.bn.com), Amazon.com and other online retailers
- Web page in the iUniverse Online Bookstore
- Author Learning Center (12 Months)

- Editorial Evaluation*
- Line Editing*
- Proofreading*
- Copyright Registration
- LOC Control Number
- Book Buyers Preview
- Google/Amazon Book Search
- Co-op Advertising
- Bookselling Promotional Materials

Editorial services are excluded from the packages and must be purchased separately.

Premier Packages $1099.00 online
$1199.00 by mail

(iUniverse carries an extremely large selection of marketing services as well, far too many to mention. They include everything from television advertisements, to video trailers, audio books, and far more. The prices are high, but have you seen the cost of a single 30 second spot on network television? Marketing is expensive!)

Chapter Fifty-Five: Jada Press
No longer publishing

Chapter Fifty-Six: Just Self Publish
A Children's Book Offset Subsidy Publisher and Author Services Company

At *Just Self-Publish!*, we are dedicated to helping you achieve success as a children's picture book self-publisher. We specialize in the creation of quality self-published children's picture books—pure and simple.

Prices:

A 32 Page soft cover, 8 1/2 x 8 1/2 costs 6.48 per book with a 25 book minimum.
A 32 page hard cover 8 1/2 x 8 1/2 costs 16.45 per book with a 25 book minimum

Larger quantities lower the price.

Coaching $145.00 per hour
Graphic Design $75.00 per hour
Author alterations $75.00 per hour
Editing/Review $95.00 per hour
Customized Illustrations - price varies with artist/illustrator chosen
Library of Congress registration $95.00
Sell Sheet (1000) $495.00
Press Release $295
Author Bio $195.00
Premium Marketing Package $795.00
-1000 2 sided full color bookmarks
-1000 2 sided full color postcards
Newswire & Internet Promotion $995.00

Chapter Fifty-Seven: Kindle

The ePublishing arm of Amazon. Completely free to publish online books.

Go to www.KDP.Amazon.com

For more information see Chapter Twelve

Chapter Fifty-Eight: Laredo Publishing

A full-service Subsidy publishing company founded in 1991. They publish high quality books aimed to educate, inspire, and entertain young readers.

Once your book project has been evaluated and accepted for publication by the Editorial Department, the process is as follows:

- You provide the text (and illustrations when available)
- We edit and proofread the manuscript
- We provide customized color illustrations of inside pages and cover
- We design the cover and the layout of interior pages
- We assign an ISBN and a bar code
- We register the work at the Copyright Office
- We send electronic files to the printer
- We print 100 copies in paperback, full color, usually perfect bound
- We keep the remaining copies to fulfill orders
- We set up the title in our Web Bookstore, Amazon and Barnes & Noble
- You receive 50% of the net profit from the books we sell

1. Evaluation and Contract

When you send your manuscript for co-edition, it is evaluated at no cost by our Editorial Department that will determine whether your book qualifies for our co-edition program. Along with an acceptance letter, we will send you our editorial feedback and a contract proposal specifying the details of the co-edition agreement. Once we receive the signed agreement, we proceed to the next step.

2. Editing and proofreading

The editor assigned to your book project will examine your manuscript, look for misspellings and grammatical errors, ensure the text consistency, clarity, syntax construction, and literary quality. The editor will take into consideration the reading and comprehension levels to make sure the text is compatible with the readers to whom it is addressed. While giving suggestions to improve the work, they will always respect your voice, vision and style. Your editor will send you the edited version for your review and approval. Sometimes the editor might consider that no changes are needed to the text.

3. Illustration and Design

The Design Department will examine your book and suggest the design and layout that best fit your work, impact and attract readers. Should you need illustrations, they will assign you the illustrator that will implement your vision and render the most appropriate illustrations for your book. You will follow the illustration process from sketches to final art.

4. Production

Upon your approval of all previous stages and once your manuscript is edited, proofread, illustrated and designed, they pass it on to our Production Department where all the details are ironed out. The production staff will produce electronic files that will be reviewed again by your assigned editor and designer to ensure that it is flawless. Before moving to the next stage, they will send you a final proof for your review. Your book is now ready to be sent to press. Once they receive your final approval, they send the book to print.

5. Distribution and Sales

Once the books have been printed, we send you 25 copies for your personal use and enjoyment. We set up the title for distribution with Amazon, Barnes & Noble and our Web Bookstores. We keep the remaining copies to fulfill orders.

You will receive 50% of the net profit from the books we sell. As the author, you have complete freedom to promote and sell your book in any way you choose. The profit from the copies you receive belongs entirely to you.

Your manuscript must meet certain quality requirements; same when illustrations are submitted along with the manuscript. Laredo Publishing does not accept all the manuscripts submitted for co-edition. Your project is evaluated by our Editorial Department that decides whether your work meets our co-edition requirements. Any author with a high quality project is important to us.
We accept fiction and non-fiction projects: children's and young adult's books, professional books, novels, poetry and memoirs among others.
We are highly familiar with the HIspanic Market. We can translate your book into Spanish to aim the Hispanic Market. We accept manuscripts in English, Spanish and Bilingual English/Spanish. We are highly familiar with the Hispanic Market.
The text must be original. We are not responsible for plagiarism.
Once your project has been accepted for co-edition and you receive the publishing agreement, please send the following:

- Your signed agreement
- Your manuscript in electronic format
- 300 dpi images, when it applies
- Book summary and Author Biography (100 words each)
- Dedication

(The above information is taken directly from Laredo's Website. Personally, I doubt I would use publisher who uses the same phrase twice in a paragraph and who doesn't catch the misspelling of the first Hispanic.

However, the website <u>might</u> be handled by someone other than the owner/operator/manager of Laredo Publishing. No prices are offered on the site, you must submit before they will advise you of their fees and charges. They are located in New Jersey not Texas.)

Chapter Fifty-Nine: Llumina Press

Llumina Press provides personalized self-publishing services including editing and marketing. Professional and out-of-print writers can get published quickly and easily. Aspiring writers can finish their works and get published, and even non-writers can turn their ideas into marketable, high-quality publications ready for distribution on the internet, in bookstores, and in specialty shops around the country.

Ready-to-Go Publishing

1. You provide finished, high resolution, X1A compliant PDF files for the interior of the book and for the cover.

2. We add in a unique ISBN and a barcode with EAN.

3. We provide you with digital proofs of your text and cover files.

4. We setup the cover and interior files for printing.

5. We provide you with a copy of the printed book.

6. We setup a webpage in our bookstore for your book so you can sell it online.

Cost: $399

Basic Publishing

1. From your Word file, we format the interior of the book. You choose fonts and style from a selection of templates.

2. We design a cover for your book from a template. You choose an image of your own or one of ours.

3. We include a unique ISBN, a barcode with EAN, and a library of Congress Control Number.

4. We provide you with digital proofs of your text and cover files.

5. We setup the cover and interior files for printing.

6. We provide you with a copy of the printed book.

7. We setup a webpage in our bookstore for your book so you can sell it online.

Cost: $499

Llumina Press is an imprint of Fast Track Publishing, handling their fiction and nonfiction books that are thoroughly edited and well-designed. Other imprints include: Llumina Kids for children's picture books, Breezeway for books published through Fast Track or Ready to Go Publishing, Metier Books for books published through Fast Track or Ready to Go Publishing, Llumina Christian Books for Christian books that have been edited, and Heart Strings for poetry books.

for publishing of books:

on-demand **Trade Paperback** - submitted online: **$799**
on-demand **Hardcover** - submitted online: **$999**
on-demand **Hardcover and Trade Paperback** - submitted online: **$1099**
(any length) and eBook distribution - **$499**

the fee covers:

Assign separate ISBN numbers for Hardcover and/or Trade Paperback versions of your book
Apply for Library of Congress numbers
Custom format (typeset) the interior of the book
Obtain a barcode/EAN for the back cover
Design an original custom color cover
Assist you in writing and editing back cover copy
Setup title for print-on-demand distribution through Amazon, Llumina, BookSensations, Books in Print, etc.
Print physical proof and overnight it to you (hardcover proof will not be bound)
Submit the title to the "Books in Print" database
Create webpage about the book and author in our online bookstore

services for Print-on-demand Trade Paperbacks and Hardcovers:

Distribution: Make your book available all over the world with extended distribution Ingram Books. This is the largest book distributor in the world, and it will make your book to some 25,000 booksellers. Please look at our partners for details. **$150**

Advance Magazine is a monthly catalog that is mailed to booksellers and libraries around th Titles are eligible to be included in Ingram Advance only once, when they are first released. will produce a short paragraph describing the title. Retail pricing information. and a black & image will also be included. We can only request that a title be advertised in Ingram at the time a title is submitted for initial set-up. The cost is **$100.00.**

Prices for publishing of books:

Print-on-demand **Trade Paperback** - submitted online: **$799**
Print- on-demand **Hardcover** - submitted online: **$999**
Print-on-demand **Hardcover and Trade Paperback** - submitted online: **$1099**
eBooks (any length) and eBook distribution - **$499**

What the fee covers:

Assign separate ISBN numbers for Hardcover and/or Trade Paperback versions of your
   book
Apply for Library of Congress numbers
Custom format (typeset) the interior of the book
Obtain a barcode/EAN for the back cover
Design an original custom color cover
Assist you in writing and editing back cover copy
Setup title for print-on-demand distribution through Amazon, Llumina, BookSensations,
   Books in Print, etc.
Print physical proof and overnight it to you (hardcover proof will not be bound)
Submit the title to the "Books in Print" database
Create webpage about the book and author in our online bookstore .

Additional Services:

Extra services for Print-on-demand Trade Paperbacks and Hardcovers:

Ingram Distribution: Make your book available all over the world with extended distribution through Ingram Books. This is the largest book distributor in the world, and it will make your book available to some 25,000 booksellers. Please look at our partners for details. **$150**

Ingram Advance Magazine is a monthly catalog that is mailed to booksellers and libraries around the world. Titles are eligible to be included in Ingram Advance only once, when they are first released. Ingram will produce a short paragraph describing the title. Retail pricing information, and a black & white cover image will also be included. We can only request that a title be advertised in Ingram Advance at the time a title is submitted for initial set-up. The cost is **$100.00.**

Editing Services:

Proofreading............$0.012 - $0.019 per word
Full Edit...................$0.02 - $0.029 per word
Rewrite.....................$$0.03 - $0.08 per word

Children's Picture Books

> *FINALLY!* It's now possible to distribute color books through Ingram. And we're gearing up to do more of them than ever. There are a few caveats, however, if your book is going to be submitted for distribution through Ingram.

   1. To get this distribution, the books have to be printed through the Ingram printer, Lightning Source. At this time, they only print paperbacks in color, so if you want hardcover, we won't be able to get Ingram distribution for it. The sizes for Ingram distributed color books are also limited: 8.5 x 8.5 **or** 8.5 x11.

   2. Color books done through POD are still very expensive to print. Often the only way to bring the cost down to a reasonable level is to order quantities of 1000 or more. However, Llumina has started its own printing company and will now be able to offer color books at prices that still allow the author to make money without purchasing hundreds or thousands of books.

After several years of working with color books and their authors, we've come up with the ideal package. In fact, we have a few of them. These packages are designed to use POD as a way to test the market for your books, and then, if sales warrant, they allow you to smoothly move on to printing the books through the offset process if this is what you want. This way you can keep your investment low until you know whether or not the books will sell.

We use a heavier paper (80 lb.) and cover (12 pt. laminated cardstock) than are used on typical POD books. In addition, while the Ingram printer binds color books with staples if they're under 48 pages, when we print these books, we perfect bind them.

Marketing Kit $199.00

Marketing Packages from $599.00 to $1099.00

Website Design from $599.00 to $1099

Video book trailer $1499.
    with extended distribution $1899.00

Children's book marketing and distribution package $999.00

eBook to Kindle. Barnes & Noble, and Apple iPad $499.00

Chapter Sixty: Lulu

One of the innovators of low-cost subsidy publishing, they've added the majority of the costs onto the price of the book rather than upfront, making publishing possible for the masses. Due to the fact that we utilized Lulu for one of our publications, we included a detailed how to guide in the section on self-publishing. Please see Chapter Fifteen for further information.

Chapter Sixty-One : Mill City Press
Author Services or Subsidy...It's your choice.

" In 2005, we knew we could build a better mousetrap. By October 2006, we did it. That fall we had two full-time employees and maybe five authors. Today, we have 27 full-time and 10 part-time employees. Our author list is more than 1,500 titles (in our Mill City Press division). In 2009, Hillcrest Media Group became the majority shareholder of Mill City Press. Hillcrest provided a powerful backend for Mill City Press and the technical expertise to grow and provide authors more and better services. For example, Hillcrest's patent-pending eBook conversion and publishing system (PublishGreen.com) has been integrated into Mill City. Being part of the Hillcrest family of publishing companies allows Mill City Press to offer much more than a single-focused self-publishing company ever could."

WHY MILL CITY PRESS?

"We believe every book should have a chance to compete in the marketplace. To ensure that, we combine our knowledge and experience in traditional book publishing with innovative book marketing. We provide real advice and help every step of the way.

- Wholesale printing costs on any size book order
- 100% royalties (after third-party retailer's fees)
- Use our ISBN or yours
- Patented eBook conversion and distribution

- Real-time sales, royalty, and inventory reporting
- Opportunities for traditional book distribution
- In-house editorial, production, and retail sales teams
- We won't sell you what you don't need or can't use

- Complete transparency - every fee is disclosed up front and we encourage you to read our contract

Publishing Packages

Basic.................$1697
Includes:
Custom Book Cover
Professional interior formatting
ISBN, LCCN, Bar code
100% Royalties
Available on Amazon, Barnes & Noble & to retail locations
Physical proof copy
5 Complimentary copies
Amazon Search inside the book
Customized website & 1 free year hosting
Google Books Submission
Copyright registration
Online author sales reports

Additional items can be added ala carte

Advanced Package.............$2497.00
Includes all of above plus:

Submission to search engines
Back Cover sales copy
Yearly book ordering fee
Returns program

Premium Package.............$3997.00
Includes all of the above plus:

Expanded distribution Program
Website Order fulfillment

Bells, whistles, bring on the band!!!

Professional Package
Includes all of the above plus

eBook creation and distribution
Basic editing up to 75,000 words

Book editing fees

Basic Editing $0.020 per word
Basic Plus $0.035 word plus $100.00 flat fee
Comprehensive Edit $0.035 per word
Publishing Prep $0.045 per word plus $100.00 flat fee

Marketing programs

Online Media Exposure $599.00
Customized Facebook Page $599.00
Amazon Exposure $699.00
Customized Twitter $499.00"

(All information is quoted from their website)

Chapter Sixty-Two:
Morgan James Publishing

Morgan James has revolutionized book publishing - from the author's standpoint. Their Entrepreneurial Publishing™ model enriches authors as well as the company. They have been a top choice as a publisher for nonfiction Entrepreneurial books since 2003 and have recently added a fiction imprint.

It is hard to determine whether they fit the small traditional press model or a subsidy model. In most ways they resemble the traditional model, BUT they basically expect the author to purchase the books for his/her business and speaking engagements. They do offer marketing and distribution avenues not generally available from subsidy publishers, they own the ISBN so they own the publishing rights. Below is information directly from their website.

"Morgan James Publishing offers you the advantages of traditional publishing as well as the time-to-market benefits normally associated with indie publishing.

We allow you to maintain your creativity of your book without demanding the rights to it. We produce high quality books. We make your book available everywhere readers buy books.

Morgan James Publishing has physical book store distribution and detailed title listing in our US distribution partners and provides coverage to over 90% of all retail bookstore outlets in the US and Canada. With channels like Ingram Publisher Services (IPS), Bertrams, Amazon.com,

Barnes & Noble, Baker & Taylor, BookSource, Powell's, etc. and detailed title listings provided to our International distribution partners.

The Morgan James Process is simple.

Your manuscript proposal will need to be reviewed by Morgan James Publishing and an author interview will need to take place.

Your manuscript proposal will be accepted, rejected or referred by Morgan James Publishing or one of our many imprints. Please note that Morgan James receives over 5,000 manuscript proposals each year, but only publishes an average of 125.

If your manuscript is one of those 3% accepted, our professional staff guides you through the publication process. We don't charge anything for publishing, and our process is clear so you know exactly what you are getting prior to submitting your manuscript. After publication, we offer marketing support that helps you find the audience for your book.

We offer the very best distribution for your book. Our extensive distribution network ensures your book is available for order at thousands of bookstores across the country. With channels like Ingram Publisher Services, Bertrams, Amazon.com, Barnes & Noble, Baker & Taylor, BookSource, and many, many more, it is no wonder Morgan James Publishing is so in demand!"

"We help you make your book stand out by providing a professionally-designed custom cover. People do judge a book by its cover. Make a great first impression with a professionally designed custom book cover. All Morgan

James Publishing books receive a unique cover that incorporates your ideas in order to give your book a custom look, all with the authors input.

Plus exclusive contracts, Paperback, Hardcover, eBook and Audio options, and one-on-one publishing support to guide you through the publishing process. Why would you want to publish any other way?

What you get with Morgan James Publishing:

World Wide Distribution: Your Book will be assigned a unique ISBN number, as well as inclusion in RR Bowker's "Books in Print", the industry's most up-to-date listing of book, spoken-word audio, and video products. Your book will also be available via online retailers like Amazon.com, Borders.com, Target.com, VirginMega.com and Waldenbooks.com and customers can purchase your book at thousands of traditional bookseller worldwide through channels like Ingram Publisher Services, Bertrams, Amazon.com, Barnes & Noble, Baker & Taylor, BookSource, etc.

Morgan James Publishing sells your books to booksellers and leading wholesalers via Ingram Publisher Services (IPS) at an industry leading 45-55% discount. Why is this important? The leading book wholesalers in the US and Canada (Ingram and Baker & Taylor) and in the UK (Bertrams and Gardners), are involved in roughly half of the trade book sales in the United States and United Kingdom. The new deeper wholesale discount means that Ingram and Baker & Taylor will resell your book to thousands of retailers at discounts of 45-55% off this list price. The deeper discount gives book retailers more incentive to sell your title. The discount and margin book stores receive is similar to traditionally published titles.

They can order replacement copies from their favorite wholesaler-whether that's Ingram, Baker & Taylor, or any other major wholesaler.

Authors with Morgan James Publishing are placed in the Ingram Advance Catalog upon release. The Ingram Advance is a monthly catalog that is distributed to booksellers and libraries around the world.

When books are first released through Morgan James Publishing, Ingram will produce a short paragraph describing the title. Retail pricing information and a black & white cover image will also be included.

Morgan James actively works with authors to help them not only maximize revenue from their book royalties, but also build new business and increase their revenue substantially through follow-on sales to their readers.

Most importantly, Morgan James brings all the benefits of a traditional trade publisher without getting in the way. "

Manuscript Submission Process and Policies

"The process that will transform your manuscript into a printed and bound book is launched at what is called The Entrepreneurial Vision™ Mastermind. In this mastermind, the people who will be working diligently to guide your book successfully through the production process, including the creative director (who is primarily responsible for The Entrepreneurial Vision™, design and schedule) and the designer (who is primarily responsible for cover art, typesetting, and proofs), discuss such matters as the entrepreneurial aspects the manuscript needs, exactly how cover art should be handled, whether any essential items from the manuscript package are missing, and the design of the published book. Soon after The Entrepreneurial Vision™ Mastermind your Author Relations Manager will contact you, in order to ask any questions we might still have about the manuscript and to tell you what the production schedule is going to be.

At this point the creative director will have the designer prepare the cover layout, and will be closely monitoring his or her work. Depending on the extent of any recommendations, the swiftness of the schedule, and several other factors, you will receive a cover proof to review.

Just about the time we are finalizing the cover of your book, you will get the page proof of the front matter (which includes the title page, Contents, Preface, etc.) to review.

The next step in the production process is typesetting. The resulting page proof, which will look pretty much like a published book, is sent to you for a thorough review, as well as to an experienced freelance proofreader. The proof may be sent in stages, and you will have a week or so to scrutinize each stage.

You will return reviewed page proof to the production supervisor, who will oversee the generation of revised proof, which will contain any changes you marked as well as typos and design errors discovered by the proofreader.

While the page proof is being checked, the index must be prepared, if desired, either by you or by an experienced freelance indexer. (If a freelancer prepares the index, you must pay for it.) At an early point in the production process, the creative director will discuss the index with you, and can give you guidance if you decide to do it yourself.

Within a few weeks of this, your completed book will be sent to the printer, and about a month later, printed and bound copies will start being shipped to our warehouse and thus will be available for purchase. You are now a published author. Congratulations!"

Book Pricing

"The book price is set jointly by competing titles, the Author and Morgan James Publishing once the manuscript has been submitted and has gone through our Entrepreneurial Vision Mastermind. The following table provides you with an estimate of what your book price should be. This table doesn't guarantee that your book will fall within this range, however, you'll know once your manuscript has been submitted and gone through production.

Manuscript Word Count	Page Count *	Recommended Price Range*
20,000 (or less)	75 (or less)	$8.95-$10.95
40,000	120	$10.95-$13.95
60,000	180	$13.95-$16.95
80,000	240	$15.95-$19.95
100,000	300	$17.95-$21.95
120,000	360	$20.95-$23.95
140,000	420	$22.95-$26.95
160,000	580	$25.95-$29.95
180,000	540	$27.95-$31.95
200,000	600	$29.95

* Estimated page count and book price. Actual book prices are determined by a competitive book analysis along with

feedback from our trademarked Entrepreneurial Vision Mastermind.

Morgan James Publishing gives you the muscle to succeed. We provide you with the tools and the one-on-one assistance to give your book the best chance at success."

Chapter Sixty-Three: Morris Publishing
Printer, short run offset

Morris Publishing® was founded in 1933 as a commercial printer. We have evolved into a specialized printer in the short-run book industry, publishing books for customers in all 50 states. Through the years we've remained family-owned and operated; Scott Morris is president of the company his grandfather founded.

Morris Publishing® has printed millions of books, including poetry, fiction, religious, how-to, and local histories, as well as books and manuals for companies and organizations. We even have a separate division which specializes in cookbook publishing. If you want to publish a cookbook, visit the Morris Press Cookbooks web site at www.morriscookbooks.com.

Morris Publishing® produces short-run books in quantities of 100 – 5,000. Our book sizes and binding styles conform to industry norms and can be tailored to meet most customers' needs. Paper and material are of the highest quality and are purchased in bulk to pass the savings to you. Since we also specialize in certain sizes and features, our prices are lower than most printers.

Base Pricing for 5 1/2 x 8 1/2 Perfect bound 100 pages

100 books 3.77 each total cost $377.00

1000 books 1.74 each   total cost $1740.00

(That's like getting 550 books for free, if you have some place to store all those books. And it does not include shipping. Yep, pesky shipping. They advise shipping is anywhere from 25 cents to 40 cents per book. Gulp. That means....400.00 more on those thousand books. Now, they ship anywhere from 30 to 100 books per box. So 1000 books divided by 30 equals...Holy Toledo....33 boxes. Where are you putting them all? Just to remind you of some of the pitfalls of self-publishing.

Morris Publishing is a printer and does not furnish any services preparing your manuscript. They don't want to begin business until you have a print ready document ready to go in PDF format, along with any print matter for front and back and your cover. This is the old-fashioned way self-publishing worked. The author handled each aspect of the process himself, contracting different people for each segment. Now it is a mix of do it yourself and contract out the parts you need help overcoming.)

Chapter Sixty-Four:
My Book Orders.com

An Imprint of the Hillcrest Publishing Group

MyBookOrders.com specializes in working with independent authors and small presses. More than 400,000 of our author's books will pass through our distribution warehouse in 2011. On average, our warehouse provides 24-hour order cycle time with 99 percent inventory accuracy. In addition, all book shipments are tracked, ensuring that customers who buy a book will know when it's arriving. By utilizing the collective weight of independent authors, MyBookOrders.com can provide pick, pack, and ship functionality never before available to small presses or individual authors. It is our mission to provide quick, accurate, and professional book fulfillment services to all our customers regardless of their size.

Website Order Book Fulfillment Made Easy

For authors who want to sell their books through a personalized online order system, we offer our services:

- Creation of an order-page specific to your book and use of our ordering system.
- Ability to sell both physical and eBook versions of your book.
- Set up of your book inventory into our warehouse and inventory management system.
- A designated customer service representative for any ordering or shipping issues your customer's experience.

- Ability to add promotional codes to track marketing efforts and provide discounts to designated customer groups.
- Set up in our author interface and access to your account to track sales numbers.
- Storage of up to 1/2 (half) pallet of books.
- Monthly royalty payments.

Service Cost: $499

Additional Sales Fees:

- $1.50 per physical book sold
- $1.00 per electronic book sold
- 4.5% of the total sales transaction

Not only can you be assured that your online orders are being taken care of by our custom built back-end administrative system and our dedicated staff of fulfillment professionals, but selling books through MyBookOrders.com instead of through Amazon.com and other retailers will earn you a higher royalty on each sale.

After your first year in the MyBookOrders.com program, there is an annual renewal fee of $199. The annual renewal fee includes another year of fulfillment service and the warehousing/storage of up to 1/2 (half) pallet of books for one full year.

Chapter Sixty-Five: **Mystic Publishing**

From the time you make the decision to contact Mystic Publishers to the moment you rip open that first box of books hot off the press, you'll find the staff has only one goal here, delivering unparalleled service at an unheard of price, resulting in unbelievable client satisfaction.

Basic Publishing Package   **$625.00**

Formatting manuscript into book form to author preferred size
3 galleys (additional galleys at $35.00 each)
ISBN (from either Mystic or Authors stock)
Registering the copyright in Authors name w/LOC
Listing the completed book with Bowker
Free Mystic Publishers website listing (This can link to your website or Mystic can take orders for you)
Quotes from 2 printers for your book
Files sent to printer of authors choice
Instructions on how to work with Amazon.com and/or the distributor of your choice
(Cover Generated for an additional fee)*

Promotions Starter Kit   **$255.00**

This starter kit contains the design & printing of the following:
100   Bookmarks
100   Postcards
100   Business Cards (additional fee for double-sided business cards)
2   11×17 posters
25   Flyers

Plus sending your manuscript or completed book for 2 reviews:
Midwest Review
The View News (A regional Las Vegas/Henderson division of the RJ, or your local newspaper)
Or 1 other (author choice) review

Combination Packages

Package #1   **$825.00**

Basic Publishing Package
Promotions Starter Kit

Package #2   **$1125.00**

Basic Publishing Package
Promotions Starter Kit
Basic Cover Design (See a la carte services for definition)

Package #3 $1450.00

Basic Publishing Package
First 150 Books**

Package #4 $1700.00

Package #1
Basic Publishing Package
Promotions Starter Kit
First 150 Books**

Package #5 $2000.00
Package #2
Basic Publishing Package

Promotions Starter Kit
Basic Cover Design* (See a la carte services for definition)
First 150 books**

* Basic cover generated by Mystic Publishers: Fee –
$300.00

** Limited to 350 pages or less, 6×9 trim size or smaller in
trade paperback editions, w/the first (5) five author
supplied B&W photos included (Does not include color
photos)

(This information is directly from the website
www.mysticpublishers.com. However, I noticed the
website is from 2009 and yet there are still blank pages
under some of the tabs. Is Mystic Publishing still
operational? Or are they lost somewhere in the mystic
cyberspace? You might want to contact them before
ordering a package.)

Chapter Sixty-Six: New Book Publishing
A Christian Subsidy Publisher

A division of Reliance Media

Our focus on Christian book publishing and marketing will help you sell more books! Lowest book publishing pricing, highest royalties and no hidden fees coupled with quality and speed of book printing are hallmarks of our service. Trust the best Christian book publisher with over 40 years in printing!

We make publishing your book simple and straightforward. No mystery. Predictable. Highly cost effective book printing and publishing. Unmatched guidance and author service. At NewBookPublishing.com, we have streamlined the book printing process for ease, speed and quality. This dream of yours is important to us, from the top of our company to the bottom…and has been since 1969. And when your book is published, we don't stop—we press on to help you promote and market your book at the highest level of excellence

Publishing Packages:

Run it Now Package............................$437.00
One on one Author support
Electronic proof
ISBN & Barcode
Listing on NewBook Publishing.com

Base Package $737.00

One-on-one Author Support
Full Color Cover/Template

Interior Formatting/Template
Electronic Proof Galley
Personalized Back Cover
Choice of Book Trim Size
ISBN & Barcode
Non-exclusivity contract
Book Listed on New Book Publishing

New Release $1157.00

All the above plus:

Custom cover- 2 choices
Custom formatting
Complimentary Author copy
Library of Congress Registration
Copyright registration
Book in Print registration
Available for bookstores to order
Amazon listing
Google Preview
Featured Page on NewBook Publishing's Book page
Process orders from NBP or Amazon

Top Seller..$1677

All the above plus:

Custom cover 4 choices
Amazon marketing, including "Look Inside" feature
Graphic insertions (up to 10)
Professional Marketing Consultation
Featured Author Page on NewBook Publishing's site
Process all book orders
1000 Business cards
100 book marks

NBP Select...$5423.00
                              (save $1000.00)

All the above....

But Wait! there's more!

Hardcover editions for reviewers
Monthly Royalty Payments and Reports
Complimentary books (quantity varies by month)
Rush (Books completed within 45 days of manuscript
submission)
Book Signing Kit
Tradeshow presentation
eBook
Press Release
Video Trailer
Social Media Package
Library Mailer
Book Store catalog placement
Book Review catalog placement

Editing Services Available

Level 1: Spelling, punctuation, spacing
corrections $0.015 per word

Level 2: Level 1 plus grammar, gender neutrality, and
abbreviations $0.025 per word

Level 3: Level 2 plus usage, syntax, and paragraph
transitions. Questions and suggestions noted in
margins
        $0.035 per word

Level 4: All of the above plus clarity, cadence/consistency, flow, sentence polishing, paragraph and chapter relocation, characterization, plot consistency, assistance with dialogue. $0.045 per word.

* Note: NBP uses Associated Press Style rather than the Chicago Manual of Style. AP is accepted for magazine and newspapers but Chicago is the style for most full length books.

Marketing Services:

(They also offer a multitude of marketing options through different venues with different media options. The one we found different from the standard promotional offerings is their Press release to 1,200 key Christian outlets nationwide. For a Christian book this is a good option but it cost $400.00. If you have another way of gaining the list, it might be wise to consider.)

Chapter Sixty-Seven: **Outskirts Press**
POD Publisher

Publishes...

- fiction (genre fiction and literary fiction)
- non-fiction (general, historic, etc.)
- self-help
- children's books
- young adult
- poetry
- cookbooks
- autobiography, biography, and memoirs
- Christian, and other religious, spiritual, and inspirational texts

Publishing Packages:

Initiation Package   **$35.00**

Applied to any package you purchase
One on One Consultation
Establish a Publishing profile to determine YOUR goals
Manuscript Evaluation
Three books free: Self Publishing Simplified, Adventures in Publishing, The Highly Effective Habits of 5 Successful Authors

Emerald Package   **$199.00**

1 Free Paperback book
5 1/2 by 8 1/2 paperback size
Cover template, color choice
Standard formatting
B & W printing

Non-exclusivity contract
Author maintains all rights
Author set retail price above minimum

Sapphire Package   **$399.00**

All the above plus:

3 free paperbacks (Woo-Hoo!)
Choice of 3 book size
Choice of 6 cover templates
Marketing tool kit
Standard webpage
Author Discounts
ISBN/barcode
Available on Amazon
Available on Barnes & Noble
Available at Outskirts Press
Ingram wholesale distribution

Ruby Package   **$699.00**

All the Above plus:
6 free paperback
Choice of 6 book sizes
Choice of 12 cover templates
    or provide your own custom cover
Baker & Taylor distribution
Worldwide distribution

Diamond Package   **$999.99**

All the above plus:
10 free paperbacks
Choice of 19 book sizes
Choice of 21 cover templates

or provide your own
Marketing Coach via email
EVVY Awards eligibility
    (an award for Colorado subsidy publishers)
Spring Arbor Christian Distribution--if applicable
3 minute audio on your Outskirts webpage
Press release
eBook edition
Discount on future book package (10%)

Pearl Package   **$1099.00**
For Picture Books

Everything included in Ruby Package plus
5 Free books
Choice of 14 book sizes
Choice of 21 cover templates or bring your own
Full color Interior
Marketing Coach
EVVY Awards eligibility
    (an award for Colorado subsidy publishers)
Spring Arbor Christian Distribution--if applicable

Also offers optional pre-production services like...

- copyediting (basic, moderate, advanced)
- ghostwriting
- copyright registration
- private label imprinting and ISBN registration
- full-color award-winning illustration packages
- the list goes on and on...

Outskirts Press offers more marketing services and products than anybody else, including...

- Amazon Kindle editions
- Apple iPad/iPhone eBook editions with iBooks distribution
- Personal marketing assistance in 5-hour blocks of time
- Book award submissions to Writer's Digest and many others
- Book video production with distribution to YouTube and others
- Custom t-shirts featuring your book cover
- Posters, postcards, bookmarks, announcements, business cards
- Virtual book tours
- Custom press releases and publicity campaigns
- Celebrity endorsements
- Global book tours for your book to venues like Frankfurt, Beijing, and the BEA (Book Expo of America)
- and much, much more!

Chapter Sixty-Eight: Palibrio
An Author's Solution Affiliate

Palibrio is the Spanish-language imprint of Author
Solutions
 Who knew? Hispanics have their own subsidy publishing
company. Great idea and makes sense that Author's
solutions realized the growth potential in this market.
  Palibrio has the clout of the leading name in independent
and print-on-demand publishing. Palibrio gives Hispanic
authors a rich selection of book packages and editorial and
marketing services to produce books with the highest
industry standards. A staff of Spanish-speaking
professionals with years of experience in publishing and
book marketing are on hand to help authors with any
concerns.

  They aim to celebrate literary art in the Hispanic/Latino.
Palibrio offers editorial services, cover design, formatting,
publishing packages, and marketing packages.

Come Up with a Plan

The first step in publishing a book is taking note of what
your goals are. List your reasons for publishing in Spanish.

Choose a Publisher

Choose a Spanish book publisher that suits your needs.
Palibrio's wide range of publishing packages and services
makes your publishing experience enjoyable, affordable,
and fast. Furthermore, beyond our publishing expertise is
our confidence of knowing the Hispanic/Latino heart.

Market Your Book

Palibrio provides guidance on marketing strategies to enhance your chance of publishing success.

For more information and to choose a package please go to: http://www.palibrio.com/

(We apologize for not printing the packages, but we do not read Spanish. There may be other publishing companies specializing in the Hispanic market, but this is the only one we found.)

Chapter Sixty-Nine: Peppertree Press
A POD "Independent" Subsidy Publisher

Julie Ann Howell, Publisher/President along with Teri Franco, Editorial Director, are proud to introduce to you a company that offers professional publishing with a personal touch! Together we have planted the book publishing seed and with great enthusiasm have launched this fine company to aspiring authors who have dreams and aspirations of turning their manuscripts into masterpieces.

Prices are not available until after you contact Peppertree. Assorted websites indicate prices ranging between $1800 to $3000, but do not indicate what is included. In a few cases they cover the initial costs and recoup their money through the back end by charging more for books they know have an audience such as anthologies. (Each author will buy at least four or five books.) They have recently contracted with a local bestselling-author and I seriously doubt she is paying them any money. It is possible that eventually the Peppertree Press will have both subsidy and traditional avenues.

Peppertree includes services such as basic word processing editing, cover design, and professional formatting. They do not have any marketing packages at this time. Based near the Ringling School of Art in Sarasota, Florida, and surrounded by artists, Peppertree has a large stable of illustrators to choose from if you are writing a children's book or to help design your book cover.

We did an in-depth interview with the owner and have included it, as well as an interview with one of her customers, earlier in the book." (See Chapter Four)

(The policy of Peppertree Press is to walk you through the entire process, helping you every step of the way. The authors we spoke to who used her services were happy with the results. The main complaint we heard dealt with the fact that Peppertree Press does not embrace the fact that they are a fee based service. Some potential customers are put off by the subterfuge. Bottom line, if you want someone else to handle the publishing aspect and have the money to make it happen, it is your decision. Choose what is right for YOU.)

Chapter Seventy: **Publish America**
A POD **Subsidy** Publisher

(No matter how much they try to deny it. Publish America makes their money on the back end sales when the author purchases the VERY costly books. The below information comes directly from their website)

1. "We publish **more new titles** than any other traditional book publisher. PublishAmerica has a history of regularly putting thousands of its titles on the market **in hardcover.**
2. We accept **more new and unpublished authors** than any other traditional book publisher in the nation.
3. We receive **more queries** from new authors than any other book publisher in the nation.
4. According to the Guinness Book of World Records, we hold the record for **the largest book signing in history.**

We are always happy when a new author finds his or her way to our door--*opportunity knocks on both sides!* If you are an author who is determined to see your manuscript become a book, perhaps PublishAmerica is the publisher for which you've been searching.

If you are interested in becoming a PublishAmerica author, please go to the website and tell us about your work. Your submitted manuscript will be reviewed by our skilled and thorough Acquisitions staff, who will determine whether or not your work has what it takes to be a PublishAmerica book.

Meanwhile, please take the time to tour our website--see who we are, what we are, and how PublishAmerica authors feel about us. Also, you may browse our online bookstore-- there are almost 40,000 titles from which to choose! No other traditional book publisher puts as many new titles in print, every day."

(Okay. While we do not make positive or negative recommendations, we need to clarify exactly what Publish America offers. First, they are NOT a traditional commercial printer. They receive their money on the backside of publishing rather than upfront as most subsidy publishers do. They are a Print On Demand company. They do not offer author discounts. The books are priced extremely high, not competitively, and you are usually committed to buying a certain amount of books. The contracts often require you use them for any second book you write. That is correct, you are often contractually obligated to publish your next book with them. I will repeat, as much as Publish America enjoys calling themselves "traditional" publishers, they are not! Have the contract looked over by a lawyer before you sign it. Check how long they hold the rights to your material. Some contracts have been for the life of the copyright. Please see our section on definitions for a deeper understanding of these conditions. This contract doesn't leave the author rights in your hands. You get to set your price over and above their minimum price. Now how many paperback books do you think readers will buy at $25.00 per book? How many are you obligated to buy? Ten books will run you around $250.00. Pay up front or after, but pay you will. And you cannot republish this book as an eBook or anywhere else until the contract is completed.

We are not saying do not use PA, but be completely aware of what you are getting. They are a backend subsidy publisher. If they owned up to it and embraced it, they would rise exponentially in our estimation as an author's service provider. Because.....

If you have no money at all to publish your book, and you have no expectations of high volume sales, and you don't plan on writing a second book, this may be your best option other than doing it yourself. Their books are of a good quality paper, printing, and binding. The template book cover choices are extensive and look good.

Just understand, they ARE a subsidy publisher, NOT a traditional publisher.

Unlike many of their fellow author services sites, they have limited marketing or distribution plans. Their website marketing plan is comprised of selling you a book on marketing tips for $25.00. If they sold marketing plans it would compromise their effort of trying to make you believe they are a traditional publisher. You will need to handle all aspects of marketing and distributing your very expensive books. But for a new author with no money and lots of ambition to market and distribute, it is a start. You can be Published!)

Chapter Seventy-One: Published.com

(This company has ceased doing business under this name, instead utilizing their parent company, the Hillcrest Publishing Group and other affiliates to offer these services. (May 2012))

"Unlike a lot of other websites, we aren't posers or wannabes. We aren't crazy (or have enough money) to think we'll be a Facebook. We creatively help authors and publishers maximize their Facebook presence, but there is no chance that some random person from your high school will find you on Published.com (unless of course they are searching for great books).

We aren't trying to be Amazon or any other online retailer. We help authors and publishers get their books found so that they can provide links to such retailers on their Published.com profile pages.

Basically, we've built our company 100% from search engine optimization and a cost-effective online marketing strategy. We didn't hire people to do it for us. We are good at it. Our sites rank high for the search terms important to us.

Authors

Promote your book to millions of people searching online for books in your genre.
Opportunities to be a featured author in your specific category and on our homepage
Opportunities to have your book reviewed by bloggers and reviewers seeking books in your genre to review
Opportunities to give away review copies of your book to build a buzz.

A link back from Published.com to your site which can help your website's ranking in search engines.
Links to up to five retailers that sell your book (including your own website)

Publishers *(with 5 or more published titles)*

Promote your titles to millions of people searching online for specific genres.

Pages on a high ranking website for all your submitted titles and authors

Opportunities to give away review copies of your titles to build a buzz

Opportunities to have your most important titles featured

Book Reviewers / Bloggers

Get free copies of books in genres you love

Create contests to give away books in order to get more visitors to your blog or review site.

Enter our "Blog Your Way to a Book Deal" and be eligible to win a $20,000 book publishing contract from Bascom Hill Books.

Get a link back to your site from a PR5 site on Google (Okay, I have no idea what a PR5 site is.   LOL)

Get free review copies of books in genres you love.

***(NOTE - This site is in no way affiliated with the publishers, editors, or authors of this book.)

Chapter Seventy-Two: Publish Green
An imprint of the Hillcrest Publishing Group

An author's service company focused on ePublishing

Offers ePublishing packages ranging from $399.00 to $1999.00

Upload your book as plain text, PDF, Word®, or InDesign®. We'll make it look great on Kindle®, iPad®, Nook® & more.

You own all files we create for your eBook.

Distribution through 31+ resellers including Amazon®, Apple iBookstore®, and Barnes & Noble®.

Earn up to 100% net royalties.

Automated conversion produces ugly eBooks. We format your book by hand.

Chapter Seventy-Three:
Rose Dog Publishing
An Affiliate of Dorrance Publishing

CHOOSE ONE OF OUR COMPLETE, TURNKEY PACKAGES

Based on our years of experience working with unpublished authors, we developed two all-inclusive publishing packages that contain elements we know are critical and necessary to properly bring a book into print. With RoseDog, you pay one price for a complete turnkey publishing services package.

BASIC ROSEDOG IMPRINT: $980

Includes professional page design, creation of an original full-color cover, e-book, bookstore and on-line availability, bookstore returns policy, toll-free number ordering and fulfillment services. *ISBN and copyright registration provided for free!* Publish in paperback or hardbound format.

BASIC ROSEDOG IMPRINT WITH PROMOTION: $1,980

Includes all of the services of the basic imprint package plus a industry leading book promotion campaign that includes the notification of bookstores and media of your book's availability.

Each Package Includes *AT NO ADDITIONAL COST*:

Bookstore Return Policy: RoseDog allows a retailer that displays our books in their bookstore to return any unsold books for full credit. No other print on demand (POD)

publisher that we know of offers this policy AT NO
ADDITIONAL COST TO THE AUTHOR.

Multiple Book Formats: Since consumption of books in a
digital format is a rapidly growing book distribution
market, RoseDog books are available to consumers in
tradtional printed form and also in digital formats. These
formats would be suitable for reading on e-book readers
such as the Amazon Kindle, the iPhone and other cellular
smart phones, personal computers, laptops, personal digital
assistants and other electronic reading devices.

ISBN and Copyright Registration: Copyright obtained in
the author's name from the Library of Congress along with
a LCCN (for qualified books) and an ISBN (International
Standard Book Number---needed for bookstore sales)
assigned.

With either package, you can add:

RoseDog Books Editing Services: a professional check for
grammar and spelling errors. $25.00 plus $2.50 per page

RoseDog Books Illustration Services: we will create
original artwork for inclusion inside your finished book
$100.00 per illustration

Publish Your Book in Full Color: perfect for children's
books, cookbooks, photo essays or any book that would be
enhanced by the use of color. We can create original full
color illustrations, too!

Publish Your Book as a Hardbound Book: Your basic publishing fee will not change, you can make use of our editing or illustration services and you can choose to have your interior pages printed in either black and white or color.

Chapter Seventy-Four:
SelfPublishing.com
An affiliate of RJ Communications and Books Just Books

From their website:

"Step #1 The first step in the book publishing process is to educate yourself. We provide you a free eBook to familiarize yourself with the process. You may also sign up for their free newsletter.

Step#2 The next step is

Editorial, Layout & Design

The second step in the book publishing process is to prepare your files for print. Selfpublishing.com offers many services to help you create the perfect file for printing.

Editorial Analysis
Obtain Single ISBN
Obtain Multiple ISBNs
Book Layout Cover Design
They have packages to assist with these steps ranging from $250.00 to $1060.00

Editing costs:

Manuscript evaluation $99.00 (Usually $249.00?)

Mechanical edit: $0.019 per word

Corrects spelling, punctuation, grammar, capitalization, and basic usage errors, as well as suggesting changes re overuse of particular words

Substantive editing: $0.023 per word

Mechanical editing plus:

Identify inconsistencies or contradictions in concepts, characterization, or plot points

Suggest rewording

Improve flow

For nonfiction organization of content, identify where citations needed, formatting of references, footnotes.

They also offer Cover design. Standard is $250.00, higher rates for hardcovers or jackets

A few other editorial tasks are available

Step #3 Printing and binding

   This is offset printing which is generally of a higher quality than POD print. There is a minimum order of 100 books. You supply the digital formatted manuscript, jpeg cover, and a check for the number of books you want. They supply them at low costs.

Our standard sample of a book of 100 pages, black and white, 6 x 9, color soft cover has a unit cost of $3.86. With

a minimum order of 100 books you would need $386.12
plus shipping and handling and don't forget the storage.

Step #4

The fourth step of the book publishing process is almost as important as the first three steps combined. 90% of Self Publishers publish their book to make money. Selfpublish.com also can provide Website Design, Press releases, online bookstore, and storage and fulfillment for your books.

(An offset printer with additional author services.)

Chapter Seventy-Five: Sirius Publications

An Author Services Company
www.sirius-books.com

Dual Exclusive E-Book and Print on Demand Contract

Summary of terms:

- You earn 70% royalties on the net profits from sale of e-books.
- You earn 50% royalties on print on demand books.
- $500 initial (one-time) fee for POD program - required by the POD service
- $25 each subsequent year maintenance fee.
- You earn 80% royalties on the net profits from sale of print books for the first year, or until you earn $100, whichever comes first.
- Payments occur on a monthly basis provided we owe you at least $20.
- This is an exclusive contract, which means you are NOT free to contract with other publishers or sell your work elsewhere.
- Your book will be published in various electronic formats.

Dual Non-Exclusive E-Book and Print on Demand Contract

Summary of terms:

- You earn 50% royalties on the net profits from sale of e-books.
- You earn 40% royalties on print on demand books.
- $500 initial (one-time) fee for POD program - required by the POD service.

- You earn 80% royalties on the net profits from sale of print books for the first year, or until you earn $100, whichever comes first.
- $50 per year maintenance fee for POD program.
- Payments occur on a monthly basis provided we owe you at least $20.
- This is a non-exclusive contract, which means you are free to contract with other publishers or sell your work elsewhere.
- Your book will be published in various electronic formats.

E-Book Exclusive Contract

Summary of terms:

- NO submission or setup fees.
- You earn 60% royalties on the net profits from sale of e-books.
- Payments occur on a monthly basis provided we owe you at least $20.
- This is an exclusive contract, which means you are NOT free to contract with other publishers or sell your work elsewhere.
- Your book will be published in various electronic formats.
- You have the option to publish in other formats, such as Print on Demand (there is a separate agreement for this option, and you are not obligated to publish in other—non-digital—formats.)

E-Book Nonexclusive Contract

Summary of terms:

- NO submission or setup fees.
- You earn 50% royalties on the net profits from sale of e-books.
- Payments occur on a monthly basis provided we owe you at least $20.
- This is a non-exclusive contract, which means you are free to contract with other non-exclusive publishers.
- You agree to submit the Work to a minimum of ten (10) e-book reviewers within the first month of its publication.
- Your book will be published in various electronic formats.
- You have the option to publish in other formats, such as Print on Demand (there is a separate agreement for this option, and you are not obligated to publish in other (non-digital) formats.)

Print on Demand Exclusive Contract

Summary of terms:

- You earn 50% royalties on print on demand books.
- Payments occur on a monthly basis provided we owe you at least $20.
- $199 initial (one-time) fee - initial setup fee required by the POD service.
- $25 per subsequent year maintenance fee

- You earn 80% royalties on the net profits from sale of print books for the first year, or until you earn $100, whichever comes first.
- This is an exclusive contract, which means you are NOT free to contract with other publishers or sell your work elsewhere.
- Your book will be published in various electronic formats.

Print on Demand Nonexclusive Contract

Summary of terms:

- You earn 40% royalties on the net profits from sale of print books.
- You earn 60% royalties on net profits for the first year or first $100, whichever comes first.
- Payments occur on a monthly basis provided we owe you at least $20.
- This is a non-exclusive contract, which means you are free to contract with other non-exclusive publishers.
- $199 initial (one-time) fee - initial setup fee required by the POD service.
- $25 per subsequent year maintenance fee
- You agree to submit the Work to a minimum of ten (10) book reviewers within the first month of its publication.
- Your obligations are to: provide us with an appropriately formatted copy of your book, provide a biography, summary and word count and other pertinent information for posting online, respond to emails, help publicize your book.
- Our obligations are to: format your book for publication, edit the book, publicize the site, post

your book in a timely manner, update the site frequently, and provide credit card transactions.

Let our professional editors enhance your document to showcase your talent even better.
Why Choose Us?
Attention to detail, one-on-one service, experience and professionalism. Our Services
The following editing services are provided
Proofreading/Copyediting
Extensive Editing/Rewriting
Critiques
Manuscript Preparation
Market Research
Cover Design
Web Page Editing
Resizing/Reformatting Existing Artwork
~~~~~~~~~~

Proofreading/copyediting
Price: $30 per hour; approximately $3 per page
Typical project: 1 hour (short story/article, 10 pages)
10 hours (novel, 100 pages and up)

Payment: We will bill you for first hour/estimate after receiving your contact form. Once estimate is agreed upon, we will bill you for that amount.

Examines and corrects for:
Errors of spelling, grammar, punctuation.
Confusing or awkward sentences.
Inconsistency of style.

Extensive Editing
Price: $50 per hour; approx. $5 per page.

Examines and corrects for all of the above (errors of spelling, grammar, punctuation; confusing or awkward sentences; inconsistency of style) in addition to editing document for clarity, logic, and content. Your editor will make sure your words say exactly what you intended. Awkward phrasing, redundancy, inconsistency, and poor pacing will be corrected. Includes a critique and consultation with the author regarding major changes.

Critiques
Price: $50 per shorter manuscript (1-50 pages); $50 per 50 pages thereafter. Payment: We will bill you for first hour/estimate after receiving your contact form. Once estimate is agreed upon, we will bill you for that amount.

Your editor will give your manuscript or proposal (three chapters and a synopsis, or a narrative outline) a thorough reading. The first twenty or thirty pages (generally the first chapter, if a book) will be line edited. Usually, you will find notations made throughout the entire ms. that can help guide you through revisions. You will receive a thoughtfully crafted letter detailing problems found in the manuscript along with possible solutions that are based on a clear understanding of what makes good writing.

If extensive critique is warranted the author will be consulted regarding further work for a further fee. Nothing further will be charged the author without his or her authorization.

Manuscript Preparation
Price: $35 per hour
Typical project: 1-2 hours (short story/article), 3 hours (novel)

Market Research

Price: $50 per hour
Length: Varies. First hour will be $25 and we will give you
an estimate of length for your project.

We do the work so you can concentrate on your writing.
We will research possible markets for your manuscript. We
will find appropriate markets and create a customized
listing for you. We can also create cover letters and labels
for each market, and even mail out your manuscripts for
you if you prefer.

Web Page Editing
Price: $15 per page for proofreading, $35 per page for
extensive editing.

Cover Design

Price: $65 for e-book cover.

$95 for print book cover
One of our cover designers will work with you to create an
attractive, professional cover for your book using existing
graphics and artwork.

If you would like something more unique, an artist can
create original artwork for $250.

Resizing/Reformatting Existing Artwork
Price: $20 flat fee per graphic. Graphics such as cover art,
author photo, or web art resized, optimized or reformatted
into .jpg or .gif. Must be in .jpg, .gif, .tiff or .bmp (bitmap)
format.

(Great graphics on this website. Basics look cut and dry.
We found no complaints on the web reference this
company.)

Chapter Seventy-Six: SkyLine Publishing
POD

A division of OmniLandBooks.com

Skyline Publishing, the POD side of OmniLand Books can help you publish your manuscript and turn it into a high-quality soft or hardback book. We can help authors with interior formatting and cover design. Your book becomes available to 25,000 retail outlets and through major internet retailers like Amazon, Barnes and Nobel. And, of course, OmniLand's online "Book Catalog" will make it easy for your friends to order your book; it's just a click away.
You submit your finished manuscript, to Skyline Publishing, P.O. Box 313,Anahuac, TX 77514, and we will work with you to get it in print in a hassle-free, step-by step process. We do not do it the same way each time because each author has different problem areas and we adjust to their needs.

OmniLand Books will assign your book an ISBN number.

We will affix the EAN barcode.

Full price for 5 X 8 paperback: $785.00 No hidden charges.

The 5 X 8 Paperback Package Includes:

Interior formatting and cover design
Worldwide Distribution Through Online Channels Such as Barnes & Noble and Amazon
Ten Paperback Copies
OmniLand Books will assign your book an ISBN number
We will affix the EAN barcode
Nonexclusive Contract

Listing in Books in Print

Self-publishing, coupled with Print On Demand (POD) services is becoming an industry standard for getting published, it allows you, the author complete control over publishing your own book. Skyline Publishing is an imprint of OmniLand Books for those who are interested in POD Self-Publishing.

Manuscript Submission Guidelines for Skyline Publishing:

Submission should be: electronic, and you should provide all pertinent information in the email message.
Hard copy manuscripts are acceptable, but author incurs a charge for transferring the file to digital. If you intend to send your manuscript by mail, e-mail or call us for instructions.

We use professional layout and design software to complete each page of the manuscript. Follow these guidelines to help make the transference process move effortless.

Create your manuscript as a single word processing document with Microsoft Word or WordPerfect software.

Use Times New Roman, Adobe Caslon Pro, or Garamond typeface.

Use Twelve-point type, and no headers, footers, or page numbering.

An 8.5" x 11" layout is a good choice, with 1" margins all around.

Chapter Seventy-Seven: Smashwords

Please see Chapter Sixteen for complete information on Smashwords.

Chapter Seventy-Eight: Spire Publishing

Welcome to Spire Publishing where self publishing a book is simple and affordable.

Your book is published with the same care and attention that it took you to write it. When you publish your book with Spire Publishing it can be designed, published and available for purchase worldwide within six weeks.

E-book publishing - now available as either an e-book publishing package or an add-on to some of our publishing packages (see eBook link for further information).

Which publishing package are you interested in?

$189.00 The Spire e-Book Publishing Package includes all of the following:

- You deliver a print ready word (.doc/docx) for the body of your book.
- ISBN assignment for archival and records purpose.
- One on one author support.
- Title set-up at e-book distributor (Kindle, SonyReader, Nook, etc).
- You keep all rights to your work.
- All sales figures collated, biannual sales reports.
- Royalty payments

$599.00 The Spire Print Ready Publishing Package includes all of the following:

- You deliver a print ready .pdf for both cover and body of your book. Learn more.

- Free Adobe InDesign templates available. Please e-mail us with your requirements.
- Design Assessment. One of our book designers will be on hand to help with design questions.
- ISBN assignment for archival and records purpose.
- ISBN barcode created and delivered to you for insertion on the cover.
- Legal deposit books printed, shipped and administered.
- One on one author support.
- Title set-up at printer.
- You keep all rights to your work.
- 3 to 6 day delivery in the UK and North America. 5 to 10 day delivery for color and hardback books.
- Bulk discounts for orders over 50 books.
- Books printed in both the USA and UK.
- Books can be produced as either a trade paperback, hardback or co lour book.
- 5 copies of your book.
- You are responsible for sales and distribution.

$699 (£479) - Spire Print Ready Plus

All the features of the Print Ready Package as well as:

- Library Cataloguing.
- Wholesale distribution through Ingrams and Baker & Taylor in North America.
- Wholesale distribution through Gardners and Bertram in the UK.
- Books available from over 25,000 on-line booksellers worldwide.
- All sales figures collated, biannual sales reports.
- Royalty payments
- 5 copies of your book.

$799 (£549) - Spire Essentials

This popular package is for authors who just want to publish a book for family and friends or who wish to take control of their own sales, for example from their personal website. *There is no wholesale or on-line distribution included in this package.*

The Spire Essential Publishing Package includes all of the following:

- Your book is created by a book designer from your final manuscript.
- Two hours design time for a custom designed cover, incorporating your own images. Library images may be purchased for a fee.
- Full color cover.
- ISBN and bar code assignment for archival and records purpose.
- Legal deposit books printed, shipped and administered.
- One on one author support.
- Copyright information page inserted into manuscript.
- Preparation of electronic proof.
- One round of author proof corrections.
- Title set-up at printer.
- You keep all rights to your work.
- 3 to 6 day delivery in the UK and North America. 5 to 10 day delivery for color and hardback books.
- Bulk discounts for orders over 50 books.
- Books printed in both the USA and UK.
- Books can be produced as either a trade paperback, hardback or color book.
- Books can be produced in either regular or large text.
- 5 copies of your book.

- Your book is created by a book designer from your final manuscript.
- Two hours design time for a custom designed cover, incorporating your own images. Library images may be purchased for a fee.
- Full color cover.
- ISBN and bar code assignment for archival and records purpose.
- Legal deposit books printed, shipped and administered.
- One on one author support.
- Copyright information page inserted into manuscript.
- Preparation of electronic proof.
- One round of author proof corrections.
- Title set-up at printer.
- You keep all rights to your work.
- 3 to 6 day delivery in the UK and North America. 5 to 10 day delivery for color and hardback books.
- Bulk discounts for orders over 50 books.
- Books printed in both the USA and UK.
- Books can be produced as either a trade paperback, hardback or color book.
- Books can be produced in either regular or large text.
- 5 copies of your book.

$999 (£699) - Spire Professional

This package is for authors who want their book to be available through the book trade and access to international distribution.

- Your book is created by your personal book designer.
- Custom designed cover, incorporating either your own images or pictures from our stock image library.
- Full color cover.
- One on one author support.
- Preparation of electronic proof.
- One round of author proof corrections.
- Title set-up at printer.
- Full ISBN allocation and administration
- Copyright information page inserted into manuscript.
- Legal deposit books printed, shipped and administered.
- Wholesale distribution available through Ingrams and Baker & Taylor in North America.
- Wholesale distribution available through Gardners and Bertram in the UK.
- Books available from on-line booksellers worldwide.
- All sales figures collated, bi-annual sales reports.
- Bi-annual royalty payments (if due) .
- You keep all rights to your work.
- 3 to 6 day delivery in the UK and North America. 5 to 10 day delivery for color and hardback books.
- Bulk discounts for orders over 50 books.
- 10 copies of your book.
- Books printed in both the USA and UK.

- Books can be produced as either a trade paperback or hardback or color softback book.

$1299 (£849) - Spire Premier

This comprehensive self publishing package comes complete with 20 paperback copies and an e-book edition of your book (black and white, no images).

- Your book is created by your personal book designer.
- Custom designed cover, incorporating either your own images or pictures from our stock image library.
- Full color cover.
- One on one author support.
- Preparation of electronic proof.
- One round of author proof corrections.
- Title set-up at printer.
- Full ISBN allocation and administration.
- Copyright information page inserted into manuscript.
- Legal deposit books printed, shipped and administered.
- Wholesale distribution available through Ingrams and Baker & Taylor in North America.
- Wholesale distribution available through Gardners and Bertrams in the UK.
- Books available to purchase from on-line booksellers worldwide.
- All sales figures collated, bi-annual sales reports.
- Bi-annual royalty payments (if due)
- You keep all rights to your work.
- 3 to 6 day delivery in the UK and North America.
- Bulk discounts for orders over 50 books.

- 20 copies of your book.
- Books printed in both the USA and UK.
- Books produced as trade paperback book.

Additional Services

$75 (£55) - Printed proof of your book before final distribution

$99 (£89) - e-book version in addition to one of the above publishing packages (black and white books only)

Spire also has the other typical author services like proof reading, marketing and distribution assistance, cover design, and formatting.
You can contact them or gain more information at www.spirepublishing.com.

Chapter Seventy-Nine: Tate Publishing
A Christian Subsidy Publisher

Tate Publishing & Enterprises, LLC, is a Christian-based, family-owned, mainline publishing organization with a mission to discover and market unknown authors.

Besides releasing your title in a traditional paper version, Tate Publishing authors also have their book released as an eBook format. An eBook is an electronic version of the paper book that a person can purchase and download to read on their computer, smart phone or a stand-alone eBook reader such as the Apple iPad or Amazon Kindle.

Children's books can also be released in 3D with illustrations jumping off the page. Other options include creating a 15 second book trailer commercial and customized website design. With such a wide variety of formats and marketing tools, this greatly increases the impact your book can have on the marketplace. We give your book the best chance for success!

We are the publisher that others are striving to emulate because we are the most author-friendly publishing house in America with the highest author royalties of anyone! When you become part of the exclusive Tate Publishing family, here are a few things you can expect:

- Beautiful custom cover designs created specifically for your book.
- Professional editing and text layout in Adobe inDesign, registered ISBN, and author copyright also provided.
- Book is set up for nationwide distribution with the largest distributor in the world, Ingram/Spring Arbor.

- Author is assigned a personal marketing representative, as well as a full-time publicist, who follows a marketing plan for every book which includes sending press releases, book signing requests to bookstores, and monitoring availability of the book at all times, as well as assisting with speaking engagements and public appearances. The marketing representative is the author's personal contact for any marketing requests and needs ongoing. (Our marketing staff remains at your service for the life of the book, and a book is forever!). Tate Publishing does not charge a fee for publishing and absorbs all the cost of production and distribution of a book. However, there are requirements regarding professional marketing and publicist representation the author is required to provide. We do expect any author who signs with us to have full-time professional book marketing and publicist representation.

- **Book can be produced in paper format, audio book format *and* eBook format.** eBooks are quickly gaining popularity as technology now allows you to read books on your smart phone, tablet, computer or a stand-alone eBook reader.

- **The option to have your book advertised on national television.** Through our award-winning multimedia department, Tate Publishing authors are now offered full production of 15 second commercials that will be aired on national television to gain an entire new level of visibility and promotion for our books and events.

- **The option to have a custom website design.** Our staff can create and host a website for the life of the book where you can update the content whenever you need.

- **The highest royalty earnings.** Authors receive 40 percent royalty from all direct sales while also benefiting from a 60 percent discount on their own personal book purchases—unbeatable in the industry! We also beat the usual 8 percent industry standard for distribution sales by offering our authors 15 percent.
- **Author retains all rights to book** as a partner for success in this exciting, unique and fulfilling Tate Publishing venture.
- **Book is available for sales on Amazon.com, BarnesAndNoble.com** and many other websites.
- **Book featured in TatePublishing.com bookstore** generating perpetual sales.

(Tate Publishing requires a manuscript be submitted BEFORE they will discuss printing and author services costs. They do not even hint at their fees, stating that less than four percent of the manuscripts submitted are accepted. This could well mean that there fees are so high that most authors can not afford to publish with them. As they do not advise what those fees are, it is anybody's guess.)

Chapter Eighty:
Third Millennium Publishing
An Author Services company

Third Millennium is a website dedicated to providing authors with the infrastructure and resources necessary to publish and sell their work themselves. We use a different model than the one with which you may be familiar from dealing with conventional publishers. Instead of purchasing the rights to publish your work and then providing you 5-10% royalties on everything we sell; with our model, you retain total control over your work. You establish the cover price, the terms of sale, how long your work will be offered to the public, and in what form. And when you make a sale, you keep all of the money in excess of credit collection and distribution costs. Typically, this means that your "royalty" is 65-75% of the full price of each book sold. Except it isn't a royalty. It is the money you earn by selling your own property to the reading public. It is your "profit."

Remember, it is *your* book. You are the sole owner of the "right to publish" and are free to use it as you see fit. Nor does Third Millennium Publishing require exclusivity concerning the books we publish. If you find two or three different avenues to market your book, then by all means, use them.

What do we get out of it? We make our money by providing you with electronic and trade paperback publishing services at substantially less cost than you could purchase them for yourself. We can afford to do this because we have already paid for all of our infrastructure and equipment, which we initially acquired for our own use, and it does not cost us very much more to allow you to use them. We provide you with access to our world-wide website, commercial bank account, credit card collection service, software, computers, printers, and specialized bookbinding equipment, all of which cost nearly $50,000 to acquire.

Specifically, in exchange for a nominal setup fee and a $1.00 charge for each book sold, we will assist you with the following:

- We will build you your very own section of the Third Millennium Publishing Web Site in which to display electronic and trade paperback copies of your books. Your section will include:
  - A web address of http: //3mpub.com/YOUR NAME.
  - A summary page listing all of your books.
  - Individual display pages for each book.
  - An author biography page.

- We will format your book into an electronic file using Adobe's industry-standard PDF format, PalmPilot format, and Microsoft Reader format and post it on the INTERNET in a secure subdirectory that will prevent anyone from accessing it unless they have paid for the privilege.
- We will provide you with credit card collection, PAYPAL, and personal check purchasing capability. Customers may order via INTERNET, toll free telephone number, or good old fashioned surface mail. When they order over the INTERNET, you instantly receive an email notifying you of that fact. We will collect your money for you and disburse it promptly at the beginning of each month. You will receive all money in excess of the actual cost of sales (the charge the credit card collection agency and bank assess for their services) plus our $1.00 fee per book.

- We have a production facility that will print trade paperback books for you, or else you can have them printed elsewhere. Unlike typical vanity presses, which require you to initially order 500-1000 books at a cost of up to $10,000 to obtain their services, Third Millennium Publishing has a minimum book order requirement of only 1 book!
- Regardless of where you have your books printed, we will provide you with two (2) complimentary trade paperback copies of your book printed in the Third Millennium Publishing production facility.

You send Third Millennium Publishing your manuscript in an electronic format that is ready to publish. That means that the manuscript should be edited, spell checked, and all corrections made before we get it. Once we receive your book, we will put it into a form that makes it easy to read on a computer screen, or in hard copy after being printed out. We will put your manuscript into the industry-standard Adobe PDF format, as well as PalmPilot and Microsoft Reader formats. We will then put the copies of your book online and provide a link to Third Millennium Publishing's credit card collection service, electronic check processing service, PAYPAL, and our toll free telephone ordering number. We will even provide an order form your customers can print out in case they are still ordering products the old-fashioned way, by mail.

We will build you your own section of our website, with your own summary page (if you have more than one book), individual display pages for each book, and a biography page. Once you have your own section, along with navigation links to easily jump between pages, we will add you to the HOME PAGE, where you will be prominently listed among the other authors.

Once you are set up, customers input their credit card numbers and receive a USERNAME and PASSWORD. These are used to access the electronic book files in a secure directory at the Third Millennium Publishing site. Having obtained your book, they have the choice of reading it on their computer screen using the free Adobe Acrobat PDF reader, Microsoft Reader, or PalmPilot reader, or printing it out. As soon as their credit card number clears the bank, the credit collection agency will send you an email notification that tells you the name of the customer, the name of the book purchased, and how much money you have made. The average response time between sale and notification is typically 30 seconds. If they use some other form to order, we will notify you of the order as soon as we receive it.

At the end of every month, we tally up your sales, deduct the costs incurred in making the sale (approximately $0.60 per electronic book or $1.00 per trade paperback sold to collect, validate, and process the credit card numbers), and then send you a check for the net proceeds.

SCHEDULE OF CHARGES :

Third Millennium Publishing will put your book online for you, display it in a manner that will enhance sales, and collect your money for you. Our charge for this is as follows:

1. Basic Hosting of Your Book on Our Web Site for Two Years:

a.	First book	-	$300
b.	Second book	-	$200
c.	Third book	-	$100
d.	Additional books	-	$100 each

2. 3MPUB charge per sale: $1.00 for electronic
books or trade paperback books printed by third parties
3. Credit charge per sale: $0.50 plus 2.6% of the
sale price
4. Monthly disbursement cost: Free
5. Cost after initial two years: $100 per book per year
6. Other charges: Sometimes when people purchase by
credit card, they will refuse to acknowledge the sale when
the bill comes due. This happens infrequently, but is a
normal part of being a credit card merchant. You, the
author/publisher, will be responsible for all credit charges
or charge-backs related to the sale of your books.

Third Millennium Publishing charges a setup fee and a fee
on each book sold. What does this money pay for?

The initial fee ($300 for hosting one book for two years,
and a declining scale for subsequent books) goes to pay for
the labor required to set up your section of the website.
This includes preparing your manuscript for publication,
building the summary page, description page, and
biography page, and setting up the money collection
service. It also goes to defray the cost of adding your book
to our site. Internet Service Providers charge for two
things: storage and throughput. Adding your book to our
web site increases it size, which in turn, costs us money.

The recurring fee ($1 per book sold) goes to cover the
impact your sales have on our throughput capacity. In
other words, when people come into the website to look at
your book, data is exchanged over the INTERNET. When
they buy one of the electronic editions of your book, that
book must be transmitted by the ISP to the customer. Since
Third Millennium Publishing pays for the number of bytes
it transmits each month; the recurring $1 fee is intended to
cover the additional cost of traffic to your pages.

There is another function the $1.00 fee per book sold performs. It makes us enthusiastic about increasing your business! Let us say that you place a book online and then sell a million electronic copies. If the book sell price is set to $5.00, then you will receive $3,370,000 in revenue from the sales, after paying credit costs and sales fees. We are happy for you! However, Third Millennium Publishing will be receiving $1 million for the same transactions, which makes us VERY enthusiastic to help you increase your sales.

Chapter Eighty-One: Trafford
An Imprint of Author's Solutions

1663 Liberty Drive
Bloomington, IN 47403
888-232-4444
www.trafford.com

As an imprint of Author Solutions, Trafford offers all the benefits of the parent company and sister companies. Every level of design, editing, marketing, promotion, and distribution is available to Trafford authors.

We have been nurturing writers into independently published authors for more than 15 years. Today Trafford's family comprises more than 10,000 authors spanning 120 countries. Our commitment to giving our authors the best possible publishing experience means that we are continually evaluating, adapting and developing our services and processes

Publishing Packages:

Trafford's Black & White publishing packages offer the best blend of publishing options available. Choose from Prime, Watermark, Elite, Signature, and Signature Bookseller and find the best publishing package for you. Starting at $799.00

Designed to give writers a practical array of publishing services at one low price, Black & White publishing packages offer essential services to authors of all genres. All packages include:
- Paperback Format
- Author Support

- Custom Cover Design
- Interior Page Layout
- Proof Corrections
- Worldwide Distribution
- Volume Book Discount
- Online Bookselling Page
- Worldwide Distribution

Trafford's comprehensive Full-Color publishing packages are ideal for authors hoping to present professional books to the marketplace. Whether your dream is to publish your art, photography or recipes, Prime Color, Watermark Color and Elite Color make it easy to get your book in print Starting at $999.00

Our Full-Color publishing packages include:
- Paperback Format
- Custom Interior Layout
- Full-Color Custom Cover
- Color Image Insertion
- ISBN Assignment
- Proof Corrections
- Worldwide Distribution
- Author Support

Their children's publishing package options are are tailored for authors who want to reach a younger audience. If you've always dreamed of publishing a children's book, Bedtime, Storyteller, and Chapters publishing packages make it easy to accomplish your goal.
Starting at $999.00

Authors can customize their experience by purchasing additional publishing or marketing services separately.

Make a child laugh, share a life lesson or expand a child's imagination with your story. All Children's publishing packages include:

- Paperback Format
- Free Paperback Copies
- Full-Color Custom Cover Design
- Interior Page Layout
- Author Support
- ISBN Assignment
- Proof Corrections
- Worldwide Distribution
- Volume Book Disc
- Online Bookselling

Chapter Eighty-Two: Tri-State Litho

National Tradebook and Publication Printer

(Their minimum for offset printing is only 50 but since we have been using 100 books at the offset printers cost estimates, we will stay with that amount.)

Quantity: 100

A softcover tradebook, 100 pages, black and white text, color cover, perfect bound

The per-book cost of our sample book is $7.30 plus shipping and handling. Don't forget your storage.

Tri State does not offer editing or marketing. They are printers. You can order promotional printed material from them and have it delivered with your books, cards, book marks, posters, they can do it.

Offset printers are an excellent solution when you are publishing a nonfiction book and plan to sell or give it away as part of your speaking platform or at seminars, and conferences. They require a digital copy of your book and cover.

Tristate recently purchased digital printers and can now print much smaller quantities.

Make a Profit!! Sell Every Book

Tri-State Litho is unlike any other printer you will ever use... Why, you ask? Our sales team will advise you to only print the quantity of books that you know you will sell or distribute in a very short time, instead of investing large quantities to try and reduce your unit cost.

Short-Run Press Runs Are Where We Are Most Competitive!

Be Careful...when buying in large quantities to reduce your unit costs on books! It has been proven that at least 25% of the books purchased become out of date while in storage or book sales weren't what they were expected and the books sit in your closet or end up remaining on the shelves. This 25% is a direct cost to your unit price. Our Ultra Short Run Book Printing allows you to maintain a very reasonable unit cost so you can realize a profit by selling all of the books you print with us. The other benefit of Ultra Short Runs is the editing and revision capabilities. Don't tie up large amounts of cash in book inventories that are out of date. Get updated information to your clients "On Demand."

Don't Over Order...Every book can be a prosperous one.

We do not insist on fixed sizes, papers or inks for your publications: Tri-State Litho can create unique customer publications in short runs at affordable prices.

The Different Printing Methods.

Our two methods of printing, digital printing and conventional offset makes us especially efficient in the Ultra short-run book printing process.

Digital Printing

Most first time authors and experienced publishers looking to test the marketability of a new title will choose the Digital Printing method for all of its obvious advantages.

With the advent of digital printing, authors can now affordably publish and print in quantities as low as 50 books with quality comparable to offset. Digital printing assures consistency throughout the printing process by reducing the possibility of human and mechanical error inherent in traditional offset printing. This is achieved by eliminating the need for film, plates and color matching inks and instead printing directly to paper from the computer disk you supply.

Advantages	Disadvantages
• affordable short run printing as low as 50 books • consistent quality printing • fast turn around, days not weeks • proof is a sample of finished book • edits are fast and affordable • complete process can be accomplished via the Internet	• only cost effective up 1000 books • photo quality good, but limited • limited to black ink for text • paper stock and size limitations • spot colors not available

• ideal for standard sizes 5 1/2 x 8 1/2, 6 x 9, 7 x 10, and 8 1/2 x 11 books • reprints from the same file • full color covers are now very affordable	

Offset Printing

Offset printing is best used for books printed in quantities greater than 1000 and require a high degree of flexibility in the finished book. Offset printing uses film, plates and inks to achieve accurate color reproduction.

Unlike digital printing, the initial setup costs for offset printing are generally high, but, as the quantity ordered increases, these costs are spread over a larger number of books, causing the unit cost per book to decrease dramatically. Offset printing makes perfect and case bound book printing very affordable in quantities between 1000 and 5000.

Advantages	Disadvantages
• cost effective in larger	• longer turnaround time

quantities • greater range of paper and ink choices • spot colors • great photo quality • fewer page size limitations • text can be any ink color	• greater setup costs • edits are costly and create delays • more steps involved in the process

How to decide on the best method to print your book:

If your book is a standard size, prints black on 50# or 60# book paper, good but limited photo quality is acceptable, the cover is either black or full color and your requirements are under 1000 books then you should choose the Digital Printing method; otherwise the Offset Printing method is generally the best way to go. If you need more information please contact Kumar Persad @ 800-836-7581 extension 444.

(Generally, Tri State accepts camera-ready copy, which must be complete, requiring no additional page design, typesetting or editing before printing. The printed page will look exactly like the copy submitted. They have limited publishing services to assist with making sure ISBN and copyright have been registered, but it is the author's responsibility to be ready to go to print when they submit their manuscript. For more information or referrals, please contact them at www.tristatelitho.com.)

Chapter Eighty-Three: U Build a Book
A Printer, Offset and Digital Press

This may be the printer to use if you have a children's book, cook book, or any book requiring color pictures or photographs.
 (When I ran their onsite price quote for our standard sample, black and white 6 x 9 trade softcover it estimated a whopping $31.55. But I also noted they had a slot for colored pages, so I entered that ten pages were color and 90 black and white. Voila! Same price.)

Creative Book Publishing

UBuildABook is a creative book publishing platform. If you have the idea, we can turn your idea into a full color, high quality book that you will cherish for years to come! We offer a great solution for self publishing and printing on demand since we do not share in any of your profits!

To build a book, supply us with your book content. You design the custom book cover and the page layout and leave the rest to us. We will take your vision and turn it into a unique and high quality book and we can do all of this very quickly

We specialize in publishing short runs (from 1 to 1000 books!), we offer custom covers and we feature full color printing. Your custom book can be made in standard sizes or custom sizes (up to 12"x12"). You can publish your own book with our Book Building Software or in *any layout* or program and we have a low minimum for reorders.)

The UBuildABook Advantage

- Use our new book building software or your own software to create your books
- Hard and Soft Book Covers. Print One or Thousands!
- Free Hard Copy Proof for orders of 40+ books
- Standard or custom sizes (up to 12" x 12")
- 7 - 10 Business Day Turnaround (quicker time is available for a rush fee)
- Book Printing & Binding done at our facility
- Low minimum and no extra charge on Re-Orders
- Full Color, Black & White or Mixed Color/Black & White
- All Workmanship Guaranteed*
- You Can Design or We Can Design

UBuildABook is a great option for anyone who is interested in showcasing their work or their lives.

(They have free software to download in order to prepare and format your book before submitting it to them for publication. U Build a Book appears to be an option for anyone publishing a book with multiple color pages.)

Chapter Eighty-Four: Vantage Press

Founded in 1949 Vantage Press is America's oldest self-publishing corporation. For more than 60 years, Vantage Press has been based in New York, helping new and established writers publish their books. Vantage Press offers a premium, full-range publishing service for a fixed fee.

We take your book seriously. We pride ourselves on our professionalism and customer service. Our staff has on average more than twenty years of experience. When you publish with Vantage Press, you will work hand-in-hand with publishing professionals who will ensure that you and your book receive service personalized in every respect.

By choosing Vantage, you are also enlisting the services of our distributor, Ingram Publisher Services. IPS is an affiliate of Ingram Book Company, the largest book wholesaler in the world. IPS exclusively warehouses, ships, and sells Vantage books. Other Ingram companies allow us to make eBook editions available and give us versatility in printing.

At Vantage we provide full-service fee-based publishing. Every author enjoys the follow inclusive services:

Manuscript preparation for editing

Thorough copyediting

Typesetting and proofs

Copyrighting (in your name) and Library of Congress cataloging

Design and production, including cover design, photo handling, and illustrations

Hardcover or paperback printing to a professional standard

ISBN (International Standard Book Number), bar coding, and listing in Books in Print

Coordinated marketing, promotion, and publicity

Full sales availability to booksellers, libraries, and wholesalers including Amazon

Warehousing, shipping, and accounting

Twice annual royalties at 50% of net sales

Additional printings to satisfy sales at Vantage's expense

How much do you charge to publish a book?

"We cannot answer this precisely until we have seen your manuscript, but generally our publishing fees range from $5,000 to $25,000. Since every book presents its own editorial and production issues that affect cost, an exact proposal can be made only when we have your manuscript in hand. We typically communicate our fee and proposal to you within three weeks of receipt of your manuscript."

You may of course pay the fee in its entirety, but our normal schedule breaks it into three approximately equal payments: upon contract signing, upon delivery of page proofs, and upon printing of your book. In some cases we also offer a flexible installment plan of monthly payments; however, the entire amount must be paid before your book can be marketed. We will do everything we reasonably can to accommodate you.

You receive at least 25 books free of charge upon publication and can purchase additional copies at a 50% discount.

(The self-proclaimed first vanity press owns what they do. They offer all author services and based upon your needs they create individualized packages that will cost you between $5000 and $20,000. No subterfuge.

Now, think about the possibilities. A known best-seller like James Patterson or Stephen King could contract with this company, pay them five grand and receive far more money than the traditional publishers pay them. Actually they could use a company like Peppertree Press for two grand and get 100% of the profits rather than the 10% to 15% they are receiving now. Are you listening traditionals? You have snubbed the new writers and soon the best sellers in your fold will snub you.)

Chapter Eighty-Five: Virtual Bookworm

POD — eBooks

     Virtualbookworm.com is one of the most established on demand publishers in the business and has been online since 2000. We offer full distribution, marketing, website design, book cover and interior design and much more.

Included in all POD Packages:

- Softcover available on white or cream paper.
- Trim Sizes for Softcover Books

Inches	Millimeters	Binding	Paper	Page Counts
5X8	203X127	Softcover	White	48-828
5X8	203X127	Softcover	Cream	48-740
5.25X8	203X133	Softcover	White	48-828
5.25X8	203X133	Softcover	Cream	48-740
5.5X8.5	216X140 (Demy 8vo)	Softcover	White	48-828
5.5X8.5	216X140 (Demy 8vo)	Softcover	Cream	48-740
6X9	229X152	Softcover	White	48-828
6X9	229X152	Softcover	Cream	48-740
7X10	254X178	Softcover	White	48-828
8.25X11	280X210	Softcover	White	48-828
8.5X11	280X216	Softcover	White	48-828

- Page counts as low as 48 and as many as 828 pages.
- Electronic proof
- ISBN assignment (author can provide own ISBN and imprint at no additional charge)
- Copyright application kit
- Book page on our website
- Barcode
- 15 free internal graphics/images (must be submitted to specs)
- Data Backup
- Full Distribution
- Drop Shipment
- Book registration through Amazon.com, Barnes & Noble, Books in Print and many others
- 50% royalties of net receipts (Approximately 30-35% of cover price on paperbacks sold through us!)
- Monthly Sales Report
- Author may purchase first order of his/her softcover edition for 50% off list price (subsequent orders at least 30% off list, but discount increases with larger orders)

Add-on Specials:

- Add our ebook package (including Kindle, Nook, and iBook for iPhone/iPad book creation) to any level below for only $65 additional!
- Extra Internal Warehousing: $100. Since we primarily utilize print-on-demand technology, we keep only a limited supply of books on hand to reduce inventory costs and keep your prices low. This sometimes causes delays if a book sells a number of copies at once. This package will cover

our warehousing costs and keep a minimum of 7-10 copies of your book in stock at all times.

Packages:

Level A: Includes all of the above services and one free book. The package includes a generic cover with an author photo and bio on the back. (The author may supply artwork for the cover as well, as long as the work is 300dpi or greater)
Level A Price: $360

Level B: Includes all of the basic services, Library of Congress number and three free books.
Level B Price: $440

Level C: Includes all of the basic services, Library of Congress number, five free books and professional cover.
Level C Price: $495

Level D: Includes all of the Level C services plus professional editing package (for up to 75,000 words).
Level D Price: $790

Level E: Includes all of Level D services, plus Bronze Marketing Package.
Level E Price: $1,110

Level F: Includes all of Level D services and the Silver Marketing Package.
Level F Price: $1,390

Level G: Includes all of Level D services and the Gold Marketing Package.
Level G Price: $1,950

(all Softcover packages have a $20 annual maintenance fee, with the first 2 years free)

What is in the Marketing Packages?

- Bronze Marketing Package: $400 (if purchased separately). Includes professional press release, 100 four-color business cards, and a personal storefront for two years!
- Silver Marketing Package: $700 (if purchased separately). With this package, we will write a press release and send it to over 200 media outlets and send review copies of your book to at least 10 major reviewers. You will also get a Personal Storefront for two years and 100 four-color business cards.
- Gold Marketing Package: $1,300 (if purchased separately). This package includes a professional press release written and distributed to over 200 media outlets, review copies of your book sent to at least 15 major reviewers, a Personal Storefront for two years, placement in Ingram's Advance Magazine, 500 four-color post cards, 500 business cards and 500 2X6" book markers.

Virtual Bookworm offers additional pricing for hardcover or illustrated books as well as some combination packages. Fees can be found on their website at www.virtualbookworm.com.

(While surfing their site I noticed that they continue the idea of "subsidy" publishing being deceitful. They actually come out and advise that subsidy publishers "charge up to $50,000 and make you purchase a large number of books." Until all the subsidy/pod/vanity publisher's accept that charging a fee for their service is not wrong or deceitful, we will continue to question the industry. The way to remove the "taint" is to embrace the fact. Shout it out. Yes, we are a subsidy publisher! We provide you the expertise to get your book printed with good quality and in much less time than the commercial traditional publishers. Yes, there are some subsidy publishers who do a shabby job, yes, some charge exorbitant rates. There are unethical "members" in almost every industry. Don't allow it to affect the companies who are offering legitimate author services for a fair price. That is the purpose of this entire guide, giving you the information to make the best choice for YOU.)

Chapter Eighty-Six: VMI Publishers
A Christian Subsidy Publisher

"VMI is a full service partnership publishing company which works with authors to go beyond just printing their manuscript. With top of line industry professionals, our authors receive the best in editing, cover design, and typesetting. But, we don't stop there! Our authors are given opportunities to make their mark through our distribution company which makes VMI titles available wherever books are sold. Our sales team visits stores sharing our titles across the country. If that is not enough, our authors have been seen and heard on national media such as the 700 Club, Phil Waldrep Ministries, American Family Radio, and more through the services of our marketing and publicity company."

(They offer no indication of their fees on their website. They advise they must have a proposal, a few sample chapters, and the completed manuscript word count. If it fits their Christian parameters, they will then inform you of the work needed and your cost for the work.)

Chapter Eighty-Seven: Voice Projects

An Author's Service company providing audio book formats

So you've completed your masterpiece -- maybe it's a novel or non-fiction; paperback or eBook -- and you're ready to have it professionally-produced as an audiobook.
Whether the book went through a mega-publisher or you're an indie author, if you hold the audio rights you've come to the right place!

Through our "work for hire" process, we'll work with you through every step in the process of converting your manuscript into spoken word with your choice of top-notch narrator. You retain all the publishing and audio rights, you decide on distribution, you keep *100%* of the net proceeds, and you choose how much or how little of our help you need along the way.

There are over 14 million paper books listed on Amazon.com, but only 85,000 audiobooks listed on Audible.com., a mere 0.6% of the market.

Over 300,000 books are published every year (not including eBook-only titles), but only about 5,000 are produced as audiobooks. This represents only 1.6% of the market

How many devices can play MP3 audio files? 2 Billion!

► iPod and all other MP3 players.
► iPhone, Android, BlackBerry, Windows, and other smartphones.
► iPad, Kindle, Nook, and other eReaders.

► Car and home stereos with MP3 CD capability.
► USB flash drives for laptops and desktop PCs.

How much will it cost to become a part of this underserved market?

The recent explosion of independent publishing is a boon to authors and readers, but everyone's busy schedules are limiting their free time to keep up with all these great new books. Combine that with the proliferation of MP3 players and smartphones, and there's a ready-made demand for audiobooks that is still greatly underserved.

The following chart shows high-level project estimates for a typical 300-page novel of 75,000 words.

Three options are given to indicate how your range of choices can affect the overall cost. ***These are rough estimates, your specific quote will be dictated by the actual length of your book and by the narrator you choose.*** Note that all estimates include production of high-quality master audio files ready to use for CD manufacturing, but do not include the cost of distribution media or marketing.

In all cases except author-narrated, you don't sign the contract and you don't pay anything until after you've reviewed the auditions and selected your narrator. At that point, we have a 25% installment plan that goes along with our progress in completing your project. You don't make the last payment until you have approved the entire audiobook from start to finish.

All prices are quoted in "per finished hour" dollars ($/fh). This way you'll have a fixed quote to work with, and it won't change regardless of how long things take behind the scenes. For example:

- Raw narration takes 1.5 to 2 times the finished length of your book, and it's typically done in a maximum of 3 - 4 hour individual sessions so the narrator's voice has time to recover and their energy level remains consistent throughout the book.
- Editing takes 3 - 6 times the finished length. An 8 hour book can require 24 - 48 hours of editing.
- Quality Control takes a bit longer than one full run through of the finished book.
- In all cases, time must be allotted for notation, review, and completion of necessary revisions and corrections.

Sample Estimate for 75,000-word AudioBook	*Option 1*	*Option 2*	*Option 3*
Obtain detailed project estimate	free		
Review custom auditions from voice talent	free		
Approve first 15 minutes of the audio file	included		
Record raw narration files for the entire book	DIY	800	1,800
Edit raw files into finished audio chapters	700	1,400	1,400
Supply one bumper music track for all chapter starts and ends	included		
Custom cover art	not included		
Provide necessary revisions and corrections	included		
Quality Control - Full run-through of finished audiobook	800	800	800
Provide necessary revisions	included		

and corrections			
Finished audio file mastering and preparation for distribution	included		
Total Estimate	*$1,500*	*$3,000*	*$4,000*

- **Option 1**
  - You supply the raw narration files (narrated by you).
  - If you need help with home studio setup or a referral to a studio near you, let us know.
  - We'll sub-contract an apprentice editor to keep your costs even lower.
  - You'll still get the full Quality Control run-through, and your finished audiobook will be produced to professional quality standards.
- **Option 2**
  - You select a talented but less well-known narrator.
  - You'll have the option to audition several voice talent before selecting one, so you'll be sure they sound great.
  - Rates range from $50 - $200 per finished hour ($100/fh example is used in the chart above).
- **Option 3**
  - You select a more well-known voice talent from the audition pool.
  - This won't be a celebrity narrator, for those we have to go through their agents and the paparazzi.

- o Rates range from $200 - $800 per finished hour ($225/fh example is used in the chart below).

For more information and a quote on YOUR book, contact www.voiceprojects.com.

Chapter Eighty-Eight Volumes

A Division of M & T Printing Group

A Canadian Subsidy Publisher

M&T was born 40 years ago in the city of London, Ontario. Within the blink of an eye, that one store in London soon turned into 5 stores in the Kitchener-Waterloo-Cambridge-Guelph area with 3 stores in London and eventually grew to become South Western Ontario's leader in the instant printing market.

Print On Demand has made it possible for authors to get their work into the marketplace without having to deal with the bigger publishing houses or the costs associated with them. The idea of selling the book first and then printing it does away with excess stock and obsolescence. Read about the services we offer below and decide between our Launch and Folio packages to determine which would best suit *your* vision.

	Launch Package $799.00	Folio Package $1699.00
ISBN Assignment	✓	✓
CIP Arrangement	✓	✓
Design an EAN Barcode	✓	✓
Include a Copyright Notice	✓	✓
2 Copies Sent to National Library	✓	✓
Online Access to Sales & Royalty Information	✓	✓
Electronic Master of the Book	✓	✓
Front and Back Cover Design	✓	✓
Book Interior Formatting	✓	✓
Proof for Review by Author	✓	✓
Archive the Book for Future Ordering	✓	✓
Available Online at volumesdirect.com	✓	✓
Purchase your Book at Print Cost	✓	✓
Available Online at chapters.ca & amazon.com	-	✓
500 Full Colour Business Cards	-	✓
500 Full Colour Bookmarks	-	✓
20 Finished Copies to the Author	-	✓
Listing in the Canadian Booksellers Assn. Magazine	-	✓
Create Press Release of the Author's Book Title	-	✓
E-commerce Ordering covered by Volumes	-	✓

What we will provide for you:

1. Consultation on the choices available to you
2. Book archival, production and distribution on demand
3. Legal and administration fulfillment
4. Partnership with design and layout
5. E-commerce, distribution, tracking and payment of royalties
6. Complete in-house printing and bindery facilities
7. 14 Docu-tech printing systems
8. IGen3 Advanced colour printing system
9. 4 Docu-Color 2045 colour printing systems
10. 8 Docu-12 printing systems
11. 21 offset presses
12. Direct Imaging Press (full colour)
13. Complete in-house coating and laminating systems
14. Complete Soft and Hard Cover solutions

Why Volumes?

1. You maintain total ownership and control of book rights
2. You choose between two robust publishing packages
3. We post press releases to thousands of potential buyers

Volumes can make your book available all over the world to major booksellers' websites. We also provide our own on-line bookstore to handle e-commerce distribution if this is the route that you choose to take.

By working with Volumes to self-publish you will:

1. Keep total control of your book. Ownership of the content and design is all yours – You keep the rights. Whether you sell the content to other publishing houses, foreign rights, television or promotion rights – You will own them all.
2. Cover layout and design at no extra cost. We understand the concept of the cover sells and will work with the cover layout until you are 100% satisfied.
3. We take the headaches out of producing the EAN bar code, ISBN number, Copyright page and Cataloging in Publication data.
4. With our state-of-the-art electronic archival system you can print the quantity you want when you want it. This new process lowers the risk that you would undertake using any other publishing process. No more administration cost for warehousing, obsolescence and interest expense. You have no extra cost for ordering on demand. You also have the ability to make revisions and updates at a later date with no additional cost.
5. We manage the royalties and pay you on a bi-monthly schedule plan. By partnering with Volumes you will reap the well-deserved rewards. When signing up with most publishing firms you will not only lose total control but you will receive a royalty payment between 6% – 8% per book. By self-publishing you can increase this royalty to over 60% of the retail price.
6. Volumes' consulting team will also sell the books to you at our print cost. When you need to sell your book in seminars, book affairs and other related

shows we will not offer a discount but sell you the books at cost. We encourage this as you take the extra time and effort in selling your book. We want you to be well-rewarded.

Writing and producing a book takes a lot of hard work. Let your hard work speak Volumes. Choose one of our two publishing packages to best suits *your* needs.

Chapter Eighty-Nine:
Wahmpreneur Books
Independent publisher of microbusiness books

Looking for the right publisher to package your latest
business book?
Wahmpreneur Books offers high-quality book packaging
and publishing services, individualized attention, and
affordable prices.

Our Self-Publishing Services:

Our basic package for publishing with Wahmpreneur
Books includes these services:

- ISBN assignment and barcode
- Book composition services
- Book cover formatting for print
- Title set up
- Listing in Bowker Books in Print
- Copyright registration
- Online and offline distribution through our
  wholesale distribution partners
- Retail sales page at the Wahmpreneur Books online
  bookstore
- Quarterly royalty payments

Total package price: $400

We also offer these optional services:

- Custom book cover design
- CIP (catalog in publication) data block

For more information please visit
www.wahmpreneurbooks.com.

Chapter Ninety: WasteLand Press

An Author's Service Company

"Use our publishing plans to make your dreams come true!

Publish with the least expensive full-service press on the Internet without sacrificing quality! Publish your book in 7-14 business days, instead of 6-12 months like our competitors, for under $250 with no setup fees! You'll receive anywhere from 5-500 books, depending on the self-publishing plan you choose. Our plans offer various combinations of printing, editorial and marketing services, including a Booksellers Returns Program."

The prices below are for books up to 125 pages. For books with additional pages, please visit the website for the price for your book. www.wastelandpress.net

Publishing Packages:

Basic $245.00

This plan is our most affordable plan aimed for the casual writer that wants to see his or her work in print. The Basic Plan includes all of the following: 5 paperback books, 20-125 page book (5x8, 5.5x8.5 or 6x9 format) set-up, online distribution via amazon.com and other online retailers via Ingram Distribution, unlimited re-prints of your book, a 15% royalty on any money received by Wasteland Press for the sale of your book, unlimited black and white pictures throughout your book, and free shipping for your 5 paperback books.

Silver $295.00

This plan is for the casual writer that wants to see his or her work in print and provide copies to friends and family. The Silver Plan includes all of the following: 2 hardback books, 20-125 page book (5.5x8.5 or 6x9 format) set-up, online distribution via amazon.com and other online retailers via Ingram Distribution, unlimited re-prints of your book, a 15% royalty on any money received by Wasteland Press for the sale of your book, unlimited black and white pictures throughout your book, and free shipping for your free hardback books.

Gold $650.00

This plan is our most popular service and for those who do not want to make a heavy investment into self publishing. The Gold Plan includes all of the following with your fee: 75 paperback books, 20-125 page book (5x8, 5.5x8.5 or 6x9 format) set-up, ISBN number including barcode, full-service marketing (including 2 books sent for review with various publications), worldwide distribution including Bookseller Returns Program in the United States, United Kingdom, and the European Union through Ingram Distribution (which will make your book available to over 5000 retail outlets, including online retailers like amazon.com), unlimited re-prints of your book, a 25% royalty on any money received by Wasteland Press for the sale of your book, unlimited black and white pictures throughout your book, and FREE shipping for your 75 paperback books.

Platinum $995.00

This plan is aimed at the serious, career minded writer who wants to establish his or her name in the book industry. The Platinum Plan includes all of the following with your fee: 150 paperback books, 20-125 page book (5x8, 5.5x8.5 or 6x9 format) set-up, ISBN number including barcode, full-service marketing (including 5 books sent for review with various publications), worldwide distribution including Bookseller Returns Program in the United States, United Kingdom, and the European Union through Ingram Distribution (which will make your book available to over 5000 retail outlets, including online retailers like amazon.com), unlimited re-prints of your book, a 30% royalty on any money received by Wasteland Press for the sale of your book, unlimited black and white pictures throughout your book, and FREE shipping for your 150 paperback books.

Ultimate $1995.00

This plan is aimed at the cost efficient minded writer, who can sell many of their own copies in the marketplace. It is also aimed at the serious, career minded writer who wants to establish their name in the book industry. The Ultimate Plan includes all of the following with your fee: 500 paperback books, 20-125 page book (5x8, 5.5x8.5 or 6x9 format) set-up, ISBN number including barcode, full-service marketing (including 25 books sent for review with various publications), worldwide distribution including Bookseller Returns Program in the United States, United Kingdom, and the European Union through Ingram Distribution (which will make your book available to over 5000 retail outlets, including online retailers like amazon.com), unlimited re-prints, a 30% royalty on any money received by Wasteland Press for the sale of your book, unlimited black and white pictures throughout your book, and FREE shipping.

"Our publishing plans include all of the following at no extra charge: cover design (we design your cover from scratch and DO NOT use cover templates), formatting service (we format your book by adding headers, pagination, and even footnotes/endnotes), one-contact Customer Service (no dealing with several individuals), and we even include editing services for most of our plans! We challenge you to find a better deal and if you do, we will match or exceed our competitor's offer! We want you to feel confident that you made the right choice in publishing with Wasteland Press by giving you honest answers to all your questions. We take pride in being an ethical business who fully discloses the entire publishing process."

Chapter Ninety-One: We Publish

An Author's Service Company

www.we-publish.com

Publishing comparison chart from their website based on a book up to 200 pages, black and white, soft cover:

Publisher	Publishing Cost *	Retail Price*	Royalty % Paid to Author	Author Earnings Per Copy Sold	Revenue Earned by Publisher Per Copy Sold	Author Earnings Per 100 Copies Sold	Number of copies to sell before you make a profit = Publishing Cost/Earnings Per Copy Sold
We-Publish	$998.00	$14.95	60%	$8.97	$5.98	$897.00	Only 111 copies!
iUniverse	$2,099.00	$14.95	10%	$1.50	$13.45	$150.00	1400 copies
Lulu	$1,429.00	$14.75	10%	$1.48	$13.27	$148.00	966 copies
Trafford (1)	$1,899.00	$17.33	25% (through Trafford online store)	$2.85	$14.48	$284.85	667 copies
Xlibris (2)	$1,699.00	$19.99	25% (through Xlibris online store)	$5.00	$14.99	$500.00	340 copies

"Our 60% royalty means - 60% of the selling price of your book. For example a 200 page book sells for $14.95, _so the author's royalty is $14.95 X 60%= $8.97 each..._"

Royalties Paid by We-Publish.com
for Publication of Kindle Version

Royalties Paid by We-Publish.com
for Publication of Kindle Version

25% Royalty Option		
Size of Kindle File	Min List Price	Max List Price
- = 3 MB	$0.99	$200.00
- > 3 MB & = 10 MB	$1.99	$200.00
- >10 MB	$2.99	$200.00
50% Royalty Option	$2.99	$9.99
No Limit on File Size		

You will receive 5 FREE copies of your printed book. (A $90.00 to $135.00 Value including FREE Shipping (ground) to a US address)

A Professional Full Color Custom Cover designed to SELL your book! ($125.00 to $200.00 Value)

The custom cover does not include any original artwork. A custom cover may include artwork provided by the author, if the artwork is supplied in a 300 dpi resolution graphic file. The size of the artwork must be proportionate to the cover size. If the author does not provide artwork, the graphic designer will use stock graphic images to create an appropriate cover design.

ISBN number assigned to your printed book
(Your book listed in Books in Print, every bookstore's source for published books)

An electronic proof of your formatted book for review and correction.

Up to 10 graphics images (300 dpi grayscale -black & white) may be included in your book FREE of charge. (A $50.00 Value)

A corrections package of up to 50 content changes made in one correction session (A $150.00 Value)

> If more than one session of changes is requested by the author, the fee for each session of changes including reopening the file, making the changes and re-formatting the book will be $50.00 plus $1.50 per change.

A FREE printed proof of your book after corrections. (This is an un-bound printed proof copy of your book including the full color cover shipped FREE of charge (ground) to a US address)

Shipping charges will be billed at cost for books shipped to international addresses

We-Publish.com will place an unspecified number of copies of your book in inventory (at no additional cost to you) to be available for immediate shipping to your readers.

An e-Commerce enabled web page (setup to accept Credit Card payments) designed to sell your book on the Internet.

We-Publish offers marketing and distribution packages as well as pre publication services. Check their website for more information.

Chapter Ninety-Two: WheatMark

Publishing a book can be a daunting process that takes time and energy away from doing what you love-- writing! There are many pitfalls to avoid that can kill your book's chances of succeeding in an already-crowded marketplace.

Wheatmark can help you write, edit, design, publish, and distribute an exceptional book or eBook. We publish fiction and nonfiction titles in paperback, hardcover, and the six most popular eBook formats: Amazon Kindle, Barnes & Noble Nook, Apple iPad, Sony Reader, Google eBook, and Kobo eReader.

We help our clients sell their titles on Amazon.com, BN.com, Apple's iBookstore, and all the other major online retailers. We also support them in their "back-of-the-room" sales and, where applicable, their sales to physical bookstores.

Wheatmark does not publish poetry or full-color illustrated children's books, except in very rare cases.

(WheatMark will not divulge their prices until you have downloaded and read their "The Author's Guide to Choosing a Publishing Service". At the end of the guide they suggest three packages but still no prices. You must schedule a consultation to discuss prices and ask questions about their services.

However, through research I found someone who stated they were charged $799.00 for publishing and copyediting was two cents per word with a $100.00 minimum. They pay a 20% royalty, if purchases are from their website it increases to 40%. This author advised they had excellent customer service.

If you're looking for a team of publishing professionals to take the pain out of the publishing for you, contact them to download the guide and investigate further at www.wheatmark.com.)

Chapter Ninety-Three: Whitehall Printing

An offset printer (This is the largest printer used by most subsidy printers nationwide, although Lightning Source is used by most subsidy publishers because it is POD.)

Quality book printing at a superb value. The fastest turnaround in the industry. Over 50 years of printing experience. Plus, the reliable service of dedicated professionals. These are our hallmarks.

As you browse our website, we hope you will learn about our excellent products and services, find easy-to-understand answers to your book printing questions, and feel completely comfortable to contact us. Our capable printing team is eager to assist you with all your book manufacturing questions and needs.

The word "partnership" is defined as "a relationship between individuals marked by mutual cooperation and responsibility." Think of us as your printing partner.

Pricing:

(By quote only, you must fill out the questionnaire indicating binding, size, paper, cover, and pages. They have a minimum order of 250 books. I used our sample book, a 6 x 9 perfect bound, 100 page book. The price for 250 books is $4.99 per book plus $113.00 estimated shipping.

If you order 5000 books the price drops to .74 cents a book **plus shipping**. Five thousand books will be rather expensive shipping (at the rate for 250 books it will cost over $2000 for shipping unless a less expensive shipping method is used) and where the heck are you going to store 5000 books? This quantity requires a warehouse for storage.)

Chapter Ninety-Four:
Wine Press Publishing
A Christian Subsidy Publishing Company

A Pleasant Word Affiliate, Partners in custom publishing since 1991

"WinePress provides all the services and representation you need to publish books people will read and enjoy."

They offer a free guide to help you subsidy publish, "Publishing Essentials." They provide editing services at three levels but do not advise their prices. You must contact them if you are interested in editing services. They also provide cover design, interior layout, illustrations, eBooks, audio books, and specialty books. Wine Press offers distribution services of fulfillment, warehousing, and accounting as well as marketing assistance from planning a strategy, publicity, online marketing, video production, and promotional materials. For any of their prices you must contact them from their website. (Remember the warning flags in Chapter Six)

"We are members of the Christian Booksellers Association (CBA) and the Evangelical Christian Publishers Association (ECPA), and we've enjoyed long-established relationships with distributors, bookstores, literary agents, editors, and publishers in the Christian market—making us the perfect publisher for both new and seasoned authors."

For more information contact them at their website www.winepresspublishing.com.

Chapter Ninety Five: **WingSpan Press**

Everything you need to publish your book in one place for one price.

- Setup and Design
- ISBN, Bar Code, Copyright, Library of Congress Number
- Worldwide Print and Distibution
- Listing on Amazon, Barnes & Noble and hundreds of online retailers
- Available to order in more than 25,000 bookstores worldwide

All for one low price. No hidden charges, no pricey add-ons.

Fast, Easy and Affordable

We'll turn your manuscript into a beautiful, professional book in just 6-8 weeks.

Your book will be listed on all the major booksellers - Amazon.com, Barnes & Noble, Books-a-Million and more than 150 others - and distributed through Ingram Book Group, the world's largest book wholesaler. Your book can be ordered virtually anywhere in the world, and will appear on internet retailers worldwide.

Now, your book can also be formatted and distributed as an eBook, including **Amazon Kindle**. Your book will be available through dozens of electronic retailers in formats readable by virtually all eBook readers - **Kindle, Nook,**

Apple iPad, Sony Reader, Adobe Digital Editions and more.

Take advantage of the eBook revolution. Get published in print *and* eBook today.

What sets WingSpan Press apart from the competition?

- Low price
- Easy to understand
- Non-exclusive contract
- You retain all Rights
- No hidden costs
- Select only the options you need
- Kindle/eBook availability
- World class customer service

What about Royalties?

You earn 20% of the retail cover price on every book you sell, without having to price your book out of the market. No percentage of the 'net', no arcane formulas

Other Services

(Okay so there are additional prices for other services, but everything seems to be out in the open and above board. Who could ask for anything more?)

Enhance your book's image and marketability with the following options.

Cataloging in Publication Data – $150

Cataloging data is a specialized language used by libraries to correctly and consistently catalog and shelve new books. (Look at the lower half of the copyright page of almost any book on your bookshelf and you'll find CIP data). Created by a professional librarian schooled in cataloging science, this adds to your book's professional look and feel.

Note that you can't make this block up yourself. The Library of Congress has created specific language and formatting requirements for this data.

Copyright Registration – $100

Note: Your book will be legally copyrighted the moment it's published, without purchasing this service. As part of the $499 setup fee, your copyright is secured under international law with the inclusion of your name and the © symbol on the copyright page.

But many authors go a step further and register their copyright with the Library of Congress. LOC registration has been viewed by the courts as *prima facie* evidence of ownership of intellectual property in the past. You might think of it as a form of insurance in case you ever have to defend your ownership of the material in court.

Image Acquisition – $50

Every author receives a design unique to his or her book as part of the $499 setup fee. If you have an image or photo that you want to use for your cover, we'll incorporate it into the design at no additional charge.
If you don't have a cover image in hand, we can help you acquire one, either by directing you to stock photo sites where there are millions of images available, or we'll find 2 images that will make a good cover for your book and let you choose between them. Once you've made your selection, we'll acquire the image for you.

We can also work with outside designers if you choose to have your cover designed elsewhere.

Manuscripts over 100,000 words——$100

Our standard $499 setup fee applies to a text manuscript of 100,000 words or less. This charge is for manuscripts between 100,000 and 200,000 words in length. If your manuscript is longer than 200,000 words, please talk to your customer service representative.

B&W interior images – $10 each;   Tables and Charts – $20 each

We'll place and size them to fit the page and add your caption.

Index Formatting – $75

We'll create and format the index of your book based on the index tags you flagged in your Microsoft Word document. If you need an index and are not familiar with this function in Word, talk to your WingSpan Press service representative about your options.

Footnotes – Cost: $100 + $.50/footnote

We'll format and position your book's footnote references. Note that all footnotes must be flagged using Word's footnote function.

Endnotes – Cost: $50

End notes appear all together at the end of the book. These are normally flagged using Word's endnote feature, but because they appear all together at the end of the book, they may just be typed text and do not require as much formatting as footnotes.

Editorial Assistance

Line Editing – $.02 per word.

It's almost impossible to edit your own work successfully. And nothing says 'amateur' like misspellings, bad grammar and poor word choice - no matter how well you may know your topic.

If done right, editing is a time-consuming process. Many companies charge attractively low editing prices, then essentially spellcheck your document using Microsoft Word. But a proper line edit does more than find obvious spelling errors. 'There', 'they're' and 'their' are all spelled correctly, so only a careful reading of your manuscript will note that one is appropriate in a sentence and the others are not. A good line edit will check for spelling, grammar, word usage, punctuation, capitalization, even sentence fragments.

An experienced grammarian will go over your manuscript twice looking for every misplaced comma to help make your book the best it can be. Every book has errors, but minimizing them is key to leaving the reader with a good impression of your writing skills.

Development Edit – $.04 per word

The developmental provides and in-depth editorial review of your work with focus on organization and writing style.

- Fiction: We'll look at voice, characterization, scene development and language. A historical romance 'reads' differently than a mystery or a modern social novel. Does your writing voice fit the genre of your book? Are the characters believable - even in the most far-reaching fantasy novel, people are people, and sometimes even aliens are people too. Do they act the way people act? Does your book adequately present a sense of place; is it descriptive?

- Non-fiction: Does your work hold together as a piece, or is it all over the road? Does your table of contents promise an easy-to-follow journey of learning and discovery, and does the text deliver? Is your writing too casual? Too formal? Does it have the authority that a reader can trust? We'll help you sound like the subject matter expert you are.

For both fiction and non-fiction, we'll review grammar, word choice, sentence construction and logical organization. We'll help you shed the clichés and generally improve your approach to your material.
After editing, you'll receive a markup copy of your manuscript with corrections and improvement areas noted, plus, a thirty-minute conversation with our senior editor to discuss ways to improve the overall quality and approach to your book.

Good writing is marketable. Bad writing is not. We'll help you improve the writing to catch and keep a reader's attention.

Kindle and other Electronic Editions

Kindle Formatting and Publication – $150

Once the print version of your book is complete, we'll create eBook and Kindle versions of it. The Kindle edition will be sold exclusively through Amazon. The eBook version is distributed through Ingram Book Group, the same company that distributes the print edition. That will make the eBook available through dozens of electronic retailers in a format readable by virtually all e-book readers - Nook, Apple iPad, Sony Reader, Adobe Digital Editions and more.

Electronic sales are growing rapidly. Join the eBook revolution.

Amazon search inside – $75

We'll create and upload an Amazon version of your book for their Search Inside program. When browsers view your book listing, they'll be able to look at a few random pages of the interior to get a sense of what the book is about and how it's written before they buy.

Google Book Search submission – $50

When people search for books on Google your book will be available for review, with links to major retailers for purchase. Buyers will be able to look at sample pages to get an idea what your book is about. Inclusion on Google also increases your internet exposure.

Making Changes to Your Book

There are two points at which you may want to make changes to your book: Before it's published, and after. It's best to review carefully and make changes *before* your book goes to print. Doing so after your book has been published is time-consuming and expensive.

Changes before Publication – $50 per round of 25 changes

When you first sign up, we'll ask you to verify that you're submitting the final manuscript that you want to see in print before we begin layout. But sometimes, when you see the book in layout form, you find typos, or even things you wish you'd said differently the first time around. Using our online change request form, you'll be able submit changes before approving your book for print. After that, changes are made, we'll provide you another pdf proof for review.

Printed Proof for Review – $50

Once layout and design of your book is complete, you'll receive a pdf version of it for review. Some people find it easier to review if they can see it as a printed book rather than viewing it on-screen or even printing it themselves. With this option, we'll print and send you a bound draft softcover copy of your book. The cost for setup and the first copy is $50. Additional copies of the same draft are $10 plus shipping.

Changes after Publication

Once your book has gone to print or has been published as an eBook, making changes requires that it be taken out of print and reassigned to a designer. Changes are made then the manuscript or cover is sent back to you for review and approval. Upon approval, the book goes through quality control again and is uploaded and its internet catalog listing refreshed so that the new version appears to online retailers. This process is expensive and time consuming, and is necessary for each published edition of your book. If you have both hardcover and softcover in print as well as an eBook, it has to be done for all 3 versions. The distributor charges us for this, and those costs are passed on to you. (for this service, Kindle and eBook are considered a single edition.)

Changes to a published book cost **$100 plus $50** per edition. For example:

Softcover only: $150
Softcover and hardcover: $200
Softcover and Kindle/eBook: $200
Softcover, hardcover, and Kindle/eBook $250

If you require a new printed first copy of the revised book, or if your changes require more than 2 hour additional edit/design time, additional charges will apply.

Marketing Services

Make a splash in the marketplace.

The key to getting sales is making your book, and yourself, known.

To get people interested in your book, you have to get them interested in you and your story. Below you'll find tools to help you do just that - get reviews, attract media, give people something to remember you by.

A couple of things are missing from this page that you'll see on many other sites. To find out why there are some things we refuse to offer, read our article on Targeted emails

Ingram Advance Magazine – $75

Advance, the flagship trade publication of the Ingram Book

Group, the nation's largest book distributor, is sent monthly to thousands of booksellers and libraries all over the world. We'll include a B&W image of your cover, retail pricing info, and a short description of your book. Titles may only be included in Advance when they are first released, so this service must be ordered prior to publication. It is not available after your book has gone to press.

Press Release – $250

A sharply crafted press release, properly placed, spreads the word, leaves a professional impression, and motivates buyers and reviewers to take a look at your book. Your release will be placed on-line through wide-distribution wire services that reach thousands of people. Unlike email spam campaigns, press wire services are subscribed to by millions of individuals and businesses looking for topics, books and interviews to be used in print, radio, television and internet media. There is no lower-cost way to get the word out to those who will actually read and notice your book.

Advance Reader Copies – $50 setup plus the cost of printing and shipping.

Sometimes known as 'advance review copies' ARCs are just that - copies of your book printed and distributed prior to publication to reviewers and other insiders to give them the opportunity to review and comment on your book before it's finalized.

Reviews and recommendations on the back cover of your book are strong incentives to buy. Plus, ARCs lend a more professional air to your review copies than just printing the manuscript at home and binding it at Kinko's. And since they are produced without ISBN or bar code info, they aren't likely to wind up for sale at used bookstores without your consent.

Review Submission Service – $300

Combining the strengths of advance reader copies with a press release, this package is the most economical way to get your book in front of people who will notice it, review it, and write about it or call you for an interview. These submissions have the added professional advantage that they arrive on WingSpan Press letterhead, direct from the publisher, individually addressed and packaged.

We'll create a press release and print 6 copies of your book. We'll send 2 copies to Midwest Book Review, the nation's premier reviewer of self-published books, plus copies to 4 other media outlets of your choice. Your best bets are outlets close to you, or ones specializing in your book's niche. Regional and local TV, radio, magazine and newspaper editors are always on the lookout for new local-interest material, and a professional package from the publisher, including your contact information, directed at them individually, is the best way to get reviews, articles and interviews that *sell books*.

In addition, we'll submit your press release to internet wire services for added exposure.

The added bonuses to this service are

- Your press release can be used elsewhere as you need it.
- Your book is already set up for Advance Reader Copies. You can buy as many as you want.

Printed Hardcover Dustjackets – $75 for a set of 25.

If you're publishing a hardcover version of your book, extra dustjackets are available. A dustjacket, without the book, is often sent along with a sell sheet about your book to stores and other outlets. Bookbuyers are used to it - many distributor's salesmen carry dustjackets only - and it saves you the cost of printing and mailing copies of your hardcover book if you're contacting a lot of buyers.

Bookmarks, postcards and business cards.

500 Business Cards	$150
500 Postcards	$200
500 Bookmarks	$250

Good quality stock branded with your book's cover, description and technical information will make a good impression on media and retail contacts, and will help brand *you* as 'Author of' your book.

Chapter Ninety-Six:
Word Association Publishers
(Another subsidy publisher with all fees and features on the front page. Makes comparisons so much easier.)

Your one-stop shop for self publishing

- Editing
- Ghostwriting
- Cover and Interior Design
- Printing, Binding and POD
- ISBN, Library of Congress, Bar Codes

- Marketing and Promotion
- Publicity
- Distribution
- Royalties and fulfillment
- E-books

Word Association offers two simple ways to self-publish your book. We don't use smoke and mirrors and we make no effort to make you think this is rocket science. The key to your choosing has to do with how many books you feel you can initially sell. Period. Here's how to gauge: If you already have a public following, perhaps you write a column for your local newspaper, or you are a public speaker, a popular chef at a well-known restaurant, a teacher, host a radio talk program, or are a religious or community leader, you will likely be able to sell more books on your own because of what you do and who you are.

Those authors who are recognized experts in their fields or those who have identified a target group for their books can expect higher sales faster. Those books will also likely be able to attract more media attention, which of course sends book buyers to the book stores to purchase even more of your books.

If you fall into this first category, your best choice is our Program A. This plan, which requires a larger initial investment for book development and production, will enable you to purchase more books at a lower wholesale cost. That means, of course, you will enjoy a greater return or profit as you sell your books. Since the initial investment you make is a one-time fee, re-prints of your book and subsequent sales will bring you an even better return.

Authors who succeed best with this plan are primarily writers of non-fiction. This not to say that an experienced or known novelist, poet, or children's book author cannot do well with our Program A. It depends upon how much effort, time, and money you can put into promoting and publicizing your book.

For those of you taking that first leap into the world of publishing without a niche audience or sales track record, we have designed Program B. This program is something of a safety net because it enables you to make the smallest investment in your book's development and production and allows you to purchase a minimal number of books–enough to get you started. You will pay a higher cost per book but you aren't risking as much money. As your book gains momentum and sales improve, you can and will eventually be able to purchase larger quantities of your book at a lower cost per book, therefore bringing your profit margin to that of Program A. The choice, as always, is yours to make at any time.

PROGRAM "A"
Publishing set up: $1200.00*

Includes:

- Cover design
- Page formatting/interior design
- ISBN and Library of Congress Number
- Listing in Books in Print
- ISBN and bar codes
- Bookstore & Internet sales/distribution
- Listing on Amazon and Word Association websites
- Promotional post cards or business cards

Book specifications:

- Size: 5 1/2 x 8 1/2
- Binding: softcover "perfect" binding
- Interior: 24 lb. white offset, black ink, text only (for photos, illustrations, graphics, see below)
- Cover: 80 lb. gloss, full color
- Suggested List Price: (determined by publisher and author)

Printing fee is determined by page count
Example - 200 Pages:

100 books: $9.60
250 books: $8.00
500 books: $7.20
1000 books: $5.60
2000 books: $4.00

For books with more or less than 200 pages, the printing charge is adjusted accordingly. We will provide you with an exact quote based on the page or word count in your manuscript.

Options:

- Marketing: $1200.00 package (see below)
- Copy editing: $0.02 per word
- Advanced editing: price quote upon manuscript review
- Photo scans: $6.00 per scan
- Color interior pages: price quote upon manuscript review
- Cover design requiring original art design: $500.00
- Book publicist: price quote upon manuscript review (see below)
- Amazon Kindle edition: $150.00
- e-pub edition for i-pad: $150.00

Manuscript submission:

*The $1200.00 base rate is guaranteed only after the manuscript has been reviewed by our staff. Manuscripts containing charts, graphs, illustrations, lists and other special features that present formatting complexities may result in increased charges. In such cases, we will notify authors of price estimates. We will return the deposit payment of authors unwilling to incur additional fees.

Authors are encouraged to submit manuscripts in Microsoft Word. We can also accept Apple Works, Word Perfect, QuarkXpress, In-Design, and PageMaker. Authors may send files as email attachment, or on CD or floppy.

Payment schedule:
50% deposit due upon signing of publishing agreement; Balance upon publication/delivery. Shipping charges for books delivered to the author are additional.

Note: *Pennsylvania residents will be charged 7% sales tax, unless author has a valid sales tax exemption certificate.*

Production schedule

Books are generally completed within 8 – 12 weeks of signing of agreement. Production schedules are approximate: they depend upon work load, and timeliness of returned proofs. The editing service requires extra time, determined by length of book level of editing. Clients are advised not to schedule any publication events until actual delivery of printed books.

Rights: Author retains all rights, including all subsidiary rights. Author holds the copyright.

Marketing & Promotion (option) $1200.00

Your Word Association Marketing Package is designed to help you light a fire, build a bridge, and start the buzz about your book. The goal is to sell your book by letting readers know what it has to offer them, motivating them to buy it, and making that purchase simple and easy. Word Association has accounts with all of the major book industry channels, including Amazon, Borders, Barnes&Noble, and also with the nation's largest book wholesalers, Ingram Book Co. and Baker & Taylor. This means that your book will be listed in the database of these large companies, making it easier for individuals and bookstores to find and order your book.

Your book will be posted and sold on www.amazon.com, www.barnesandnoble.com, www.borders.com, www.wordassociation.com, and other internet websites.

We also complete and submit the Advanced Book Information (ABI) form, ensuring that your book will be listed in Books in Print. It's the most important directory in the book industry.

Basic marketing package materials include:

- (5) promotional copies of your book
- (25) News Releases
- A sample cover letter
- (100) 2-sided Business Cards
- (100) bookmarks
- (50) 2-sided post cards
- (5) 11 x 17 full color posters
- (5) 8 ½ x 11 full display card
- (25) promotional book covers with author bio and photo

Also available upon request are price quotes for:

- Pre-publication copies of your book
- Oversized posters and banners
- Additional quantities of any of the above materials
- Personalized catalogue envelopes

PUBLICITY

For authors who want to take their marketing activity to the next level, we partner with Sherry Frazier at Frazier Public Relations for author publicity programs. Sherry creates custom publicity programs and marketing plans designed to bring nationwide attention to the author and book. She also works with the author to seek awards, greater distribution of the book, book reviews, endorsements, speaking engagements, press/book tours and national and local media campaigns. Website, press kits and any copy needed to help "sell" the book are created as part of an overall author program. Please contact us for more information about publicity for your book. We will be happy to set up a telephone meeting between you and Sherry to discuss your goals. You can read more about Frazier Public Relations at www.FrazierPublicRelations.com.

Confab Marketing & Design is a Pittsburgh, PA based marketing and design agency that specializes in brand development, social media marketing and public relations with emphasis on small to medium sized businesses and individual brands. Whether you're a seasoned writer or being published for the first time, we'll develop an effective communications and marketing strategy that is consistent with your goals and objectives. We offer a complete social media marketing plan for writers that includes a custom "Author's Official Website," Facebook, twitter and Youtube optimization and a Hollywood style movie trailer that brings your book to life! When you partner with the team at Confab Marketing & Design, you can be sure we will make your brand Unique...Entertaining...Empowering...Consistent!

Order Fulfillment

When we fill orders for your book, Word Association charges a flat fee of 35% of the net sale for all of the services that fall under the general category of order fulfillment. These services include: 1.) order taking: phone, fax or email. 2.) packing, shipping. 3.) invoicing and credit card processing. For orders to wholesalers, this fee increases to 45%.

PROGRAM "B"
Publishing set up: $1200.00*

Includes:

- Cover design

- Page formatting/interior design
- ISBN and Library of Congress Number
- Listing in Books in Print
- Barcodes (for price and ISBN)
- Bookstore & Internet sales/distribution
- Listing on Amazon and Word Association websites
- Amazon kindle edition available for $150.00 additional
- Promotional post cards or business cards

Book specifications:

- Size: 5 1/2 x 8 1/2
- Binding: softcover "perfect" binding
- Interior: 24 lb. white offset, black ink, text only (for photos, illustrations, graphics, see below)
- Cover: 80 lb. gloss, full color
- Suggested List Price: (established by publisher)

AUTHOR ROYALTIES: 30 PERCENT

In Program B, Word Association pays authors a royalty of 30% of the purchase price of the book. For example, a book with a list price $20.00 will earn the author $6.00, if it is sold at the full list price. If the book is purchased by a re-seller (either a bookstore or other re-seller) the author royalty is 30% of the invoice. Example: if the re-seller takes a 50% discount on a book with a list price of $20.00, the author's royalty is 30% of $10.00, or $3.00.

If a re-seller requires more than a 50% discount, the royalty we pay authors on these sales is reduced to 20%.

Author royalties do not begin until a book has achieved $25.00 in total sales. At that point, authors receive a royalty report and a check once every quarter for the first year. After the first year the frequency of royalty reports depends upon how active book sales are. At the very least, we issue royalty reports once a year.

Options:

- Marketing: $1200 package (see below)
- Copy editing: .02 per word
- Advanced editing: price quote upon manuscript review
- Photo scans: $6.00 per scan
- Color interior pages: price quote upon manuscript review
- Cover design requiring original art design: $500.00

Manuscript submission:

*The $1200.00 base rate is guaranteed only after the manuscript has been reviewed by our staff. Manuscripts containing charts, graphs, illustrations, lists and other special features that present formatting complexities may result in increased charges. In such cases, we will notify authors of price estimates. We will return the deposit payment of authors unwilling to incur additional fees.

Authors are encouraged to submit manuscripts in Microsoft Word. We can also accept Apple Works, Word Perfect, QuarkXpress, In-Design, and PageMaker. Authors may send files as email attachment, or on CD or floppy.

Editing

Editing is one of the most important services we offer here at Word Association. That's why it is at the top of the list. The criticism that is most frequently leveled at self-published books is that they are not subject to the same rigorous editing as books that are published by "traditional" publishers. There is a lot of truth to this criticism. When we receive a manuscript at Word Association, we let you know up front if we think the editing is sub-par. If it is, you have the choice of either finding your own editor, or using one of our editors. Or you could go to a vanity press that doesn't give a whit about quality editing.

Do you have a story, an essay, a novel, or a poem about which you would like to have a professional critical opinion? Word Association offers writers several levels of service: we can critique an entire manuscript or as few as two pages of a manuscript. The critique includes grammar, usage, punctuation, style, organization, and development as well as overall effectiveness and impact. Our fee for creative/critical editing is $9.00 per manuscript page (8 1/2 x 11, double-spaced), with a minimum of 25 pages. Note: We estimate that the average manuscript will require about one hour to edit four pages. If after reviewing your manuscript we determine that more or less time will be required than is customary, we will notify you of a fee increase or reduction. Light copy editing will be billed at a rate of .02 per word, while editing that requires actual rewriting and follow-up review will be billed on an hourly basis of $36.00 per hour. If you have any questions about our editing service, simply e-mail Dr. Tom or call him at 1-800-827-7903.

(Word Association appears to have covered everything. Their information speaks for itself.)

Chapter Ninety-Seven: Word Pro Press
Offset Printing Service

WORDPRO Press specializes in short- to medium-run book, chapbook, catalog, and cookbook printing. Our customers can print from 100 to 5,000 copies of a publication in color and/or black/white using our all-digital state-of-the-art facilities. We deliver on-demand turnaround, professional quality, and quick response, at a very low cost. All of our standard books are printed on 60# smooth white opaque paper and include a laminated spot color cover (using one or more colors).

WORDPRO Press is a wholly owned subsidiary of THE WORDPRO, a large service bureau and digital printer located in Ithaca, NY. Founded in 1978, The WORDPRO has printed books, manuals, catalogs, and much more for customers throughout the world.

The Press serves the self-publishing segment of the book market, and also prints books and manuals for companies, organizations and other publishers

Base Price for our sample book: 6 x 9 Black & White 100 pages, soft cover color perfect bound
*Note Word Pro does not offer 6 x 9. Their closest size is 5 1/2 x 8 1/2. They also only provide spot color covers as standard. Full color is additional.

Book printing cost is $3.30 per book for 100 books (minimum order.)

(We found no editing services, cover design services, or marketing service on the website. They did however claim, "The WORDPRO Press is associated with Amazon.com and this gives authors who self-publish through us an advantage. You can have your book listed for sale on the Amazon.com web site. To do so, you must have an ISBN Number and set a retail price for the book."

I thought anyone could list their book on Amazon, you just pay a small annual fee. I presume the fee is waived due to their association with Amazon, otherwise why mention it.)

Chapter Ninety-Eight: Word Clay
An Author's Solutions Company

"We're focused on publishing books for authors. As you familiarize yourself with the Wordclay DIY self-publishing wizard, you'll come to appreciate the attention to detail that Wordclay affords. And, best of all, you can self-publish as many books as you like...for free, compliments of Wordclay.

In addition to our FREE DIY self-publishing wizard, we also offer a variety of services to help you create, distribute and promote a marketable book. We realize you could do it all on your own, but we're here to offer assistance when you just don't have the time or patience to publish your book alone.

Editing Services:

Manuscript Evaluation............	$275.00
Content Editing......................	$0.06 per word
Copy editing..........................	$0.03 per word
Cover Design..........................	$499.00
Custom Cover design..............	$999.00
Cover template.......................	$275.00
Bring your own Cover................	$49.00
Interior Formatting....................	$325.00
WordClay ISBN..........................	$99.00
BYO ISBN................................	$135.00

(No marketing packages found nor did they direct users to other sister affiliates for more extensive marketing options.)

Chapter Ninety-Nine: Xlibris

1663 Liberty Drive
Suite 200
Bloomington, IN 47403

888-795-4274   www2.xlibris.com/

An Author's Solutions Affiliate

Advantage Package - $299

A streamlined service that enables you to publish a quality
paperback book at an affordable price. Advantage is an
especially good choice for those authors who want to publish
a book for their friends and family or who simply want the
satisfaction of having a printed version of their work.

Design and image features:

- Choice of three cover templates
- Choice of two interior templates
- Allowance of cover art and author photo (supplied
  by author)

Production features:

- Availability of your book in paperback format
- One paperback author review copy
- Assignment of ISBN

Post-publication features:

- Book and author web pages in the Xlibris online
  bookstore – you control the content
- Quarterly royalty payments

Basic Package - $499

This economical service provides multiple options and includes all the elements required to turn your manuscript into a quality paperback book. Your book will be listed in the industry's leading distribution network and available to order in more than 25,000 retail outlets worldwide including Amazon.com, BarnesandNoble.com and the Xlibris online bookstore.

Design and image features:

- Choice of eight cover templates
- Choice of five interior templates
- Allowance of cover art and author photo (supplied by author)

Production features:

- Availability of your book in paperback format
- One paperback author review copy
- Assignment of ISBN
- Registration with Books In Print database
- Ability to track book production progress through our website
- Author Service Representative who provides support throughout the publication process

Post-publication features:

- Five paperback copies
- A complimentary paperback book of your choice from the Xlibris Bookstore
- Worldwide distribution

- Registrations with online booksellers through national distributor
- Online book sales and royalty accounting
- Book and author web pages in the Xlibris online bookstore – you control the content
- Quarterly royalty payments

Marketing features:

- 50 bookmarks
- 50 business cards

Professional Package - $899

The Professional Service combines our most popular publishing features into a more robust package. It includes all the services of the Basic package plus more books, more marketing materials, more design options and hardback availability. Authors using the Professional service may customize elements of the interior templates to create an interior that is truly unique.

Design and image features:

- Choice of eighteen cover templates
- Choice of nine interior templates
- Allowance of cover art (up to 3 images) and author photo (supplied by author)
- 25 allotted interior graphics and tables

Production features:

- Availability of your book in paperback format
- Availability of your book in hardback format
- One paperback and one hardback author review copy
- Assignment of ISBN
- Registration with Books In Print database
- Ability to track book production progress through our website
- Author Service Representative who provides support throughout the publication process

Post-publication features:

- Ten paperback copies
- A complimentary paperback book of your choice from the Xlibris Bookstore
- Worldwide distribution
- Registrations with online booksellers through national distributor
- Online book sales and royalty accounting
- Book and author web pages in the Xlibris online bookstore – you control the content
- Quarterly royalty payments

Marketing features:

- 50 bookmarks
- 50 business cards
- 5 posters

Custom Package - $1599

The Custom service breaks through the boundaries of the Advantage, Basic and Professional services and presents an ideal package for the author who has a clear artistic vision of the way their book should be presented. As a custom author, you communicate your ideas directly to our designers to create something truly exceptional. Enjoy all of the services offered in the Professional service plus five hardback books and more marketing materials and services.

Design and image features:

- Customization of cover and interior
- Consultation with cover and interior designer
- Allowance of cover art (up to 5 images) and author photo (supplied by author)
- 40 allotted interior graphics and tables

Production features:

- Availability of your book in paperback format
- Availability of your book in hardback format
- One paperback and one hardback author review copy
- Assignment of ISBN
- Registration with Books In Print database
- Ability to track book production progress through our website
- Author Service Representative who provides support throughout the publication process

Post-publication features:

- Ten paperback copies
- Five hardback copies
- A complimentary paperback book of your choice from the Xlibris Bookstore
- Worldwide distribution

- Registrations with online booksellers through national distributor
- Online book sales and royalty accounting
- Book and author web pages in the Xlibris online bookstore – you control the content
- Quarterly royalty payments

Marketing features:

- Web Design - Starter
- 50 postcards
- 50 bookmarks
- 50 business cards
- 5 posters

Premium Package - $2999

Premium service. Premium value. This package provides all the elements of Custom, plus everything you need to create a bestseller. It is the perfect choice for authors who want to deliver a fully customized, first-class book to a vast marketplace. In today's competitive publishing environment, the Premium service provides authors with the tools they need to design, customize, distribute, and market their manuscript.

Design and image features:

- Customization of cover and interior
- Consultation with cover and interior designer
- Allowance of cover art (unlimited) and author photo (supplied by author)
- Unlimited number of allotted interior graphics and tables

Production features:

- Availability of your book in paperback format
- Availability of your book in hardback format
- One paperback and one hardback author review copy
- Corrections Service
- Data Entry Service
- Copyediting Service
- Indexing Service
- Assignment of ISBN
- Registration with Books In Print database
- Ability to track book production progress through our website
- Author Service Representative who provides support throughout the publication process

Post-publication features:

- Twenty paperback copies
- Five hardback copies
- A complimentary paperback book of your choice from the Xlibris Bookstore
- Library of Congress
- U.S. Copyright Registration
- CD Archive
- Worldwide distribution
- Registrations with online booksellers through national distributor
- Online book sales and royalty accounting
- Book and author web pages in the Xlibris online bookstore – you control the content
- Quarterly royalty payments

Marketing features:

- Web Design – Starter
- Press Release Campaign – 100 outlets
- Book Review Campaign – Pro
- E-mail Marketing Campaign – 200,000 recipients
- 50 postcards
- 50 bookmarks
- 50 business cards
- 5 posters

Executive Package - $5999

Enjoy all the benefits of our Premium Package plus up to 125 books. This VIP package gives you even more marketing tools and materials to help give your book the maximum exposure it deserves. Set your own book price, enjoy unlimited customization options, coincide the launch of your book with an advanced webpage design and an extensive marketing bundle all designed to give your book the competitive edge it needs to take the market by storm.

Design and image features:

- Customization of cover and interior
- Consultation with cover and interior designer
- Allowance of cover art (unlimited) and author photo (supplied by author)
- Unlimited number of interior graphics and tables

Production features:

- Availability of your book in paperback format
- Availability of your book in hardback format

- One paperback and one hardback author review copy
- Corrections Service
- Data Entry Service
- Copyediting Service
- Indexing Service
- Assignment of ISBN
- Registration with Books In Print database
- Ability to track book production progress through our website
- Author Service Representative who provides support throughout the publication process

Post-publication features:

- Seventy-five paperback copies
- Twenty-five hardback copies (or exchange for 50 paperbacks)
- 1 leather bound edition (The Consul)
- A complimentary paperback book of your choice from the Xlibris Bookstore
- Set Your Own Price
- Library of Congress
- U.S. Copyright Registration
- CD Archive
- Worldwide distribution
- Registrations with online booksellers through national distributor
- Online book sales and royalty accounting
- Book and author web pages in the Xlibris online bookstore – you control the content
- Quarterly royalty payments

Marketing features:

- Web Design – Regular

- Press Release Campaign – 500 outlets
- Book Review Campaign – Pro
- E-mail Marketing Campaign – 1,000,000 Recipients
- 250 business cards
- 50 postcards
- 50 bookmarks
- 5 posters

Platinum Package - $12,999

The Rolls-Royce of publishing – the Platinum Service offers an exclusive world of publishing privileges and benefits. You'll enjoy true 24/7 ultra-personalized service, up to 300 books plus five beautifully leather bound, library-edition books, the ability to set your own price and an incomparable assortment of marketing options. This is a luxury service that delivers unprecedented opportunities including an advertisement in The New York Review of Books, Bookstore returnability and maximum online exposure.

Design and image features:
- Customization of cover and interior
- Consultation with cover and interior designer
- Allowance of cover art (unlimited) and author photo (supplied by author)
- Unlimited number of interior graphics and tables

Production features:

- Availability of your book in paperback format
- Availability of your book in hardback format
- One paperback and one hardback author review copy
- Corrections Service

- Data Entry Service
- Copyediting Service
- Indexing Service
- Assignment of ISBN
- Registration with Books In Print database
- Ability to track book production progress through our website
- Author Service Representative who provides support throughout the publication process

Post-publication features:

- Two hundred and fifty paperback copies
- Twenty-five hardback copies (or exchange for 50 paperbacks)
- 5 leather bound Consul editions (or exchange for The Ambassador)
- A complimentary paperback book of your choice from the Xlibris Bookstore
- Bookstore returnability
- Set Your Own Price
- Library of Congress
- U.S. Copyright Registration
- CD Archive
- Worldwide distribution
- Registrations with online booksellers through national distributor
- Online book sales and royalty accounting
- Book and author web pages in the Xlibris online bookstore – you control the content
- Quarterly royalty payments

Marketing features:

- Advertising in The New York Review of Books Journal

- Newswire
- Web Design – Advanced
- Press Release Campaign – 1,000 outlets
- Book Review Campaign – Pro
- E-mail Marketing Campaign Targeted – 1,000,000 Recipients
- 300 business cards
- 300 postcards
- 300 bookmarks
- 30 posters

Chapter One-Hundred: Xulon Press
A Christian Subsidy Publisher

Xulon Press is the largest, most experienced Christian owned and operated print-on-demand self publisher of Christian books.

We utilize lightning-fast print-on-demand digital technology to publish your book. We make your Christian book available through the largest distribution network of 71,000 retail and library customers globally, plus online at Amazon and Barnes & Noble. In less than 90 days your Christian book will reach a readership of thousands, making you a leading author in the field of Christian self publishing! And with our 100% royalty rate paid to authors for all bookstore sales, you keep most of your hard-earned money!

As the original print-on-demand self publisher for Christian authors, we have helped thousands of writers and authors get published, people just like you, from pastors to professors, housewives to businessmen, missionaries to novelists. We have more experience than all other self publishing houses combined!

Publishing Packages:

Tribute $999.00

Includes:

Paperback format, Custom Cover, Interior formatting, 10 Image Insertions, Choice of book size, electronic proof, ISBN, Online bookstore page, Google preview, support team, author & royalty account center, Professional marketing specialist, royalties, nonexclusive contract, 1 free copy of book

Debut   **$1799.00**

Includes all the above plus:

5 free copies of book, 10 image insertions, copyright registration, online distribution, international distribution, bookstore distribution availability, Books in Print listing, eBook formatting and distribution, editorial diagnostic

Showcase   **$2399.00**

Includes all the above plus:

10 free book copies, 20 image insertions, Lifetime book return service, Espresso book machine, advertisement in 1 edition Christian Book Browser Catalog, book exhibited at the International Christian Retail Show.

Premier   **$3799.00**

Includes all the above plus:

15 free books, 30 image insertions, advertisements in 2 editions of Christian Book Browser Catalog, book exhibited at the International Christian Retail Show, press release, rush service, professionally designed banner advertisement posted on Christianity.com and Crosswalk.com with a guaranteed 10,000 views, a "Featured" video trailer posted on Youtube and Facebook.

Elite   **$6499.00**

Includes all the above plus:

25 free books, 40 image insertions, advertisement in 5 editions of the Christian Book Browser Catalog, book exhibited at the International Christian Retail Show and the Christian Product Expo Tradeshows, professionally designed banner advertisement posted on Christianity.com and Crosswalk.com with a guaranteed 20,000 views, a "Blockbuster" video trailer posted on Youtube and Facebook, a book signing kit, basic copy edit up to 50,000 words, an author website.

Note: *Packages are for Black & White interior books only. Please call for a custom quote on Color books. Special offers cannot be combined with other offers. Free books shipped to mailing address within the United States, Canada and the United Kingdom only. Shipping and handling will be charged to all other countries.*

Xulon also offers Add On services covering editing, formatting, marketing, distribution, and promotional materials. Visit them at www.xulonpress.com

Section Four

Chapter One-Hundred-One: Writing Good

We wish to leave you with a small dose of humor.
Please take note and understand this is the "opposite" of
writing well.

Rules for Writing Good

1. Each pronoun agrees with their antecedent
2. Verbs has to agree with their subjects.
3. Don't use no double negatives.
4. A writer mustn't shift your point of view.
5. Don't use a run-on sentence you got to punctuate it.
6. Avoid redundancy.
7. Don't repeatedly reiterate over and over.
8. About sentence fragments.
9. Don't use commas, which aren't necessary.
10. Don't abbrev.
11. Check to see if you any words out.
12. Eschew esoteric verbiage.
13. Computer spell Czechs are imperfect.
14. Never use a preposition to end a sentence with.
15. Use apostrophe's right.
16. When dangling, don't use participles.
17. Never leave a transitive verb just lay there without an object.
18. a sentence should begin with a capital and end with a period
19. Watch out for irregular verbs which have creeped into our language.

20. Profanity sucks.

21. Be more or less specific.

22. Understatement may be better.

23. Exaggeration is a billion times worse than understatement.

24. Analogies in writing are like feathers on a snake.

25. Go around the barn at high noon to avoid colloquialisms.

26. Even if a mixed metaphor sings like a canary, it should be thrown out with the bathwater.

27. Last but not least, lay off cliches.

Chapter One-Hundred-Two:
Writer's Resources

The Writer's Sherpa, LLC, is an editorial consulting firm that helps aspiring nonfiction authors write books that establish expertise, attract new clients and opportunities, and share their story in a powerful way. If you're struggling to get your ideas out of your head and onto the page, visit www.writerssherpaprograms.com to sign up for the free "Jump Start Your Book E-course!"

Publishing Poynters
Book and Information Marketing News and Ideas
Sign up for Dan's weekly newsletter for all the latest news @
http://parapub.com/sites/para/resources/newsletter.cfm

WriterProfits.com is designed to give writers and authors the encouragement,
tips and tools needed to build professional, profit-focused writing careers.
You'll get advice on what to charge, how to promote your services or books,
where to find clients and agents... and more! Start building your writing
business today by visiting: www.writerprofits.com.

http://hollylisle.com Holly Lisle sold more than thirty
novels to a string of the biggest publishers in the US and
abroad, hit multiple best-seller lists, has been translated into
more than a dozen languages, has won and was nominated
for awards...and walked away from commercial publishing
to self-publish a series of writing courses, as well as her
own novels. You can find her and her work (and her
reasons) here: http://hollylisle.com and
http://howtothinksideways.com

Armchair Interviews
Passionate book reviews and author interviews
Armchair Interviews has been reviewing books since 2005.
They only review books they hand pick, using prequalified
reviewers. The book reviews are honest, reliable, and
always respectful (even if they don't love the book). The
book reviews are all about the books. Period. St. Martin's
Press, Harper Collins, Random House and others ask them
to review their new titles as do independent presses like
Five Star Publications and Bascom Hill Books. While they
do not review every book they are pitched, they encourage
publicists, publishers of any size, and authors interested in
having a book reviewed, to complete the online book
review request form. There are NO fees, although if they
accept your book to review, you must send a hard copy of
the book. Find more information at
http://www.armchairinterviews.com/

Voice Projects
Your book on audio CD's, MP's, USB, or tape.
The recent explosion of independent publishing is a boon to
authors and readers, but busy schedules limit their free
time. There's a ready-made demand for audiobooks that is
still greatly underserved.

In order to help meet that demand, VoiceProjects.com offers independent production of audiobooks. Our one-time flat-fee model lowers the cost of entry for authors and rights holders, and allows you to keep **100%** of the net proceeds from your books.

We'll work with you through every step in the process of converting your manuscript into spoken word with your choice of top-notch narrator. You retain all the publishing and audio rights, you decide on distribution, you keep **100%** of the net proceeds.

Inquire at Mail@VoiceProjects.com or go to our website at http://www.voiceprojects.com

The TBA Lounge
An author's marketing site
http://thebestauthorslounge.com/
Promoting authors and providing readers with amazing bools in evry genre.
Find out how TBA Lounge can take you from Best author to Best-selling author
Listen to them on Blog Talk Radio Mondays @ 8pm
Blogtalkradio.com/tbalounge

Radioearnetwork.com
An internet radio station, Radio Ear Network now has a listening audience of 10 million in 148 countries worldwide. They recently syndicated the Author's Connection and Forever Write, weekly author's interview shows hosted by Susan Klaus.

PersonalCovers.webs.com
Cover designs for the financially challenged
Working with you to understand YOUR concept for the cover of your book, Personal Covers will create two to three designs, consulting with you to make any necessary

adjustments. Prices start at $150.00 for custom designed covers, not subsidized templates. Most covers are completed for less than $300.00. They also offer website creation, formatting, editing, and ghostwriting at remarkably low costs.

I would be remiss if I did not advise you of the opportunities that await you if you become a client of **Published! An Affiliate of Village Voices**. We are an author services company assisting you from start to finish. As the Manatee group leader of the Florida Writer's Association, I honed my craft under the motto "writer's helping writers." We offer manuscript evaluations, both copy and content editing, general coaching, and ghostwriting. When you decide to try your hand at self or subsidy publishing, we can offer advice or help you with formatting and cover consultations. Already published? Sales dismal? We offer marketing suggestions, help you discover your niche market, and show you how to use social media to reach the maximum readers who are your focus market.

We plan to publish annual addendums to *Published!* in order to cover the ever-changing landscape of nontraditional publishing. If you know of author services companies we missed or discover some of those included in this first volume have closed, please contact me at DGould497@aol.com.

I also want to suggest that writers, especially newer writers, contact and join local writing associations and critique groups. Here in Florida we are blessed with an excellent statewide group, the Florida Writer's Association, that not only promotes "writers helping writers," they hold one of the best annual conferences in the nation. Conferences have an enormous amount of information available for every level of expertise, but for the new writer they are worth

every penny paid and so much more. I urge you to locate
all writing associations in your area, and choose one that
appeals to you. It might be one that applies directly to your
genre, or maybe it is held in a spot that calls you to a "learn
and earn" vacation, (the annual conference in Hawaii is one
of the largest, attended by both novices and best-sellers.) If
you write thrillers, SleuthFest, held in South Florida might
be your best choice. Use search engines, ask your local
librarian, sign up for "writer's newsletters."
STUDY the craft of writing from beginning the writing
process through editing, formatting, query letters, agents,
and synopses. Then study the publishing options and
marketing methods and choose those that are best for you.
The resources in our digital age are endless. For each site
that disappears or goes out of business, five new companies
join the fray. It has been said that we all have a book in us.
It makes it harder to stand out, but if you really want to
write, then learn the craft, and let your imagination soar.

Thank you for your patronage.

Dona Lee & Al Musitano
"Plotting Success"

www.ingramcontent.com/pod-product-compliance
Lightning Source LLC
Chambersburg PA
CBHW080548090426
42735CB00016B/3182